COLOR IN INTERIOR DESIGN

COLOR IN INTERIOR DESIGN

John F. Pile

McGraw-Hill
New York   San Francisco   Washington, D.C.   Auckland   Bogotá
Caracas   Lisbon   London   Madrid   Mexico City   Milan
Montreal   New Delhi   San Juan   Singapore
Sydney   Tokyo   Toronto

Library of Congress Cataloging-in-Publication Data

Pile, John F.
    Color in interior design / John F. Pile.
        p.   cm.
    Includes bibliographical references and index.
    ISBN 0-07-050165-3 (hardcover)
    1. Color in interior decoration.   I. Title.
NK2115.5.C6P46   1997
747'.94—dc21   96-47590
                                         CIP

McGraw-Hill

A Division of The **McGraw·Hill** Companies

10 11 12 13 14 CTP/CTP 12 11 10 9 8

ISBN 0-07-050165-3

The sponsoring editor for this book was Wendy Lochner, the editing
supervisor was Christina Palaia, and the production supervisor was
Suzanne W. B. Rapcavage. It was set in Helvetica by North Market Street
Graphics.

Pinted and bound by CTPS

McGraw-Hill books are available at special quantity discounts to use as pre-
miums and sales promotions, or for use in corporate training programs. For
more information, please write to the Director of Special Sales, McGraw-Hill,
Two Penn Plaza, New York,NY 10121. Or contact your local bookstore.

Contents

Preface

In planning my 1988 book *Interior Design,* I allotted one chapter to the subject of color. While writing that chapter, it became clear that this was a subject sufficiently large and complex to deserve an entire book of its own. A search of available color books revealed that, although there are innumerable books about color, none seemed to focus on the color concerns relating to interior design.

Most color books, including the many excellent ones that are listed in the bibliography of this book, deal with color in a theoretical, even scientific way, or are focused on specialized fields other than interior design. There are books on color in the fine arts such as painting and print making, color in photography, and the use of color in commercial fields such as packaging and marketing. Interior design has been left to learn from such books as best it can. Students, professional designers, and interested amateur designers have therefore had to deal with color through trial and error and such suggestions as can be culled from the existing color books or from the often misleading hints offered in popular home furnishing magazines.

In interior design education, some schools offer a color course based on general color theory as a part of a foundation art program. Others do not make color the subject of a particular course but rather expect, quite optimistically, that it will be adequately treated as part of general interior design courses that must deal with planning, drawing, rendering, and the many technical issues that design of complex interior spaces involves. As a result, color often comes as an afterthought.

It is sometimes suggested that color cannot be taught—that it is a strictly intuitive matter that must depend on an inborn talent that some people have, much as musical talent appears in only some limited portion of the total population. It cannot be denied that some people seem to have a particular skill for dealing with color, but the assumption of this book is that anyone can become sufficiently able in working with color to do work of great excellence. It is the myth that only the talented can deal with color that leaves many students and many amateur designers intimidated, hesitant, and dependent on the advice of salespeople or friends in making color decisions.

In this book, the basics of color theory are offered, but the special effort made here is to relate such theory to the specific needs of interior design. The reader is, of course, free to skip the theoretical material and go directly to the chapters that deal with suggested routines that will make work with color practical and move to preparing color schemes that will be attractive and useful.

Almost everyone finds working with color highly enjoyable if it is undertaken without fear of mistakes and with confidence that good results are not dependent on some mysterious gift that only a few people possess. In addition to design students and professional designers, almost everyone makes color decisions relating to the interior spaces where they live and work. Buying furniture, carpet, or drapery, choosing a paint color, hanging a picture, or placing an object all involve a color decision, whether it is taken consciously or not. The aim of this book is to provide a basis for such decisions that will lead to satisfying results. Every professional designer needs to make such decisions on a daily basis, but good color is within the reach of anyone who cares to give that matter some serious attention.

ACKNOWLEDGMENTS

Appreciation is in order for the many individuals and firms that have provided advice, illustrations, and other forms of help in the preparation of this book. The following have been especially helpful.

Louis Beal
Berger-Rait Design Associates
Lisa Burke of the office of Michael Graves
Shashi Caan
Alfredo De Vido
Norman Diekman
Flavia Destefanis of Vignelli Associates
Michael Graves
Gwathmey Siegel & Associates Architects
Paul Heyer
Robert D. Kleinschmidt
Jim Morgan
Jin Bae Park
Powell/Kleinschmidt
Suzanne Sekey
Robert Siegel
Judith Stockman
Swanke Hayden Connell Architects
Yatsuto Tanaka
Venturi and Scott Brown and Associates
Vignelli Associates

Many photographers have also contributed in helpful ways. Photo credits are given with the captions of each photographic illustration. All charts, diagrams, and drawings are by the author except as otherwise credited.

Also, the staff at McGraw-Hill was very helpful, including Wendy Lochner, sponsoring editor; Suzanne Rapcavage, production supervisor; and Pattie Amoroso, editing supervisor liaison.

COLOR IN INTERIOR DESIGN

1
Introduction

The use of color is central to all work in interior design. Whether the designer is a trained professional interior designer, an architect, a decorator, or a householder dealing with home interiors, decisions about color are a major factor in the success of any project. There is a vast literature dealing with color, ranging from scientific studies, through color theory relating to fine art, to picture books dealing with interior design and decoration. Although there are chapters dealing with color in almost every interior design text-book, there is no recent book that focuses on the interior designer's use of color. This book is planned to fill that need.

Practical work with color can be approached on a strictly intuitive level, through adaptation of color use in existing projects, recent or historical, or on a basis of theoretical study. This book is intended to support each of these directions, or a combination of all three. In many schools of art and design, courses are offered in color in terms that most often focus on two-dimensional art—painting and graphic design. When offered as part of *foundation art,* that is, basic courses intended to serve all areas of art and design, their theoretical basis is seldom related to interior design practice in a way that supports the practical needs of students and interior design practitioners.

In this book, color theory is presented as a basis for development of practical methods for making color decisions, planning color schemes, and converting schemes to practical execution in real materials. In working with color, there are no fixed rules, no absolutes of right and wrong, no formulas that can be relied on to assure successful results. Any way of working that yields desired results can be satisfactory. Any theoretical basis that aids color planning can be useful. This very openness tends to make work with color seem problematic—difficulty arises because the absence of firm rules makes everything seem too easy while outstanding results remain difficult to achieve.

Each reader of this book can decide how it will be most useful. For the experienced designer, much of the information will be familiar, while illustrative examples may offer stimulation. It is always useful, when viewing a successful result, to try the exercise of relating what is seen to theory through analysis using charts such as those provided in Chapter 10. Making such charts for existing examples may not seem necessary, but thinking through the relation of reality to an abstract chart can aid the making of fresh, new schemes. Design students may find it helpful to review whatever color theories they have encountered and to then try the methodical steps suggested in Chapters 6 through 9 in dealing with school design problems. Gradually, as experience develops, some steps will become second nature and hardly require any thought. Steps can be skipped entirely as they become mental processes that lead directly to satisfactory results.

It is also intended that this book will be useful to nonprofessional readers who may want advice and encouragement in making color decisions relating to home or office interiors. There is a range of possible situations extending from the need to select a paint color or a new carpet to the complete interior design of a room, an apartment, or a house that can be dealt with without professional assistance. Amateur interior design can be interesting and enjoyable, but it can also be frustrating and difficult. Probably the most important aspect of such work is successful selection of color. It is also the aspect of interior work most fully within the reach of the amateur designer requiring no special skills in drawing or knowledge of construction. It is also a primary territory for disappointment. Interiors that are unattractive, depressing, or irritating have most often come to these unhappy states through badly chosen color. Some thought and organized planning in this area will yield superior results. This book is intended as a guide in that direction.

There have been many attempts to discover facts about color use, relationships between color choices, and emotional impact or meaning. Various experiments have developed suggestions about what colors will be most suitable to the various functional roles that interior spaces are intended to serve. The recommendations generated by such studies are reviewed here in Chapters 11 and 12, but it should be understood that this material is to be viewed as a collection of suggestions and hints that may be helpful, but that need not be considered as findings based on absolute truths. The reader is invited to follow these leads as long as they prove helpful and useful, but can feel free to ignore any suggestions that run counter to an otherwise successful effort.

It is a pleasant fact that most designers, professional or otherwise, find working with color enjoyable. From childhood onward, almost everyone finds pleasure in looking at colored objects and materials. Books of samples are inherently attractive, and watching the ways in which colors interact as they are placed in relationships has some of the pleasant sense that comes from musical harmonies. Dealing with samples of real materials with their differing weights and textures is similarly pleasant. It is only a certain nervousness that comes from fear of failure based, perhaps, on the myth that success with color requires some mysterious inborn talent that can make work with color seem frustrating and difficult. If that unease can be put aside, work with color can become the most rewarding aspect of any design project.

The color present in the natural environment offers a source of stimulus and inspiration well know as the basis for much of artists' work and as an aspect of the natural world almost universally enjoyed. It can be assumed that the human ability to perceive color developed as an aid to adaptation to the environment which was, for most of human experience, entirely natural. The modern, humanly created environment is still perceived by the same physical and mental processes that were developed to aid in the understanding of nature. It is not surprising that the colors of nature are generally a source of pleasure and satisfaction.

Figure 1.1 A pleasant landscape may be dominated by tones of blue and green in a harmonious relationship. (*Photo by John Pile.*)

Landscape is commonly thought of as dominated by the cool colors, green and blue, with the sky characteristically blue, the tones of grass and trees green. In fact, sky color varies greatly from the blue of a clear noon, to various tones of gray and white produced by clouds and haze, and the pinks, oranges, and reds of dawn and sunset. Grass and leaves are green in summer, but tones of yellow and tan appear as grass dries, and leaf colors change in autumn to the varied tones of yellow, orange, and red that are particularly exciting and pleasing. Earth colors range through tones of gray and brown to lighter tans and yellows. Snow can make land surfaces white or near white. Water is commonly thought of as blue, but the tones of oceans, lakes, and rivers can vary into blue-greens, greens, tans, browns, and near blacks according to changes in climate, weather, time of day, and degree of clarity. Ice formed on the surface of water can be near white, gray, almost black, or a range of colors reflected from the sky and other elements. (See Figures 1.1 through 1.5.)

Flowers are well known to present a wide variety of colors including warm tones of red, orange, yellow, and violet along with some cool blues. Such colors as rose and violet take their names from the flowers that exhibit those colors. Berries and fruits are full of color and also often provide the names used for colors such as lemon and orange. Nuts appear in a range of tans and

Figure 1.2 Sky colors, although typically blue, may include pinks and oranges according to weather and time of day. (*Photo by John Pile.*)

Figure 1.3 Rocks may be gray, brown, or, as in this location, shades of red. (*Photo by John Pile.*)

Figure 1.4 Leaves, green in summer, turn to tones of yellow, orange, and red in autumn. (*Photo by John Pile.*)

Figure 1.5 Water, itself colorless, may appear blue (from sky reflection) or, with different light conditions, gray, green, or brown. (*Photo by John Pile.*)

Figure 1.6 Flowers can be of many colors. Roses may be white, yellow, or red, but it is a particular pink that has taken on the name *rose color*. (*Photo by John Pile.*)

Figure 1.7 Fruits are of varied colors. Oranges and lemons have given their names to the colors that characterize them. (*Photo by John Pile.*)

browns. Fish, animals, and birds are full of color. The appealing colors of many foods come from their natural origins. The cut surfaces of lemons, oranges, tomatoes, and melons, the reds and browns of most meats, and the colors of breads and cakes made through processing of natural substances are strongly appealing. The browns and tans of many larger animals are widely varied, and the white of polar bears, the stripes of zebras, and the black of many creatures make a zoo a colorful place. Eggs can be the clear white or tan of the familiar food-shop offering or may have more varied colors relating to various birds, such as the blue of the robin's egg. The white and yellow yoke of the egg interior are a familiar sight. Bright colors appear among insects, birds, and fish while human beings vary in color tones from pale pink through tan and brown tones to near black. Hair and eyes are of many colors among varied species, both human and animal. It

Figure 1.8 Apples may be green or yellow, but red is thought of as their typical color. (*Photo by John Pile.*)

is interesting that the colors of nature seem to appear harmonious and pleasing in almost every context, offering endless suggestions for planned color use. (See Figures 1.6 through 1.11.)

Many of the colors available for human use also have their origins in natural sources. Stone, clay bricks and tiles, the wood used to make a vast variety of objects, animal products, such as leather and wool yarns, other yarns, such as cotton, linen, and silk, are all natural products that can be used in their natural colors. Dyes derived from natural materials (berries, bark, and wood chips, for example) are varied in color and are generally more pleasing in tone and in relationships than the artificial dyes made by chemical processes.

Designers can be both challenged and inspired by observation of natural color in the effort to assemble environments for human use in the modern world that will be as pleasant and stimulating in color terms as the natural world. It is not safe to assume that this will be an inevitable result of the use of varied color. Thought and planning are needed along with careful observation and some theoretical knowledge if designed color is to be the source of satisfaction that lies within its potential.

Figure 1.9   Some berries include colors in their names, as with blueberries or blackberries. These berries are red. (*Photo by John Pile.*)

Figure 1.10   The colors of insects, moths, and butterflies can be spectacular. (*Photo by John Pile.*)

Figure 1.11 Animals and birds show off some of the most beautiful of natural colorings as does this macaw. (*Photo by John Pile.*)

Figure 2.1 The pleasantly colorful interior of this dining room is part of a hotel, the Volksenåsen in Oslo, Norway. (*Photo by John Pile.*)

2
Color in Interior Design

It is obvious that color is a key aspect of successful work in interior design. A space that presents a pleasant and appropriate impression through the use of color generates an almost inevitable favorable reaction (see Figure 2.1). Conversely, even a space that is well planned and equipped but drab and indifferent or unpleasant in color terms will be depressing and disappointing. Although work with color is almost universally found to be interesting and enjoyable; there is a certain tendency to be hesitant in dealing with this matter, which is thought to rely so much on taste, or, even more intimidating, *good* taste.

In design schools, it is often noted that students avoid color and material selection, preferring to work with the planning aspects of design and with constructional details while putting off color planning until the last minute when there is no time to make wise and thoughtful decisions. Similarly, those without design training who face decisions relating to their own home environment will often hang back from color decisions and ask the advice of salespeople (who may be totally unqualified to give such advice) in preference to trusting their own judgment.

In order to trust one's judgment in color matters, whether one is a design professional, a student, or a design amateur, it is helpful to develop experience through work with color in abstract exercises and in planning schemes that are strictly experimental. In such desktop color planning, there are no risks. No money is spent on items and work that may turn out badly. Instead, color may be tried out, alternatives considered, changes made at no cost and with hardly any effort.

If this book has any one primary message to offer, it is the suggestion that such advance planning of color relationships is essential to successful color use. No one would undertake construction of a building without having plans (the so-called blueprints) on paper. Even music is most often composed and written out on paper before performance is attempted. Improvisation is, of course, possible in music, and in color scheming as well, but improvisation is generally only successful when the improviser has developed skills that are based on planned and organized methodology.

To feel fully at ease with color, the reader is invited to proceed through a series of chapters here that begin with the

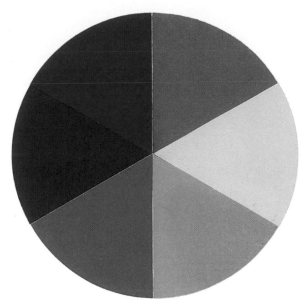

Figure 2.2   The ring of six rainbow colors, red, orange, yellow, green, blue, and violet; each is generally recognized as having a distinct identity.

basics of scientific study of the physical phenomena which generate the perception of color and then proceed to the various color systems that have been devised to attempt an orderly understanding of the ways in which color appears to viewers. These basics may or may not be useful in the work of devising actual color schemes, but awareness of them establishes a foundation of mental understanding that supports confidence in practical work. Color terminology is clarified by awareness of the scientific and systematic study of color.

The next step in mastering color involves desktop work with color samples that can be assembled into schemes to be considered for application in real (or imagined) interior spaces. Schemes can be developed to demonstrate the various kinds of relationships that have come to be recognized as successful through studies of what is usually called *color harmony*. It is often useful in this study to also demonstrate the unpleasant or discordant results

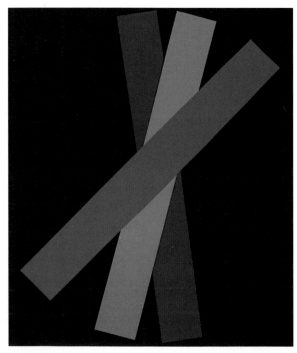

Figure 2.3   The three additive primaries: red, green, and blue.

Figure 2.4   The three subtractive primaries: red, yellow, and blue.

Figure 2.5 Achromatic colors: white, grays, and black.

that can be generated all too easily by a mistaken choice of one or more elements in a scheme under development. The step that follows involves finding real materials for the various elements of an interior that will match the abstract tones selected in the preceding step. Whenever possible, actual samples of these materials are assembled, still on the desktop, to demonstrate that a charted basis for a successful realization has been assembled. Chapters 10 to 18 deal with a variety of color topics that can be helpful and supportive in making color decisions.

Before going on, some preliminary notes on the terms to be used will be useful. The terminology of color can be somewhat complex, and many color terms are used loosely in general conversation. Exact definitions are given for the terms used by various color theorists in the development of color systems in Chapter 4. Unfortunately, various systems use slightly different terminology. Before going into the details of color systems, it will be helpful to make use of some color terms with generally accepted meanings as follows:

Color. A characteristic of light or of surfaces or objects that is perceptible to human vision and that is described by various color names, such as *red* or *blue*.

Basic colors. The most generally distinguishable colors are the spectrum (rainbow) hues of red, orange, yellow, green, blue, and violet (or purple). Although sometimes claimed not to be colors, black, white, and gray are also usually thought of as basic, readily distinguished colors. (See Figure 2.2.)

Primary colors. Colors that cannot be created by mixture of other colors. The primaries of light are red, green, and blue; those of pigments and dyes are red, yellow, and blue. (See Figures 2.3 and 2.4.)

Secondary colors. These are colors formed by mixture of two primaries. In pigments and dyes, the secondaries are orange, green, and violet. In mixing colored light, the secondaries are blue-green, violet, and (somewhat surprisingly) yellow created by the mixture of red and green.

Tertiary colors. Tones formed by mixture of a primary and a secondary, such as red-orange or blue-green.

Chromatic colors. Any colors other than white, gray, and black.

Achromatic colors. Black, white, and gray. (See Figure 2.5.)

Figure 2.6 The three subtractive primaries paired with the secondaries that are their complements: red with green, blue with orange, and yellow with violet.

Hue. The quality that gives an identifying name to a chromatic color. Light or dark versions of some hues are given special names, such as pink for light red or brown for dark tones of red, orange, and yellow.

Lightness and darkness. The degree to which a color reflects light. Light colors reflect much of the light falling upon them and may be called *pale* or *pastel.* Dark colors reflect little light. A series of tones made by mixing white and black can form a scale of grays from light tones made up of much white and little black to dark tones made from much black and little white. Tones in the middle of such a scale are called *medium.* A similar scale can be made up for chromatic colors.

Complementary colors. Colors appearing opposite in character in such pairs as red and green, orange and blue, and yellow and violet (see Figure 2.6). Mixture of a pair of complementary colors will produce a gray or

Figure 2.7 Six tints made from the primaries and secondaries lightened by admixture of white.

Figure 2.8 Six shades made from the primaries and secondaries darkened with admixture of a complementary tone or of black.

Figure 2.9 Six color hues regarded as *warm*.

Figure 2.10 Seven hues regarded as *cool*.

similar tone having no strong chromatic hue.

Neutral colors. Neutral tones are produced by mixture of complementaries. Mixture of a chromatic color with an achromatic color will partially neutralize the resultant color.

Tints. Light color tones produced by a mixture of a chromatic color with white or light gray. (See Figure 2.7.)

Shades. Darker color tones produced by a mixture of a chromatic color with black or dark gray. (See Figure 2.8.)

Bright colors. These result from mixture of chromatic color with little or no achromatic color.

Dull colors. These colors result from mixture of chromatic color with a complementary color, with achromatic color, or both.

Warm and cool colors. Colors near the red end of the spectrum are designated as warm, those near the violet end as cool. Red, orange, and yellow are warm colors; green and blue are cool colors. Violets may be either warm or cool according to their relative content of red and blue. Grays and other neutrals may be called warm or cool according to their content of warm or cool chromatic color. (See Figures 2.9 and 2.10.)

With these definitions in mind, the chapters that follow will progress from theoretical issues to the practicalities of making up usable color schemes.

3
Vision, Light, and Color

Color is universally experienced as an important aspect of vision. Although almost everyone sees the colors of the sky, earth, grass, flowers, and all other visible objects, and although there seems to be general agreement about what these colors appear to be, exactly what color *is* can be somewhat puzzling. We tend to think of it as a characteristic of an object or a surface—but it can be demonstrated that the same object can appear different in color under various circumstances. A scientific approach to the study of color has brought about an understanding of what color is, so that any study of color must now begin with knowledge of the basic physical principles that underlie all color effects.

Whether we choose to define color as the mental or psychological impression created in the mind of a viewer by a particular observed object or surface, or we define it as the stimulus that produces such mental impressions, is a matter of choice. Like the question of whether a falling tree in the forest makes a sound if no one is present to hear it, whether color is the stimulus or the sensation produced by the stimulus is a semantic (or perhaps a philosophical) mat-

ter. In scientific terms, the choice makes little difference. All color study must begin with understanding the workings of the human eye.

THE EYE

The human (and many animal) eyes are devices for collecting information in a form that can be delivered to the brain (see Figure 3.1). Such visual information is collected by the ability of the eye to convert experiences of light into signals that can be transmitted to the brain by nerve impulses. The lens of the eye focuses light onto the sensitive retina much as the lens of a camera focuses light onto the surface of the film or plate. Without light, neither the camera nor the eye can operate. We cannot see in total darkness; to see well, we need adequate light falling on the scene we wish to view. How much light is adequate is a matter that concerns lighting designers but is incidental to this discussion. The light of a candle or a match makes vision possible under limited circumstances. The light of the sun in daytime is more than adequate for vision in most familiar situations.

How the eye and brain convert the images that the lens casts on the retina into an understanding of three-dimensional reality is a complex matter constantly under study in the field usually called *visual perception.* In this book, we are only concerned with the single aspect of that process that deals with the perception of color. It is known that the retina of the eye is made up of light-sensitive receptors called *rods* and *cones* because of their physical shape. The rods and cones vary in their sensitivity to different colors and are capable of conveying to the brain information that includes, along with the detection of light stimulus, the color of that light. We not only see a flower, a box, or a wall, we see a *pink* flower, a *blue* box, a *yellow* wall. Since the only stimulus that the eye deals with is light, it becomes clear that light is itself a carrier of information that the eye and brain can interpret as color.

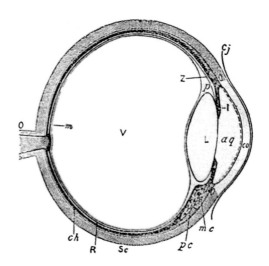

Figure 3.1   The human eye in cross section.

LIGHT

Physicists have arrived at a clear understanding of what light is and a further understanding of the characteristics of light that relate to color. Among the various forms of physical energy, *electromagnetic radiation* involves transmission of energy in the form of a pulsation or wave. The *frequency* of the wave (the number of waves occurring per second) can be given as the number of *cycles per second,* or *CPS,* also now given the name *hertz.* Because electromagnetic frequencies are very high (in a range of 400 to 800 million million), it is more convenient to use another unit which defines wavelength.

Since electromagnetic energy travels at a constant speed, a wave has a length that varies in proportion to the frequency of the wave. The higher the frequency, the shorter the wavelength. The unit used to describe wavelength is the *angstrom,* or *nanometer* (abbreviated nm). One millimeter (about ¹⁄₂₅

inch) is equal to one million nanometers or an angstrom. Cosmic rays, gamma rays, and X rays are of very short wavelengths. Long wavelengths are used for radar, radio, and TV transmission. The term *light* is used to describe electromagnetic energy with wavelengths between about 100 and 5000 nm. Although called light, ultraviolet radiation (100 to 380 nm) and infrared radiation (780 to 5000 nm) are not visible to the human eye. (See Figure 3.2.)

THE VISIBLE SPECTRUM

The eye is sensitive to light energy in the range of 380 to 780 nm. Within this range, different wavelengths give rise to the sensations of color. A particular wavelength is interpreted as light of a specific pure color. A basic color name is given to light with wavelengths that are close together. When all wavelengths of visible light are present, the light is perceived as white or colorless although, in fact, all colors are present in white light. A prism has the ability to break up a beam of white light into its various colors as the various colors are bent at slightly different angles when they pass through the glass of the prism. A laboratory instrument

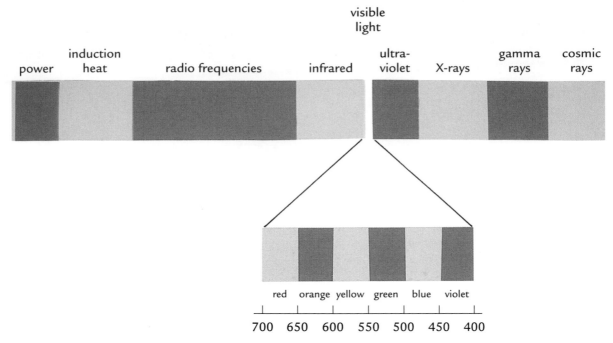

visible
light

| power | induction heat | radio frequencies | infrared | ultra-violet | X-rays | gamma rays | cosmic rays |

red   orange   yellow   green   blue   violet

700   650   600   550   500   450   400

Figure 3.2   The energy spectrum with the spectrum of visible light shown enlarged.

called a *spectroscope* provides a narrow slit through which a band of light is passed to a prism, which breaks the incoming light beam into a rainbowlike band called a *spectrum* (see Figure 3.3). The colors of the spectrum produced by sunlight appear, in order of their wavelengths, in the familiar sequence red, orange, yellow, green, blue, violet. These successive colors are in a continuous sequence, each color shading into the next without sharp separation. The wavelengths at the center of each named color zone are approximately as follows (see also Figure 3.4):

Red	700 nm
Orange	600 nm
Yellow	580 nm
Green	530 nm
Blue	470 nm
Violet	400 nm

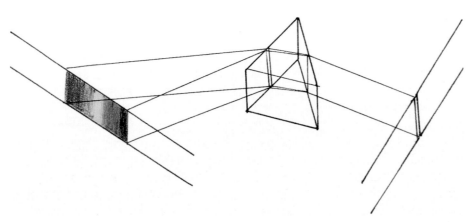

Figure 3.3   A beam of white light passing through a glass prism is broken up into the sequence of hues identified with the rainbow.

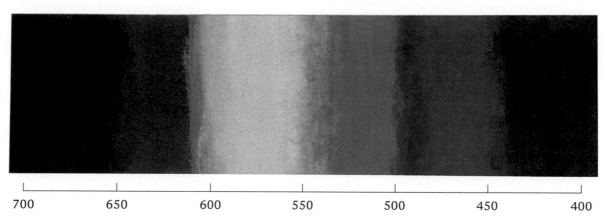

700	650	600	550	500	450	400

Figure 3.4   The colors of the spectrum result from the differing wavelengths of light as separated out by the process of refraction in a prism. The numbers of the scale here represent the angstrom number for the wavelengths at the marked points.

The colors at the red end of the spectrum, red, orange, and yellow, are generally thought of as *warm,* while green, blue, and violet are thought of as *cool.* Blacks, grays, and other neutrals such as brown can be described as warm or cool depending on whether they contain some admixture of warm or cool spectral coloration.

When heated to a temperature that produces glowing light (incandescence) various elements emit light at a particular wavelength. Gases can be made to glow by passing a high-voltage electric current through them. Light produced in these ways is of a particular pure color that will appear as a narrow line if viewed with a spectroscope. The red of neon light, the yellow of sodium light, or the blue of mercury light is readily observed where these gases are used in light fixtures and for street lighting. Since the sun is made up of all elements in the form of glowing gases, its spectrum is a continuous band of all colors.

The colors ordinarily observed are not *pure,* that is, of one particular wavelength, but are rather a mix of wavelengths near that of the clear or pure color. The usual six color names are given to colors that fall within a band of the following approximate widths:

Red	650–700 nm
Orange	600–640 nm
Yellow	560–590 nm
Green	490–550 nm
Blue	440–480 nm
Violet	390–430 nm

The gaps of 10 nm between colors represent the transitional zones of the spectrum where one color fades into the next. These transition colors are often given combined names, such as yellow-green, and may be called tertiary colors as discussed in Chapters 4 and 5. Also, note that the bands of color vary in width, with the yellow band narrowest at 30 nm and the green band broadest at 60 nm.

Some color theorists prefer to divide the spectrum into seven basic colors adding indigo between blue and violet with wavelengths between 440 and 450 nm. The more usual view finds this to be the portion of the blue band closest to violet. Since color naming is, to a degree, subjective, the decision about the exact point where red blends into orange or green into blue is somewhat arbitrary. As a practical matter, there is wide general agreement about the meaning of the names of the six major colors of the spectrum.

DAYLIGHT

Daylight, although it is always made up of all colors, varies with time of day, season, and latitude in the balance of colors. The light of a clear day at noon is quite different in color characteristics from the light of dawn or of sunset. Cloudy day daylight is quite different from full sun, and winter light is different from that of summer. The white light of a clear day noon contains a mix of all colors at near-equal intensity. At dawn or sunset, light at the red-orange end of the spectrum becomes more prominent as atmospheric haze in the air cuts down the presence of colors at the blue-violet end. Cloudy day light is weakened in reds by the filtering action of clouds and so appears somewhat bluish. Since all colors are still present in such altered sunlight, the eye can still see all colors—a blue box still looks blue at sunset, a red box looks red on a cloudy day. The human brain also makes a correction in the perception of color so that the relationship of colors does not seem to change significantly even in light that is not evenly balanced in color. This effect, called *color constancy,* is a form of adaptation in which the eye and brain adjust to ambient conditions to bring them into a form most useful for understanding. It is an effect familiar when putting on or taking off sunglasses in which tinted glass alters the balance of color.

ARTIFICIAL LIGHT

Artificial light is produced by a number of sources that differ in color characteristics. The flames of candles and oil or gas lamps are weak in colors at the blue end of the spectrum. Incandescent electric light has this characteristic to a lesser degree. Each of these light sources produce light in which all of the spectrum colors are present although in a balance different from that of daylight. An interior lighted by incandescent electric light will appear orange in tone when viewed from a daylit exterior, but after the eye has had time to adjust for a few minutes, the color of the interior will seem normal.

The mercury-vapor and sodium lights sometimes used for street and highway lighting have a totally different color content. They produce a spectrum that shows only narrow lines of color with blanks in between. As a result, color cannot be observed in normal relationships under such light. Under sodium streetlights, everything has the color of the light itself and so appears as shades of gray seen under orange light. Fluorescent light, now in wide use because of its economy, shares the characteristics of both the continuous spectrum of incandescent light in the light produced by the phosphors on the inner surface of the tube and the discontinuous spectra (lines) produced by the glowing gases in the tube. A number of versions of fluorescent tubes have been developed with color characteristics that attempt to approach normal daylight, but none are totally successful. Neon light produces line spectra of pure color (as in the bright red and other color tones used in signs) and a white neon light can be produced by a mixture of gases in the glass tube, but all such light, because of its discontinuous spectra, distorts perception of color. Artificial light sources have been developed that deliver a mix of all colors similar to that of daylight called *full-spectrum lighting.* Some experimenters believe that such light is physiologically desirable in addition to being an aid to true color vision. At present, full-spectrum artificial light has not come into wide general use, and its merits remain a subject of some debate.

In understanding the differences in the spectra produced by various light sources, it is helpful to study charts that present in graphic form the relative intensities of the

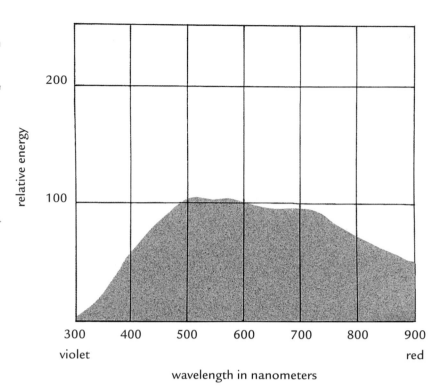

Figure 3.5 A graph showing the distribution of varied light wavelengths in normal noon daylight. Violet is on the left, red on the right. Note that all wavelengths are present with the strongest colors in the central portion of the spectrum. Since all wavelengths are present, such a spectrum is continuous.

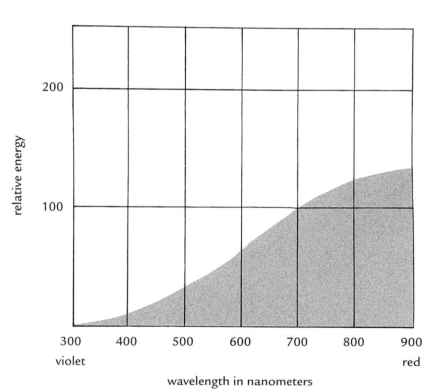

Figure 3.6 A graph showing the color distribution of the wavelengths present in typical incandescent, artificial light. Note that the warm (yellow, orange, and red) wavelengths are stronger than those at the cool end of the spectrum. The strongly warm color of incandescent light results from this emphasis.

wavelengths of light. Such charts are developed by making accurate measurements of the intensity of light across the spectrum and then showing the relative intensity at each point in a graph. The continuous spectrum of daylight is shown as a smooth line. The daylight of dawn or sunset rises in the red-orange range and drops somewhat in green-blue wavelengths. A graph of incandescent light shows a similar rise in the warm color tones. The graph of gaseous discharge lights such as neon, mercury, or sodium vapor shows narrow bars or *spikes* with blank spaces in between—these are the discontinuous spectra of such light sources. A graph of fluorescent light combines a smooth curve with a number of spikes. Manufacturers of lighting sources (bulbs and tubes known as *lamps* in the industry) make graphs of this type, which are available as an aid in comparing their products. (See Figures 3.5 through 3.9.)

COLOR TEMPERATURE

In an effort to make the color characteristics of light easily expressed in a single number, the concept of *color temperature* has been developed. Through laboratory measurements, a number is generated that expresses the degree of *warmness* or *coolness* of a particular light source. The unit used is a *kelvin*. High kelvin numbers indicate cool light, lower numbers indicate warm-toned light. A norm for a standard daylight has been selected as 4870 K (kelvin). Incandescent lamps produce light at about 2800 K. Color photographic film is balanced for light of a particular color temperature—if used under light of a different kelvin rating, photos will appear too warm (reddish) or too cool (bluish). If the film rating does not match the light in use, correction filters are used to adjust the color of light to match the sensitivity of the film. (See Figure 3.10.)

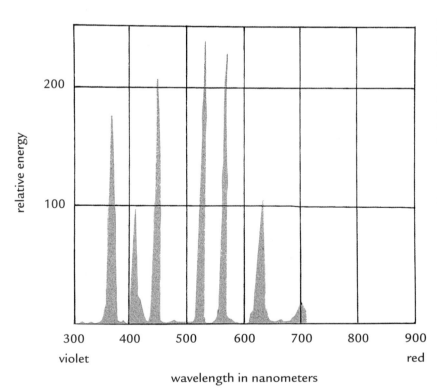

Figure 3.7   Mercury discharge lamps emit strong color at the wavelengths that characterize the mercury spectrum. The spikes of the graph occur at these wavelengths, while no light at all is present at the wavelengths between spikes. Such a spectrum is discontinuous.

Figure 3.8 Sodium-discharge lamps also show a discontinuous spectrum with a concentration in the yellow portion of the spectrum.

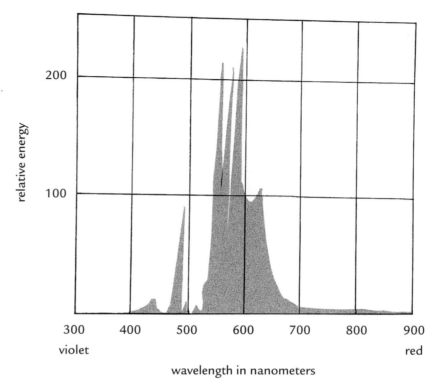

Figure 3.9 Fluorescent light has a spectrum that mixes continuous and discontinuous spectra. The smooth curve represents the continuous spectrum of light that comes from the phosphors that line the tube, and the bars represent the discontinuous spectra created by the gases in the tube.

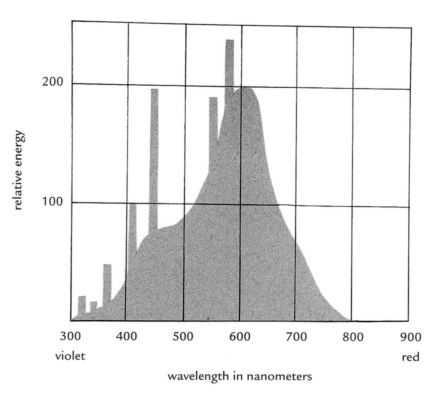

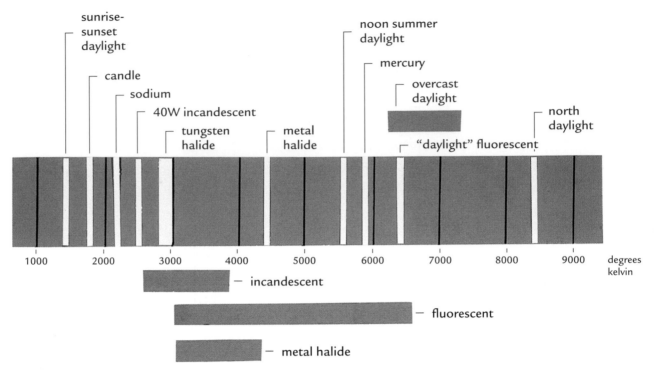

Figure 3.10   A bar chart showing color temperature in Kelvin. White bars show the color temperatures of various typical light sources. The longer bars show that the range of color temperatures from some sources can vary widely.

Another rating that gives some idea of the effect of light on color perception is the *color rendering index* (CRI), which is a single number on a scale from 0 to 100 that rates a light source according to how accurately it illuminates a full range of color. A perfect light source would have a value of 100 CRI. Standard incandescent light has a CRI of 95 or better, fluorescent light falls in a range from 48 to 90 according to the type of tube. In contrast, sodium and mercury gaseous discharge lamps have ratings as low as 21.

In spite of the changing color of daylight with time of day and season, the effect of color constancy makes the relationships of colors satisfactory under all normal daylight. Incandescent light, as might be expected from its high CRI, also is generally satisfactory in its rendition of perceived color. The various types of fluorescent lighting vary considerably and tend to introduce some distortion of colors as perceived.

Low CRI numbers suggest a light source that may distort color relationships quite drastically. The effects of lighting that alter the appearance of colors is known as *metamerism.* When working with color, it is desirable to work under lighting that will be the same as that anticipated in the completed space being designed. If both daylight and artificial light will be in use at various times (as is common with many interiors), it is wise to view a proposed color scheme under both types of lighting.

COLORED LIGHT

Strongly colored light can be produced by the glowing gases of neon, but is more often the result of filtering a white or near-white light. A glass, plastic, or gelatin filter holds back all colors except the one that gives the color its name. A deep red glass, for example, holds back all colors but red.

Many color filters are of less-intense color and so let all colors pass through, but hold back colors other than the color of the filter to some extent. The pale yellows or greens of sunglasses are of this type. Colored lightbulbs use a filtering color on the surface of the bulb that changes the light emitted to a mild or strong color tone. In theater lighting, strongly colored filters are used to produce light that is strongly red, green, or blue so that various color effects can be produced on the stage.

INTERIOR LIGHTING

Most interior spaces are lighted by daylight, an artificial light that is intended to be similar to daylight, or a combination of the two. Such white light appears as normal and makes color vision possible. Aside from the color of light itself, the color seen by the eye is usually thought of as the color of objects, surfaces, and materials. We speak of red brick, a yellow rose, or a blue automobile without giving much thought to the characteristics of these things that makes us see their colors. Objects become visible in light because they reflect the light that falls on them in various ways. It is that reflected light that the lens of the eye focuses on the retina to form images that are used by the brain to generate the sensations that we call seeing. When light falls on any object or surface, the way it reflects that light will vary in a number of ways. One of those ways is that it turns the ambient white light into colored light which arrives at the eye carrying with it the information that makes it possible to recognize the resulting color sensation.

LIGHT REFLECTION

The reflection of light may be of several kinds (see Figure 3.11). The reflection of a mirror keeps the arriving rays of light in their original arrangement, and so reflects back

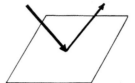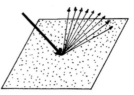

Figure 3.11   Light striking a surface, if not absorbed, is reflected. If a surface is highly polished, light rays are reflected in a single line so as to form the image-like reflections from mirrors and smooth, glossy surfaces. Matte surfaces reflect light in a scatter pattern in all directions.

a sharp image without altering color (unless the mirror itself is colored). Such sharply formed reflections are characteristic of polished metals and can occur to some degree with other smooth, glossy surfaces such as those of glass, some highly polished materials such as dark stone, or from the surface of still water. Most surfaces have some degree of roughness or irregularity that causes arriving light to be reflected in all directions or scattered. Such surfaces are called *matte* or *flat,* and even most glossy surfaces scatter reflected light so as to break up mirrorlike reflection. Rays of light coming from all directions are scattered in all directions so that those arriving at the eye of a viewer are no longer arranged so as to create a reflected image—instead the viewer sees the object or surface with characteristics such as shape, size, and position, but also with the characteristics of color. The color of the incoming light has been colored by the reflecting surface through *absorption.*

LIGHT ABSORPTION

If a surface absorbs all light falling on it, it will appear to be black. Actually, such a perfect black can hardly exist. One can still recognize the shape and details of a black object because it reflects *some* light, however little. Most blacks actually are imperfect in that they not only reflect some light, but that they do so with some degree of

Figure 3.12 Black, although lacking in strong chromatic color, is never pure, in the sense of absorbing all color. Blacks are described as warm or cool according to the hues which modify them.

color selectivity, reflecting a small bit of color so that one can speak of *warm black* (reflecting some reddish tones) or *blue black* (see Figure 3.12). If a surface reflects all colors it will appear to be white. The whites that one sees as colors of paints or materials are also generally imperfect in that they absorb a small part of the light falling on them and so reflect a white tinted with whatever color tone they absorb the least of. Strong color occurs when the reflecting surface absorbs all or most colors except one. That one color then becomes what is thought of as the color of the object. A red apple is colorless in the dark, will have no color under pure blue or green light, but becomes red under white light because its skin absorbs all colors but red. As with black and white, such absorption is never perfect. The red apple reflects *mostly* red light, but it will also reflect some light of other colors. An object that reflects both red and violet light will appear as red-violet (or purple) in color. An object that reflects both red and green light may appear as brown or warm gray according to how much of which colors it absorbs and reflects.

How much of the light falling on a surface that is reflected determines whether the surface appears light or dark. A mirror reflects almost all of the light falling on it, while a white surface reflects a high proportion of light; black reflects very little, and other colors may reflect more or less light according to how light or dark they are. It must be noticed that pure or intense colors

of various hues reflect different percentages of light. A clear, bright yellow reflects a high percentage while bright reds or blues reflect less. The percentage of reflectance of colors in use in interiors influences the brightness of a space for any given level of illumination. Lighting engineers need to know the reflectance percentages of the colors of major surfaces in an interior as an aid to calculating required lighting. A space with dark (low reflectance level) surfaces requires more light to provide adequate illumination than an identical space with light (high reflectance level) surfaces.

Manufacturers of paints and other surface materials often provide data on reflectance values expressed in percentages with 100 percent representing the theoretical level of total reflectance and 0 percent indicating total absorption. Even without laboratory measurements of reflectance levels, it is fairly easy to estimate percentages of reflectance. Typical values are as follows:

White	85 percent
Light gray	35 percent
Dark gray	15 percent
Black	2 percent
Bright red	15 percent
Bright yellow	60 percent
Bright blue	10 percent
Purple	6 percent

The reflectance of other color tones will be at levels comparable to those listed that are of a similar brightness (see Figure 3.13).

COLOR IN INTERIORS

In a typical interior, color will be seen in every element present—walls, floor and ceiling, objects such as furniture, acces-

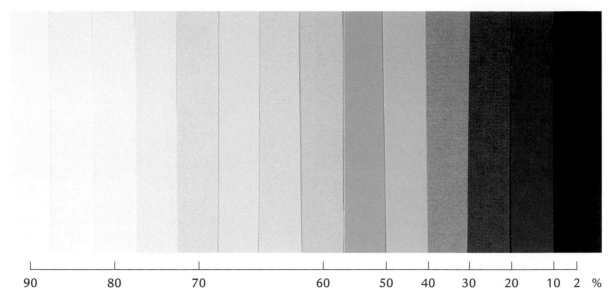

90   80   70   60   50   40   30   20   10 2   %

Figure 3.13   Various colors reflect differing percentages of the light falling on them. The scale indicates the percentage of incident white light that will be reflected by each color, ranging from those most reflective at the left to those least reflective at the right.

sories, artworks, upholstery fabrics, curtains or other window treatments, and even, if they are present, in the clothing of human occupants. Windows may introduce areas of outdoor color or may appear as dark reflecting surfaces at night. Lamps or light fixtures may appear as areas of intense color, actually sources of light. Sunlight or lamps may create bright areas of light which can reflect the colors of the surfaces they fall on to other surfaces and objects. Brightness can vary widely from floor to ceiling and in various parts of a space according to proximity to windows or artificial light sources. Objects cast shadows, forming areas of color that appear darker than the same colors receiving strong light. All of these effects make the selection of color for a complete interior very complex. It is an important element in the skills of the interior designer to be able to visualize such complexities in a way that makes it possible to make good decisions about color—decisions made in an office or studio—that will translate into a satisfying finished project.

COLOR INTERACTION

Although the color reflected from a surface or object of a particular color under a given light source will be a fixed quality, how such color *appears* to a viewer can vary considerably as a result of a number of effects known to color theorists and readily demonstrated by illustrative examples. When making color selections, it is helpful to have these effects in mind so that effects seen in a chart of samples do not distort judgment, and so that effects that will occur in a finished space can be allowed for. Such effects are sometimes called *distortions* or *illusions,* but these terms are really misleading since the effects in question are entirely normal and predictable. The following list summarizes a number of these effects.

• The size of the color area influences the way color is perceived. A small sample may appear lighter, darker, more or less intense than the same color applied to a large surface (see Figure 3.14). A chart

Figure 3.14   The large color sample shown at the left against a dark background appears lighter than the small sample shown on the right against a light background. Both samples are, in fact, identical and are of the color shown by the bar at the center.

Figure 3.15   The effect of simultaneous contrast makes the small neutral-gray sample on the left appear cool placed on a warm background, while the identical gray sample on the right appears warm in contrast to its cool background.

showing the colors available for a particular automobile gives little idea of how an actual car will appear in each color. Selection of textiles, carpet, and wall color from small samples can lead to unpleasant surprises when the large color areas are seen. It is wise to inspect a large sample of such materials before making a final choice.

• *Simultaneous contrast* is the term used to describe the effect that adjacent areas of color have on one another. In general, an area of color will seem to shift

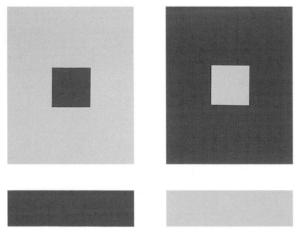

Figure 3.16   A dark tone placed on a light background appears darker than it is, while the light tone placed on a dark background appears lighter than it is.

toward a hue complementary to that of an adjacent area. A gray seen adjacent to or superimposed on an area of red will appear greenish, while the same gray, seen against an area of green, will appear reddish (see Figure 3.15). This effect is also seen with more chromatic colors—green will appear more intense (more green) when adjacent to red, less intense when placed adjacent to blue. The blue shifts the green toward its complement, orange, and so neutralizes the green color to some degree. The studies and artworks produced by Josef Albers with the title *Interaction of Color* (1963 and 1971) demonstrate such effects fully. In Albers's studies, areas of uniform color seem to shift in tone near an edge where they meet another, contrasting color creating a fringe of seemingly varied color. (See Figures 3.16 through 3.19.)

The effect called *successive contrast,* or *afterimage,* is another form of simultaneous contrast in which the contrasting colors are seen successively in time rather than adjacent in space. It occurs when, after looking at a strong color for a period of time, if vision is shifted to a white surface, the white will appear to be colored as a complementary of the first color. The same effect occurs (somewhat less obviously) when vision is shifted from one color to another (see Figure 3.17). After looking at red, green will look more intensely green; after looking at blue the same green will appear dulled.

Such effects can occur in interior spaces. A green carpet, for example, will appear brighter adjacent to a red (or pink) wall, duller if adjacent to a blue or green wall—a shift caused by simultaneous contrast. When walking from a space of intense color into an adjacent space of neutral colors, the neutral space will appear tinted with the complementary of the color of the first space. When passing from a vestibule or anteroom with strong red color, for example, an adjacent room of white and neutrals will appear greenish for a short time.

• Advancing and receding colors can distort perception of distance and can be used to modify perceptions of spatial relations. Warm colors tend to appear closer than they are, cool colors appear farther away. Dark colors tend to advance (seem closer), light colors to recede (seem farther away). Intense colors advance, more neutral colors recede. These effects interact so that a dark red seems to advance more strongly than a pale pink. The darkness of

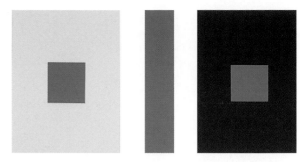

Figure 3.17   A medium tone placed on a light background (*at left*) appears darker than it is, while the same tone placed on a dark background (*at right*) appears lighter than it is. Both small samples are the same as the bar at the center.

a dark blue may make it advance more strongly than a pale orange. In interiors, the apparent shape of a space can be somewhat modified by these effects. A long, narrow room, for example, can be made to seem more normal in proportions if the end walls are given a color that is warm, deep, and intense while the side walls are given lighter, less-saturated colors. A low ceiling will seem less oppressive if its color is light while a high ceiling can be made to seem lower by a dark color such as dark blue, gray, or black. Selection of materials with

Figure 3.18   The light tone placed on a dark background (*at left*) appears lighter than it is, while the dark tone placed on the lighter background (*at right*) appears darker than it is.

Figure 3.19   The dark background on the left appears darker than it is in contrast to the light sample at its center. The dark background at the right, in contrast, appears lighter than it is in relation to the dark sample at its center. The effect is most pronounced at the edge where the background meets the superimposed sample.

Figure 3.20   The same color can appear different when seen in a matte or flat finish (*left*) as compared to a gloss finish (*right*).

strong color can also lead to such effects, intentionally or not. A room lined with dark wood paneling will seem smaller than it is because of the warm, dark color of all four walls. The same room will seem much larger with walls painted pale green. Dark colors tend to make objects appear smaller than they are, while light colors have the opposite effect.

• Texture and the nature of surfaces, as previously discussed, can seem to alter color. In general, the rougher a texture, the darker its color will appear. This results from the effect of shade and shadow cast by the elements of material that form the texture. A smooth textile will appear lighter in tone than a heavily textured fabric dyed the same color. Some textures, by catching light from one direction, reflect ambient light to some degree while developing darkening shadow in the other. The color of such materials can seem to vary with the direction of light and angle of viewing. Color is least modified when the colored surface is smooth but not reflective—a true flat or matte. A surface that is polished or coated so as to produce surface reflection is described as *glossy*. Gloss modifies color by placing a layer of what is often called *veiling reflection* over the actual color, and so diluting it (see Figure 3.20).

This will tend to both lighten color and reduce its intensity or saturation. This effect is easily demonstrated by placing a sheet of glass or transparent plastic over a sample of flat color. Many yarns in common use for woven textiles and carpets include fibers that are glossy. Their effect is to introduce a degree of *glitter* that alters the appearance of the basic color.

As a practical matter, a sample color can only be judged with certainty if the sample has the same texture and gloss as the finished surface. A sample of a flat colored paper used to identify a dye color for carpet, for example, can give an unanticipated result.

• *Additive mixture,* or *fusion,* is the term that refers to the way different colors in small areas appear to mix or fuse when seen at a distance great enough that the eye cannot separate them. A textile woven of yarn in two colors, for example, will seem to be of one solid color when seen from a distance (see Figures 3.21 and 3.22). Red and blue, for example, will seem to be a solid purple. Strong colors that are complementary will be seen as a gray or brownish neutral. Red and green, for example, combine in this way. A small material sample of wallpaper, for instance, with a small pattern of stripes, dots, or figures may appear to take on a solid color that is a mixture of the colors of the pattern when seen from a distance.

• *Vibration* is the visual effect that occurs when strongly contrasting, bright colors are placed adjacent to one another (see Figure 3.23). The eye focuses different colors in slightly different planes. It cannot, therefore, focus totally sharply on bright red and bright green if they are adjacent. The lines of meeting become seemingly blurred and the colors seem to vibrate. This is an effect that has been exploited effectively in painting by the artists whose work has come to be known as *op art*. While this effect is rarely encountered in interior spaces, it may account in part for the com-

Figure 3.21   A multicolor weave (two colors in this case) viewed at a close distance.

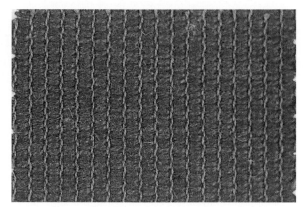

Figure 3.22   The same multicolor textile, seen from a distance, appears to take on a single color as a result of the two tones mixing together.

monly observed sense of harshness or disharmony in color schemes that juxtapose strongly contrasting colors.

COLOR BLINDNESS

Strictly speaking, while not an effect of color, *color blindness* (or, as it is sometimes called, *color weakness*) should be mentioned since it is a matter for occasional concern in interior design work. Total color blindness, an inability to see color at all, is actually very rare. The kind of color blindness that is not so unusual is an inability to distinguish certain pairs of colors, which are both seen as tones of gray. The colors most often confused are red and green. Oddly, such limited color blindness is often not obvious to those with this condition, while others, who may have difficulty working with color, wonder if color blindness is the cause of their problem. There are test charts in which figures of one color are shown against backgrounds of another color in such a way that the figures are easily seen by those with normal vision, but are invisible to those who are color blind, making the diagnosis of color blindness very simple. In practice, color blindness does not interfere with work in

interior design to any significant degree. Most colors are readily distinguished and even the colors confused appear as different tones of gray so that color blindness rarely leads to any serious errors. People who know that their vision is impeded in this way may wish to avoid the colors often confused or may ask for comment from a person with normal vision as a check against any possible problems.

Figure 3.23   Sharply contrasting tones of complementary colors can produce the effect called vibration, where, at the edges of the colors, the inability of the eye to focus both tones in the same plane produces an effect of movement. Here red and green vibrate with this effect.

4
Color Systems

The complexities of color perception, the problems of understanding color interaction, and the difficulties often experienced in working with color have led to a number of efforts to develop a systematic organization in which every possible color can be defined and all possible relationships studied. Isaac Newton (1642–1727) observed the action of a glass prism as it split up a beam of white light into a rainbowlike spectrum, and he deduced that white light is a blend of all colors. It is not surprising that it was in the development of scientific thinking in the eighteenth century that the first formal studies of color theory surfaced. The German poet-philosopher-scientist Johann Wolfgang von Goethe (1749–1832) published *Zur Farbenlehre* in 1810, which was an early effort to bring the confusing realities of the subject into systematic order. In 1840, an English translation entitled *A Theory of Colours* by Charles Locke Eastlake was published. Unfortunately, Goethe rejected Newton's sound understanding of the basic physics of color and substituted an interesting but erroneous theory based on two primary colors, yellow and blue, which he viewed as modifications of white

and black. He observed correctly that the combination of yellow and blue would produce green, but he was unable to account for red, a color that cannot be mixed from any others. Goethe proposed the arrangement of the six colors, red, orange, yellow, green, blue, and violet, in that order and observed that, when arranged in a circle, the colors that can be mixed fell between colors on either side that cannot be mixed. He was thus the inventor of the color circle or color wheel which is basic to most modern color theory and is a major topic in Chapter 5.

The somewhat different behavior of colors of light and colors of surfaces, whether natural tones of materials or those created by pigments and dyes (discussed in Chapter 5 as additive and subtractive color), seems to have confused the development of color theory and still creates some confusing distinctions in the various color systems currently in use. Interior design is largely concerned with the colors of surfaces, objects, and materials, whether natural or created with paints, dyes, and other colorants. This is *subtractive color,* which results from the way various substances absorb color from white light and reflect back only the limited color which can be given a name.

It seems to have been the English theorist David Brewster (1781–1868) who first established the basics of subtractive color by defining primary colors as those that cannot be mixed from any other colors. The three subtractive primaries now most generally accepted are red, yellow, and blue. Mixtures of the possible pairs of these colors generate the three secondaries, orange (red and yellow), green (yellow and blue), and violet or purple (blue and red) (see Figure 4.1). The three primaries and the resulting secondaries are readily observed in the spectrum produced when white light passes through a prism. They occur in a logical order that places the secondaries between the primaries which make them up; violet appears at the end of the band beyond blue. The spectrum order is thus (see also Figure 4.2):

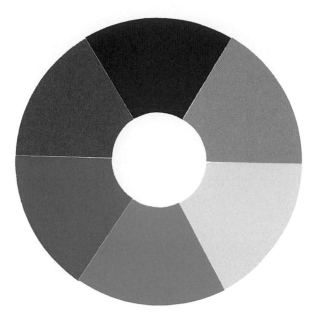

Figure 4.1   The six colors most readily identified here arranged in the circle that places violet next to red.

red, orange, yellow, green, blue, violet

These strong and clearly defined colors and the blends that fall between them place all clear and intense colors in a logical order and, when bent into a circle, create the color wheel that Goethe proposed. In it, violet falls between red and blue, confirming the logic of this arrangement. It is, however, obvious that variants of each color are possible, lighter or darker tones, or tones that have been dulled by mixing. An effort to make sense of these realities has led to an understanding that defining any observed color requires placement within three separate scales, often called *three dimensions.* These three scales are as follows:

Hue: A term for the position of a color along the band of the spectrum. The six colors previously named are hues, and the colors that fall between the named six are also hues that can be defined in physical terms based on the wavelengths of the light energy that creates them.

Value: This is the usual term for the lightness or darkness of a particular color sample. There can be a dark blue or a light blue of exactly the same hue. In general, a sample of a particular hue can be made lighter by mixing with white, darker by mixing with black. It is usual to make up a scale of equal steps from white to black, a *gray scale,* to define the value of a color by matching its lightness or darkness to a step on the scale.

Saturation, chroma, or intensity: These are each terms for the purity of a particular color. When an intense primary, secondary, or intermediate color of the spectrum is made lighter or darker by the addition of white, black, or gray, or when it is dulled by the addition of a color remote from it in the spectrum, it will become less pure, or intense, and is therefore called

Figure 4.2   The six colors, three primaries and three secondaries, in a ribbon in rainbow order.

Figure 4.3   A chroma or saturation scale of red in a series of steps from maximum saturation on the left to a desaturated tone at the extreme right.

desaturated, or *of a lowered chroma* (see Figure 4.3).

Each of the color systems in current use deals with these three aspects of color in a methodical way. The following summaries of several systems give an idea of their similarity and differences.

MUNSELL SYSTEM

Albert Munsell (1858–1918), an American artist and teacher, developed this system which was first published in 1915 and is still available in publications, charts, and samples. Any color sample is defined by its hue, its value, and its chroma (saturation). Hues are designated by letters (*R* for red, *BG* for blue-green, etc.), values are designated by numbers from 1 to 9 with the value of black as 1, white as 9, and values in between as numbers that correspond to

steps in a value scale of grays. The Munsell system is made confusing to some degree because the scale of hues is divided into five principal colors—red, yellow, green, blue, and purple—instead of the three primaries and three secondaries that seem to conform more logically to the observed spectrum. Between each pair of principal colors there is an intermediate hue with a two-letter designation. The number 5 precedes the letter identification of each of these 10 hues. Hues intermediate between these 10 are identified by additional numbers so that steps from green to blue, for example, are designated 5G, 7.5G, 10G, 2.5BG, 5BG, 7.5BG, 10BG, 2.5B, 5B. A diagram makes these steps somewhat more clear. A full color circle of 100 hues is generated.

The circle of hues forms the horizontal plane of an arrangement in which the scale of values from 1 to 10 becomes a vertical central axis. The most saturated sample of each hue is placed at a distance from this axis that leaves room for a series of numbered steps of saturation (chroma) outward from the gray of the value scale (see Figure 4.4). The most intense chroma is given the number 14 while the most neutral step (closest to gray) is given the number 2. The notation for a particular sample is given in the order hue, value/chroma. Thus 5R 5/8 indicates a tone that has a hue of red, a value of 5 and a chroma of 8. This will be a tone of medium value with a saturation about halfway between maximum chroma and neutral gray. If all possible samples are arranged in logical progression, a *color solid* results that is somewhat like a sphere, but, since some hues reach maximum chroma in more steps than others and maximum chroma is reached at different levels of value with different hues, the resultant solid is not so much a smooth globe, as a somewhat lumpy stepped solid (see Figure 4.5). A chart for a particular hue is the result of slicing this solid in a vertical plane and displaying half of the solid from the neutral axis

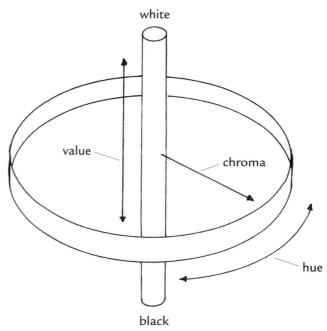

Figure 4.4   The basic concept of the Munsell system uses steps of value arranged along a vertical central axis, from black at the bottom to white at the top; hues arranged in a circle with maximum saturation (chroma) at the outer rim; and steps of saturation moving downward from the outer rim toward the center axis.

Figure 4.5   A Munsell color solid with all colors arranged in accordance with the plan in which hue is arranged in a circle, value up and down a center axis, and chroma (saturation) in steps from the center outward. The irregularity of the form results from the ways in which different hues vary in their steps of value and saturation levels.

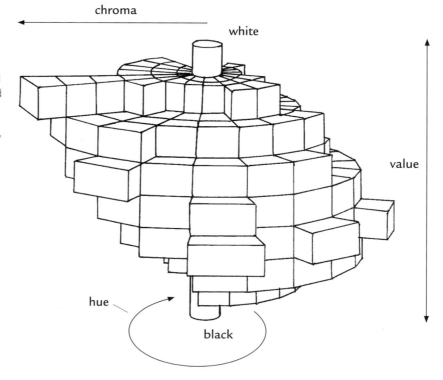

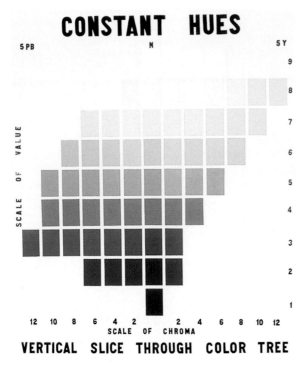

5 PB   N   5 Y

SCALE OF VALUE

12 10 8 6 4 2   2 4 6 8 10 12
SCALE OF CHROMA

VERTICAL SLICE THROUGH COLOR TREE

Figure 4.6 A slice through the Munsell color solid shows a single hue in a range of values (the vertical direction) and saturation (the horizontal direction).

to maximum chroma. The samples line up the possible steps of chroma and each level of value (see Figure 4.6).

The Munsell system has proven to be useful and practical, but most users prefer a modified version in which there are three primaries and three secondaries with all hues designated by combinations of letter as discussed in Chapter 5. Thus modified, the Munsell system offers an excellent systematic basis for understanding all subtractive color phenomena.

Munsell color materials are currently distributed by the Macbeth Division of Kollmorgan Instruments Corporation of New Windsor, New York. Available materials include charts on loose-leaf pages that assemble into a notebook-format color atlas. Removable (and replaceable) color chips are provided: about 1300 in matte finish and 1600 in a high gloss (see Figure 4.7). Additional groups of near-neutral and

pastel colors are also available. Various teaching aids include three-dimensional model units that present the theoretical color solid in realistic form (see Figure 4.8).

OSTWALD SYSTEM

A second well-known system has some similarities to the Munsell system along with some major differences. Wilhelm Ostwald (1853–1932) was a German scientist who attempted to create a consistently logical system in which all colors would be placed in an orderly pattern. As in the Munsell system, hues are arranged in a circle in spectrum order with *four* primary hues (see Figure 4.9). These four, red, yellow, green, and blue, are placed at the quarter points of a circle and intermediate secondaries are introduced halfway between each pair (see Figure 4.10). The full sequence of eight hues is as follows:

red, orange, yellow, leaf green, sea green, turquoise, ultramarine, purple

Two additional steps are inserted between each of the eight hues creating a total of twenty-four hues. A gray scale forms the center axis of the Ostwald color solid with eight steps between black at the bottom and white at the top which are lettered *a* for white to *p* for black. In Ostwald's view, any possible color is the result of the mixture of a pure hue with white and black. The hues are given numbers from 1 to 24. To identify a particular color tone, the number of the hue is followed by two letters, the first indicating the level of white added, the second letter the level of black. For example, 10pa indicates hue 10 in its purest form since the level of white *p* means no white at all and the level of black *a* means no black at all. The designation 10ec would be the same hue plus white at level *e* and black at level *c,* that is, considerable white and much less black. A light but considerably

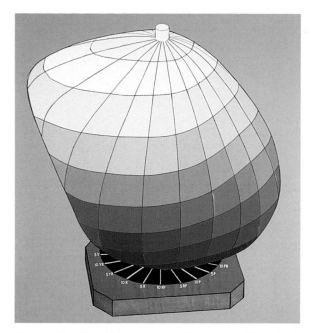

Figure 4.7   The Munsell color atlas opened to a typical page.

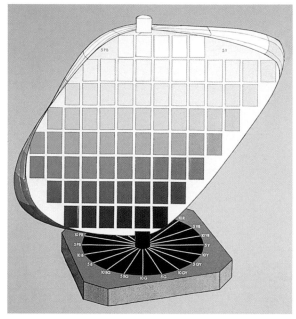

Figure 4.8   The Munsell color solid in the form of a three-dimensional model.

neutralized tone of the basic hue would be thus identified.

The Ostwald system creates a color solid of two cones (see Figure 4.11); slicing a half vertical section reveals a triangle with white at its top apex, black at the bottom, and a saturated hue at the third apex. Twenty-eight tones appear in the triangle with lighter tones (*tints*) in the upper half, darker tones (*shades*) in the lower half, and with the vertical bands moving from pure hue at the outer apex to near neutral nearest to the neutral axis. The Ostwald system forces pure hues to the equator of the solid so as to avoid the irregularity of the Munsell solid, but as a result, the steps of gradation between adjacent tones are greater for some parts of the hue charts than for others. As a practical matter, since the Ostwald system generates 680 distinct tones, this is not troublesome. It is the choice of four, rather than three, primaries that seems of questionable logic, and the number and letter designations used are inconvenient to learn and remember.

Figure 4.9   The four primaries identified in the Ostwald system add green to the more usual three primary tones.

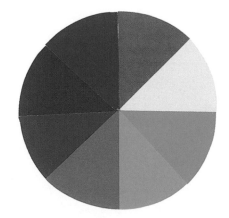

Figure 4.10   The Ostwald system creates an eight-color wheel with four primaries and four secondaries.

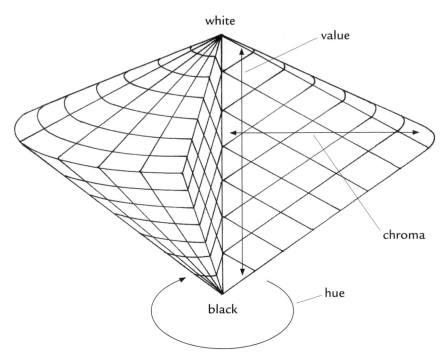

A number of other color systems have been developed, each with its own special merits for certain applications. Although the Munsell and Ostwald systems have, with modifications, proven most useful in interior design, it is of interest to have some knowledge of several other systems.

DIN SYSTEM

The German organization responsible for many standardization programs in industry, Deutsches Institut für Normung, is the source of the DIN color system which identifies some 900 standard colors. Red, yellow, green, and blue are viewed as primaries with each color classified by hue, saturation, and lightness. It is widely used in European industry.

CIE SYSTEM

The system developed by the Commission Internationale de l'Eclairage is particularly suited to scientific application dealing with the color of light sources and the reflection and transmission of light by objects in numerically quantifiable terms. It is most useful in the matching of colors under various light sources in laboratory applications.

OAS SYSTEM

The Optical Society of America has developed a set of Uniform Color Scales (OAS-UCS) consisting of 558 standard color samples which are conceived as spaced in uniform steps of variation in each color attribute. Colors are represented by spheres which can be clustered so as to build up a color solid having the form of a three-dimensional polyhedron. The conceptual basis of the system is complex and of more theoretical than practical value. In practice it is generally similar to the older Munsell system.

KÜPPERS SYSTEM

This system is developed in Harald Küpper's 1972 book *Color: Origin, Systems, Uses*. It makes use of a color circle of six primaries, red, yellow, green, cyan, blue, and magenta. The introduction of the dye names *cyan* (a slightly greenish blue) and *magenta* (a red-violet) relates to the generally accepted system of color printing in which four halftone plates are used that overprint a grid of tiny dots using the *process color* inks, yellow, cyan, and magenta, plus black. The fact that the appearance of virtually any color can be generated by the three ink colors (other than black) creates a basis for regarding these as the three primary colors. In the Küppers system, the six-color wheel is further elaborated by the introduction of intermediate steps to generate a twenty-four hue wheel similar to that of the Ostwald system. The Küppers color solid is a six-faced form, similar to a cube but with faces that are diamond-shaped rather than square. The Küppers system attempts a variation on the Brewster or Prang systems in an effort to take into account the behavior of additive color and so has particular bearing on matters relating to color lighting and color printing.

GERRITSEN SYSTEM

Frans Gerritsen in his 1975 book, *Theory and Practice of Color,* develops a theory based on the ability of the retina of the human eye to distinguish red, green, and blue. These hues are therefore designated as primaries while yellow, cyan, and magenta (the process colors of color printing) are viewed as secondaries, each sensed by two of the retinal receptors. This relates best to the understanding of the phenomena of color light—that is, to additive color. With the six primaries and secondaries arranged in a circle, additional steps are introduced to create eighteen hues or (with additional intermediates), fifty-four hues. Values are developed as steps of reduction of intensity of the primaries. Neutrals result from the mixing of the three primaries, which, at full intensity, produce

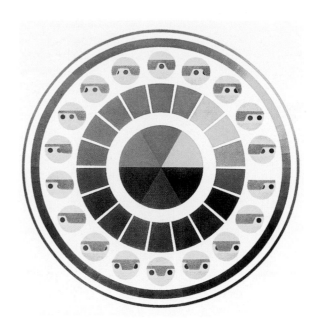

Figure 4.12   A chart from the Gerritsen system with diagrams that show the relative strength of the three additive primaries which form each hue.

white; grays result as the intensity of the primaries is reduced but maintained at an equal level. (See Figure 4.12). This accords with the behavior of additive color (light) mixing but generates the unusual pairing of complementaries as follows:

blue-yellow
green-magenta
red-cyan

NCS SYSTEM

The Swedish Natural Color System is based on the study of color perception by Ewald Hering (1834–1918). It defines six natural color sensations as red, yellow, green, blue, black, and white. The chromatic colors are arranged in a circle with nine intermediate steps between each of the basic four, making forty hues. For each hue, a triangular chart is developed with the pure hue, white, and black at the three vertices. Each side of this triangle is divided into 10 steps so that each triangu-

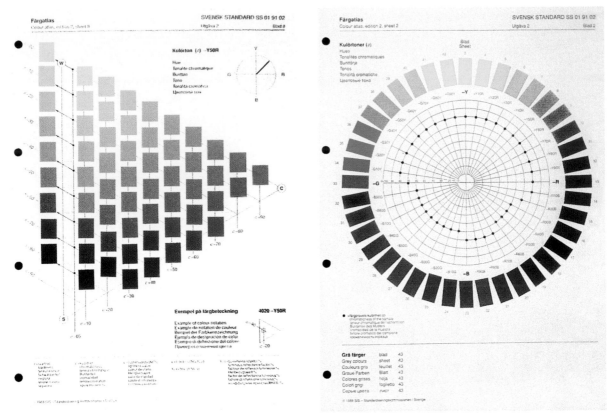

Figure 4.13 *a* and *b*   Charts from the NCS system as it appears in that system's color atlas.

lar chart is made up of 66 colors. The 40 hue charts thus contain 2640 distinct samples. A color atlas has been developed, and 1526 of the colors are produced as colored papers suitable for use in design work (see Figure 4.13). Materials for practical use of the NCS system are available from the Swedish Standards Institution of Stockholm, Sweden. The NCS system shares many characteristics of the earlier Ostwald system including the theoretical color solid of two cones, one inverted over the other. It differs in the extent of its scientific base and in the ready availability of related materials of practical value.

COLOR-AID SYSTEM

This system provides high-quality colored papers in a range of tones organized in a way generally based on the Munsell sys-

tem. A range of 220 colors, offered in several formats, has recently been expanded to 314 tones, each identified with letters designating hue and numbers for tints and shades. A particular paper, for example, is identified as BGB hue, (the most saturated tone of blue-green-blue) or BGB tint 1, 2, and so on or shade 1, 2, and so on. The number of tints and shades provided for each hue is usually 3 or 4, depending on the hue. There are a total of 34 hues, 100 tints, 47 shades, an additional 114 pastel tones, an additional range of 17 grays, black, white, and 9 additional intense colors that fall outside the range of the basic system. Each tone is available in single 18 × 24 inch sheets, and all tones are available in sets of swatches in 6 × 9, 4½ × 6, and 2 × 3 inch sizes. Several partial, selected sets are also offered in addition to charts and an explanatory booklet. The Color-Aid products are readily available and convenient for desktop use. (See Figure 4.14.)

PAUL KLEE AT THE BAUHAUS

As a teacher at the Bauhaus in the 1920s, the great modern artist Paul Klee (1879–1940) was responsible for teaching the basic introductory course comparable to the foundation art courses now taught at many American schools of art and design. In his notebooks, he left a detailed record of his approach to the development of a theoretical color system having much in common with the systems previously discussed, but using an imagined color solid in the form of a sphere with a vertical axis of values and an equator formed by a color circle using three primaries and three secondaries equally spaced around the circle. Saturation is understood to be maximum at the outer equatorial rim and diminishes inward toward the neutral value at the central axis. Klee's diagrams that appear in his published notebooks (notes of November 1922) illustrate this color organization with great clarity and elegance.

COLOR SYSTEMS IN PRACTICE

It is somewhat surprising to note that, in spite of the many carefully developed color systems, no available system seems to be ideally suited to interior design work. The teaching of color in design schools and the color work of most practicing designers is generally based on a hybrid approach that uses the concepts common to all color systems but not tied to any system in complete detail.

A designer does not ordinarily have any need to fit color decisions to the terminology of a system—colors are selected and communicated through actual samples or

Figure 4.14   A sample book showing colors from the Color-Aid system.

specification of specific products or materials. The value of study of the most practical of the color systems comes from the way in which they organize the variabilities of color so that selections can be made in an orderly and logical way, and so that color schemes can be developed on the basis of a systematic awareness of color principles.

In the study of color harmony as discussed in Chapter 5, awareness of the color wheel is essential to understanding such terms as *primary* or *secondary.* The types of color schemes that are the subject of Chapter 7 are similarly based in color system theory. Such terms as *analogous, complementary,* and *triad,* as applied to schemes, are only understandable on the basis of a color wheel and the terminology of a color system. Since each system is somewhat different, it is necessary to choose the most useful aspects of the systems that best relate to interior design work. The Munsell system is widely regarded as the most practical except for its use of four primary colors. A modified form of the Munsell system is most often taught in design schools and so has become the usual basis for color work in interior design. In this book, such a system will be assumed to be most practical and understandable. In the interest of clarity, it is summarized here.

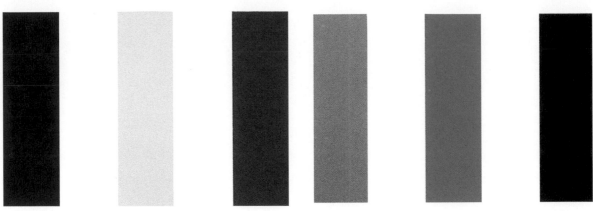

Figure 4.15   The three primaries: red, yellow, and blue.

Figure 4.16   The three secondaries: orange, green, and violet.

SIMPLIFIED COLOR SYSTEM

It is common practice to think of color in terms that are based on Munsell, but that accept three, rather than four, primary colors and that substitute a simplified vocabulary for the notation of the Munsell system. The terms and concepts of this approach are as follows:

> *Color* can be described in terms of three aspects, or *dimensions.* These are hue, value, and saturation or *chroma.*
>
> *Hue* refers to the position of a color in the spectrum or color wheel. It gives the color its basic name, such as red, blue, or green.
>
> There are three *primary hues,* red, yellow, and blue. Between each pair of primaries, there is a *secondary hue* made by mixing the primaries on either side of it. The three secondaries are orange, green, and violet. Additional hues called tertiaries and quaternaries are intermediate steps between the six basic hues. (See Figures 4.15 and 4.16.)
>
> *Tertiaries* are named by combining the names of the primaries and secondaries that they fall between, for example, red-orange, abbreviated

> RO. *Quaternaries* are identified by three-letter abbreviations, such as BVB for the hue between blue-violet and blue. (See Figures 4.17 and 4.18.)
>
> Hues that are opposite or near opposite in position on the color wheel are *complementaries.*
>
> *Value* is the term for the level of lightness or darkness of a color as compared to a scale of grays ranging from black to white. Colors at the upper range of the scale are called *light,* those near the middle, *medium,* and those near the bottom are *dark.* Colors made by mixture with white may be called *tints.* Colors at the lower end of the scale made by mixture with black or a complementary may be called *shades.* (See Figure 4.19.)
>
> *Saturation* or *chroma* is the level of intensity or purity of a color. A pure hue is at the highest level of saturation. Saturation is lowered by addition of white (to make a light color), of black (to make a dark color), of both white and black (to make a grayed color), by the addition of a complementary or near complementary (to make a partially or totally neutralized color), or by the

Figure 4.17 The six tertiaries, each between neighboring primaries and secondaries.

Figure 4.18 The 12 quaternaries, each between a tertiary and an adjacent primary or secondary.

Figure 4.19 A gray scale of values in steps from the lightest (close to white) to the darkest (close to black).

addition of a combination of such admixtures. A color of high intensity (saturation) is often called *bright* while one of low saturation may be called *dull*. The word *pale* suggests a light value at low saturation, while *deep* indicates darker value at high saturation.

While this simplified view of systematic color does not provide the precision of identification attempted by more scientific color systems, it serves well in practice. Designation of a color in Munsell notation, such as 7BG 5/4, while precise, does not readily bring a color tone to mind. Similarly, an Ostwald designation, such as 5gc, is hard to interpret. Use of familiar words tends to be more readily understandable. Designations such as *light, bright blue* or *dull, dark red* may not be precise, but they bring a color tone to mind without reference to charts or diagrams.

It should be noted, as the Munsell color solid clearly demonstrates, that various hues reach maximum saturation at differing levels of value. Maximum saturation of yellow, for example, occurs at a fairly light value. Blue and violet of maximum saturation occur farther down the value scale.

COLOR TERMINOLOGY

Identification of colors is complicated by the fact that, in ordinary speech, terms are

Figure 4.20 Tints (*above*) and shades (*below*) give little hint of the hues from which they originate. Red, yellow, and orange are the basic hues from which these tints and shades are derived.

used that do not separate the three determinants of a particular color sample, and these terms often do not include identification of hue (see Figure 4.20). Light red of medium to low saturation, for example, is usually called pink. Darker shades of violet are commonly called purple. Tones at the lower end of the value and saturation scale are usually called by such names as deep tan, brown, warm gray, or cool gray. Very light values of low saturation are often called cream, beige, light tan, or even white with some modifier to generate such terms as off-white, bone white, or antique white. More fanciful terms, such as oyster shell or moonglow, have no generally accepted meaning and can only be interpreted by reference to a color sample chart, usually the chart provided by a particular manufacturer of paint or some other color product.

Many color names, although not defined by exact specifications, are sufficiently widely accepted to be useful in many contexts. Where a name refers to a familiar object that has a consistent color, the name becomes generally useful. Two of the names for basic hues have such a reference. Orange is the name of a fruit, violet that of a flower. Although not all oranges or all violets are of identical color, there is enough consistency to make these terms widely understood. Other such color names include:

Fruits:	lemon yellow
	lime green
	apricot
	peach
Flowers:	rose
	primrose
	violet

Some color names are the names of particular pigments or dyes. These are familiar names to artists working with oils or watercolors:

Pigments:	vermilion
	yellow ochre
	sienna (raw or burnt)
	umber (raw or burnt)
	cadmium (red, orange, yellows)
	chromium (yellows, green)
	cobalt blue
	cerulean blue
	aureolin (cobalt yellow)
	ultramarine (blue)
	sepia
	viridian (green)
Dyes:	Prussian blue
	indigo
	madder (rose or brown)
	alizarin (red, crimson)
	cyan
	magenta

Other color names refer to people who were inventors or users of a particular color, such as Hooker's green, Vandyke brown, or Veronese green, or to place names, as in French blue, Antwerp blue, Venetian red, or Pompeiian red.

Other color names in general use and understood as having fairly consistent meanings might include the following:

scarlet
crimson
claret
burgundy
russet
maroon
rust
flame
pumpkin
gold
mustard
salmon
chartreuse
citron
jade
emerald (green)
leaf green
sea green
olive (green)
olive drab
turquoise
azure
sky blue
navy (blue)
midnight blue
slate (blue or gray)
plum
mulberry
mauve
lavender
beige
buff
sand
oyster (gray)
putty
khaki
gunmetal
charcoal (gray)

More fanciful names are commonplace in fashion-related fields and the product color designation used by various manufacturers. Color charts for paints, tiles, carpets, and other materials are filled with such names as lotus pink, raven, teal, moonglow, ambrosia, saffron, sage, cocoa, coffee, brick, granite, and tobacco. While such terms suggest a color tone that can be guessed at with some probability of correctness, only a sample can assure accurate understanding of the intended meaning.

SPECIAL COLOR ISSUES

There are a number of special color effects that the established color systems do not deal with effectively. The colors defined by systems are always assumed to be solid tones of uniform flat or matte (not glossy) color applied to a smooth surface. The perception of a color tone can be modified by various situations that depart from this norm. Among these—one that is commonplace in interior design work—is the effect of gloss surfaces. In theory, when lighted so as to avoid reflection, a glossy specimen of a color should appear identical to a matte sample. In practice, a glossy surface can modify a color perception to a considerable degree. There are degrees of gloss, such as the semigloss, usually offered in paints as an alternative to flat and high-gloss, and comparison of samples will show the slight color shifts that each level of gloss introduces.

Metallic colors also present problems of classification. Actual metals, such as gold, silver, copper, brass, bronze, aluminum, and chromium, each have a particular color characteristic. The names of metals are sometimes given to a color tone apart from the metallic effect, but paints, inks, and papers are available that imitate the color qualities of metals with considerable success. Metals, especially when polished, reflect the light that falls on them, acting, to a degree, as mirrors. Polished chrome is often called *mirror chrome* because of its mirrorlike reflection of all light falling on it. Silver and aluminum similarly reflect all colors of light. Other metals absorb most color and reflect only a limited range of hues. Gold and brass reflect slightly orange-yellow light creating the characteristic golden tone. Copper, when polished and protected from tarnish, reflects a more nearly orange tone. Bronze appears as a metallic brown. Aluminum appears silvery when polished, but oxidizes to a dull gray; it is often finished with a process called *anodizing* that prevents oxidation and dulling but can introduce colors in a range from yellows (that simulate gold or brass) through browns and blues (that retain metallic reflectional qualities) to solid black. Metallic paints use an admixture of a powdered metal that may simulate metal or may introduce a metallic glitter in other colors.

Transparent and translucent materials such as glass and plastic can also produce effects of color. A clear glass or plastic passes all colors equally, but colorants added to these materials filter out some hues and give the material the color of the hues that are allowed to pass through. Slight tints are often used for glazing to reduce heat and glare. Sunglasses are a familiar use for strongly tinted glass or plastic. Colors such as green or yellow alter the color of objects seen through them, although, if the coloration is not intense, human vision tends to make a correction that allows colors to be seen at near normal appearance. Intense coloration of a transparent material filters out all hues except those that give the material its hue. Such colored glass is commonly used to give color to a light source, as in theater lighting where glass, plastic, or gelatin filters color white light to produce strong color. A striking use of colored glass is its role as the basis for the art of stained glass, well known for its development in medieval church design (see Figure 4.21). The light passing through a stained glass window takes on the colors of the glass, sometimes casting colored patterns on floor or wall surfaces. Stained glass generally uses many colors so that the overall impact on interior spaces is not usually that of a single hue but rather a color tone that is resultant from the various glass colors present. Glass of an intense single hue is rarely used in interior design practice but is familiar in such special applications as traffic lights and warning and exit lights.

Colored mirror combines the effects of metallic reflection and colored glass. The silvering of a mirror normally reflects all colors equally through clear glass, but if a tinted glass is substituted, the ambient light is colored by passing through the glass twice. Blue, pale orange, or bronze tinted mirrors have had some popularity in some recent periods. Neutral tinted mirrors lower the intensity of mirror reflection without altering the balance of colors significantly.

MIXED COLOR EFFECTS

While color systems deal with solid colors, many color effects encountered in practice involve colors made up of several tones that, when seen at a distance, appear to form a single color. Textile weaves, for example, often use yarns of several colors that can be observed individually when looking closely or under a magnifier, but that, when seen at normal viewing distances, appear to merge. Blue and red yarn, for example, may be seen as purple. Many textiles that appear to be gray, brown, or tan turn out, when viewed under a magnifying glass, to use a number of colors that mix in the eye and mind of the viewer (see Figures 4.22 and 4.23). The effect of such mixtures is often more lively and attractive than a single, solid color of a seemingly matching tone. This effect, often called *broken color,* was well known to the

Figure 4.21 Medieval stained glass in the windows of the church of St. Chapelle in Paris. Brilliantly colorful glass projects color patterns into the church interior. (*Photo by John Pile.*)

impressionist painters who used intense colors in small strokes closely juxtaposed in order to get a more luminous tone than would result from mixing the paints before application.

Similar color effects can be observed with many materials that appear to be of uniform color at a distance but that actually are made up of small elements of various colors. Stones such as granite, ordinary concrete or cement, woods with grain patterns, and many synthetic materials demonstrate such effects of mixed color. Various painting techniques, such as sponging a second color onto a base tone, graining, or marbleizing painted surfaces can also introduce color mixture that can appear different from the actual colors in use. Small-scale patterns in woven or printed fabrics, in carpet, and in wallpaper

have a similar ability to blend their colors so as to appear as one tone that is an average of the separate colors actually present.

EFFECTS OF TEXTURE

Color systems also deal with color as it appears on a smooth surface. In practice, many surfaces have a texture that results from a surface that is not uniform but is rather made up of high and low points. Some textures are large enough in scale to be quite obvious, as with roughly troweled plaster or textured fabrics, but other textures are small in scale and therefore hardly noticeable. Bricks and tiles, stone, wood, and many other materials that appear smooth will exhibit, under a magnifying glass, a surface of small pits or projecting

Figure 4.22   Yarns in several colors woven together, as seen close up.

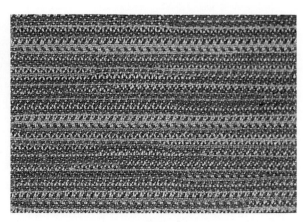

Figure 4.23   The same textile seen from a distance causes the yarn colors to blend together into what appears as a single tone.

granules or fibers. More obvious textures are created by textured or stippled paints and by fabric or plastic wall coverings that may also include elements of varied gloss, as in woven materials using both matte and glossy yarns. The color of all textured materials is modified in some degree by the texture. The pits of a porous material and the granules of a rough material create shadows that darken and desaturate the basic material color. The angle at which light falls on a textured material can increase or decrease such effects. It is often noted that paint of a particular color appears to change color when applied to a textured surface. The basic color is being modified by the effect of the texture on the ambient light as it is reflected toward the eye of a viewer.

USING COLOR SYSTEMS

Understanding systematic color concepts is an aid in planning color schemes, but the translation of a scheme conceived in system terms into an actual interior application involves recognition of the special color effects previously discussed. In practice, the translation of an abstract color scheme into real materials for use in a real space is a complex matter involving creativity and judgment. That step is the subject of Chapter 9 which follows detailed discussion of schematic planning in Chapters 5 through 8.

5

The Color Wheel

It is important to understand a basic issue involved in all theoretical studies of color: the reality that colored light behaves somewhat differently from colored pigments or materials. While the color that reaches the human eye is always in the form of colored light, that light may have been colored at its source, or it may be light reflected from a colored surface or object. In the first case, the color seen results from mixing various colors of light to produce light seen as having a certain color. In the second case, the color seen results from the action of colored materials, pigments, or dyes which have absorbed all color from the available light except the color which appears as a characteristic of that material, pigment, or dye. The mixing of colored light is called *additive color,* and the mixing of pigments or dyes and the colors that appear as inherent in materials is known as *subtractive color.*

ADDITIVE COLOR

Because the mixing of colored light is not a common or important aspect of most familiar color use, the behavior of additive color is not commonly familiar in everyday experience. The light under which objects are generally observed is generally thought of as white or colorless, although, as discussed in Chapter 3, both daylight and artificial light may have color characteristics that vary considerably from an ideal or pure white. Still, the light that is normally primary or ambient in an interior space is usually not so strongly colored as to be thought of as having a particular hue. Lightbulbs with a tinted glass envelope are used occasionally—perhaps to give an effect of candlelight—but strongly colored light, of an intense red or blue, for example, is usually found to be unpleasant. The most common use of colored light is in stage lighting. Theater stage lights are generally provided in banks of primary colors separately controlled so that the lighting designer can obtain any color effect by mixing light colors.

It is a surprise to discover that the primary colors of light are red, blue, and green (see Figure 5.1). Mixing all three creates a white or colorless light. Red and blue are mixed to generate a violet, while yellow results from the mixture of red and green. This last fact is the most striking

Figure 5.1 The additive primaries: red, green, and blue.

characteristic of additive color. It can be demonstrated by projecting beams of red and green light onto a white surface so that they partially overlap (see Figure 5.2). The overlap area will be brighter than either the red or green area and, if the intensity of the beams is equally balanced, a clear yellow will result. If the red beam is stronger than the green (or if the green is dimmed), an orange will result, while a green stronger than the red will produce a yellow-green mix. The white produced by all three additive primaries can be tinted by increasing the intensity of one of the three colors or by reducing that of one or both of the other two.

In theory, a multicolor lighting installation could provide for a similar possibility for variation of light color in any interior, but the cost of such arrangements and the complications of control make this an arrangement almost never used. Additive color has, therefore, little practical impact on the use of color in interiors. Colored light only appears occasionally, as when colored glass is used in windows or when a strong light reflects from a wall surface of strong color. A bright red or blue wall, for example, if struck by a beam of sunlight, can reflect light having enough coloration to modify the apparent color of nearby objects. Such effects are often noticed in color photographs, a face in a portrait photograph may appear to have a greenish skin tone as a result of reflection of sunlight from a grassy lawn or field. While this may be noticed in a photograph, in reality, human vision seems to compensate for such effects so that they are rarely noticed.

In interior design, the elements that generate color, the materials, pigments, and dyes that color walls and floors, textiles, and furniture all offer subtractive color so that systematic study of color for interiors is rarely concerned with additive color and concentrates almost entirely on the phenomena of subtractive color.

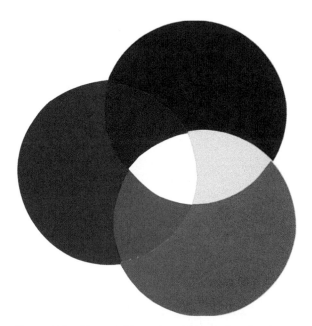

Figure 5.2 The additive primaries, overlapping in a simulation of the effects in which red plus blue produce violet, blue plus green produce blue-green, and, most surprisingly, green plus red produce yellow. The three colors of light together produce white, or colorless light.

SUBTRACTIVE COLOR

Objects or surfaces that reflect all colors of light equally are seen as being colored white. Objects and surfaces that absorb all colors of light (therefore all light) are seen as being colored black. In practice a pure or perfect white or black is a virtual impossibility. A comparison of various samples of white paint or paper will reveal many different tones of white that are the result of some colors of light being slightly absorbed so as to generate a slight tint, the result of the unbalanced presence of colors in the light reflected from the sample. Similarly, a black surface or object absorbs most light but reflects back enough to make it possible to discern details of a black object. If that limited reflection of light includes more of one color tone than another, the black will seem slightly shaded toward that color. A warm black absorbs cool (blue, green, and violet) colors more completely than it does warm color tones and so reflects back enough warm-colored light to modify the effect of total blackness.

In working with subtractive color, it is usual to turn to a systematic organization of colors of the sort developed by the various color systems discussed in Chapter 4. The arrangement of colors in a rainbow spectrum in the order established by the physics of light energy wavelengths dictates the familiar order:

red, orange, yellow, green, blue, violet

Of these six colors, three cannot be produced by any mixture of other colors; these are red, yellow, and blue, the colors that are therefore called *primaries*. The other three colors, orange, green, and violet, can each be created by a mixture of two of the primaries and are called *secondaries*. The primaries that can be mixed to produce orange and green are those that stand adjacent to them in spectrum order: red and yellow to make orange, yellow and blue to make green. Violet results from the mixture of the adjacent primary blue and the primary farthest away in the spectrum, red. In order to display each secondary between the primaries that generate it, it is necessary to bend the spectrum around so that violet stands adjacent to red so as to

Figure 5.3   The subtractive primaries: red, yellow, and blue.

be between red and blue (see Figures 5.3 and 5.4). This results in the spectrum being changed from a straight band into a circle. This arrangement, usually called a *color wheel,* is basic to several of the color systems discussed in Chapter 3 and is a useful concept in understanding many color concepts.

THE COLOR WHEEL

Having arranged the three primaries and three secondaries in a circle (or hexagon), it can be noted that additional gradations can be generated by mixing any primary with the adjacent secondary. This creates six more colors, producing a wheel of twelve hues (see Figure 5.5). These intermediate steps are called *tertiaries* and are designated by names made up of the names of the hues mixed to create them:

red-orange
yellow-orange
yellow-green
blue-green
blue-violet
red-violet

Figure 5.4a The primaries red plus yellow produce the secondary orange.

Figure 5.4b The primaries yellow plus blue produce the secondary green.

Figure 5.4c The primaries red plus blue produce the secondary violet.

Notice that in naming the tertiaries, it is usual to give the name of the primary first followed by the name of the secondary.

A circle or wheel with 12 hues forms a good basis for understanding most color concepts. By adding additional steps between each pair of adjacent hues in the 12-color wheel, it is possible to generate a circle of 24 colors (see Figure 5.6). The added, intermediate colors can be designated as *quaternaries.* Naming the additional intermediate steps is awkward so that, when they are used, it is usual to give letter designations to each hue. Thus,

> Y   = yellow
> YG   = yellow-green
> YYG = a hue resulting from a mixture of yellow and yellow-green

While logical, such designations are somewhat inconvenient. It is not easy to visualize the hue that will be designated OYO, VRV, or VBV without some careful thought. It is also not firmly established what order the letters should be given in such three-letter color designations. YYG and YGY are two ways of designating the same hue. Since each intermediate hue must fall either between a primary and a tertiary or between a secondary and a tertiary, it is logical to standardize giving the letter for the primary or the secondary first followed by the two letters for the tertiary. Thus YYG is the correct letter order for the intermediate between yellow and yellow-green. Other names for hues can be used, of course, such as turquoise, rose, or lemon, but the exact meanings of such terms are not clearly established so that different people may not agree as to what they mean. Efforts to standardize color naming through color dictionaries, where each possible name is attached to a sample or a letter and number specification using one of the color systems, have been attempted, but have proved to be of limited value.

A 24-color wheel can be further elaborated with intermediate steps producing a 48-color wheel which begins to approach a wheel with an infinite number of gradations in which each hue blends into its neighbors

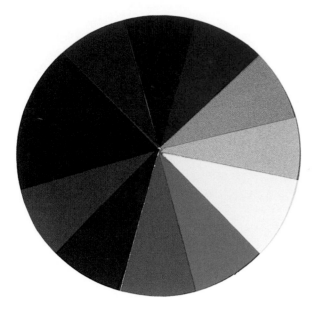

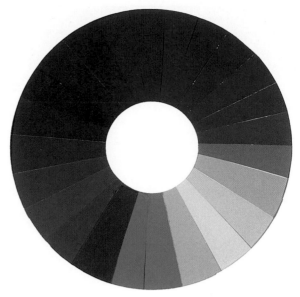

Figure 5.5   The primaries and secondaries, with the addition of intermediate (tertiary) steps generate a 12-color wheel.

Figure 5.6   Adding 12 intermediate steps generates a 24-color circle.

without discrete steps just as the hues of the spectrum do. For most practical purposes, 12 or 24 hues are satisfactory and manageable in verbal discussion. A color wheel is useful in arriving at an understanding of a number of color relationships and the associated terminology.

MONOCHROMATIC COLOR

The obvious definition of the term *monochromatic* is *one color.* Monochromatic color schemes are inherently safe in that there can be no clashing of poorly chosen hues. The one hue that gives such a color scheme its name may be used at various levels of intensity, in tints and shades all based on a single theme color. Monochromatic schemes tend toward monotony and so are often relieved by the addition of an accent color that contrasts with the theme color. If such contrasting accents are of significant importance, the scheme will no longer be truly monochromatic but will fall into one of the other color relationships.

A monochromatic scheme in which a single hue is used with a single, consistent intensity is sometimes designated as a *monotone* scheme. An all-white scheme, for example, or an all–pale blue, will be a monotone version of monochromatic. Such monotone schemes are, as a practical matter, difficult to achieve because some elements of a real space will almost inevitably vary to some degree from any one precise color tone.

ANALOGOUS COLOR

Hues that are close together in a color wheel are somewhat similar and tend to seem closely related and therefore visually harmonious. Such closely related colors are called *analogous,* and color schemes that use them are referred to as *analogous* schemes. The colors that form an analogous relationship will usually fall within one-fourth of the full color circle, that is, within three or four segments of a 12-hue circle or six or seven segments of a 24-hue circle

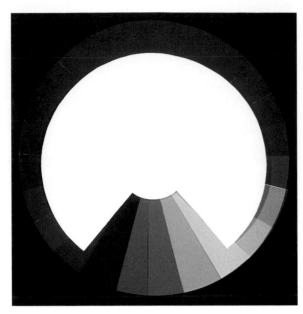

Figure 5.7　An overlay disk with a cut-out of slightly less than a quarter circle exhibits an analogous grouping of hues.

(see Figure 5.7). Some discussions stretch the definition of the term analogous to include colors within half of a full color circle, but the more remote colors included in this way will actually fall outside the limited relationship that is reliably harmonious. It is possible to view all of the possible analogous relationships by using an actual color wheel with an overlay disk that has one-fourth (or slightly more than one-fourth) cut away. Rotating the cutaway disk over the color wheel will display a sequence of analogous relationships.

An analogous scheme does not need to include tones reaching around a full one-fourth of the color circle. A narrower segment, one-sixth of the circle, for example, is also usable and will tend to be safer, that is, more certainly harmonious than a wider segment. A segment as narrow as one-twelfth of the wheel will, of course, become monochromatic since it will include only one hue or parts of two adjacent hues of a 12-color wheel.

It is often suggested that in developing analogous color schemes, one hue should be chosen as a dominant, or *key,* color with related colors near it on the color wheel used in secondary ways and reduced in area or in intensity. The key color may be centered between neighboring related colors, or the related colors may all be on one side of the key color as long as they are within one-fourth of the full color circle.

Typical analogous color schemes might, for example, use blue-green as a key color together with blue and green (the hues on either side of blue-green), or the blue-green key color could be used with green alone or with green and yellow-green, adjacent colors on one side of blue-green. A scheme that used only blue-green (in various levels of intensity, tints, and shades), however, would be designated as mono-chromatic rather than analogous.

COMPLEMENTARY COLOR

The color wheel is useful in demonstrating the concept of complementary color. It is generally felt as an intuitive reaction that certain colors are opposite to one another. Red and green are the obvious example, chosen as the universally recognized indicators for stop and go because of this sharp contrast. Such a pair of colors are called complementary and will be found in positions directly across the color wheel. Blue and orange, yellow and violet are also complementary pairs, each made up of one primary and one secondary color, the secondary formed by the mixture of the two other primaries. Pairs of tertiary colors can also have a complementary relationship: blue-green, for example, is complementary to red-orange. (See Figures 5.8 through 5.12.)

By making up a disk similar to that previously suggested for viewing analogous relationships on a color wheel, it is possible to view all possible complementary pairs (see Figure 5.13). This disk will have

Figure 5.8   Complementary colors such as red and green lie on opposite sides of the color circle.

Figure 5.9   Blue and orange also form a complementary color relationship.

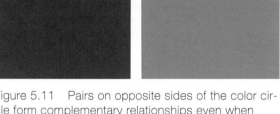

Figure 5.10   Yellow and violet are a third complementary pair.

Figure 5.11   Pairs on opposite sides of the color circle form complementary relationships even when shifted from primary-secondary positions. In this pair, a blue-green is complementary to an orange-red.

wedge-shaped cutouts of about one-twelfth the circumference of the circle placed on opposite sides of the disk. As it is rotated over a color wheel, the possible complementary pairs will appear in the two cutouts. This exercise becomes particularly interesting if performed with a 24-color wheel where some more subtle complementaries will be seen: BBV opposite YYO for example, or GYG as complementary to RRV.

Complementary color schemes, often called *contrasting* schemes, are generally felt to be lively and active and, when the complementaries are used at a high level of intensity in nearly equal quantities, can become strident and harsh. In practice, successful use of complementary colors usually places one of the complementary

pair in large areas at low intensity with the other tone in more restricted areas at a higher level of intensity. It is also sometimes suggested that any harshness in a complementary color scheme be reduced by neutralizing each of the basic pair of hues slightly with the addition of the other (complementary) hue. A typical scheme might use large areas of pale green with smaller areas of a bright red. Adding some red to the green tones to make them slightly grayish and adding some green to the red to dull it slightly will tend to soften such a scheme.

In general, complementary schemes are well liked. Each of the hues balances and gives relief from its complementary in some way that seems to offer visual and psychological satisfaction. Pairs of comple-

Figure 5.12 Tints and shades form complementary relationships when their basic hues are in opposite positions on the color wheel. Thus, the upper pale yellow and violet are complementary as are the tan (based on yellow) and brown (based on violet) shades below.

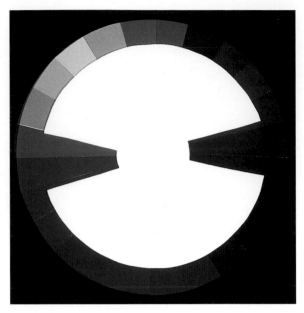

Figure 5.13 A disk with cut-outs on opposite sides, when placed on the full color wheel, can demonstrate all possible complementary relationships of fully saturated hues.

mentary colors at high levels of intensity are usually best reserved for small areas that will be seen for a limited time. The colors of flags and sports uniforms are often of this kind. For more extended viewing, complementaries are most agreeable if one or both of the tones are of lesser intensity or are restricted in area.

Split Complementaries

A variation on complementary color schemes comes about when a hue on one side of the color wheel is used with two hues on the opposite side of the wheel that are about equidistant from, but still close to, the complement of the first hue. Red, for example, might be used with two greens, one more bluish in tone, the other more yellowish. A disk to demonstrate split-complementary relationships on the color wheel would have one cutout about equal to one-twelfth of the wheel's circumference on one side and two separate cutouts on the opposite side, each about one twenty-fourth of the circumference and displaced

a short distance on either side of the point directly opposite the first cutout. The relationship of the colors that make up such a scheme is roughly that of a letter Y with a fairly narrow top opening. (See Figure 5.14.)

Split-complementary schemes afford more variety and flexibility than direct complementary schemes, but many of the same comments apply. The tones on one side of the wheel (usually on the side that is split) are most often used in larger areas at reduced levels of intensity while the single hue opposite can be of higher intensity but in smaller areas. If the two tones on the split side of the wheel are far apart, the scheme will become a *triad,* a different type of color relationship discussed later.

Double Complementaries

Still another variation on complementary schemes develops when a pair of hues near one another, adjacent or somewhat separated, are used on each side of the color wheel in a symmetrical arrangement.

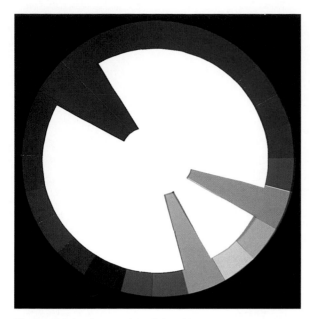

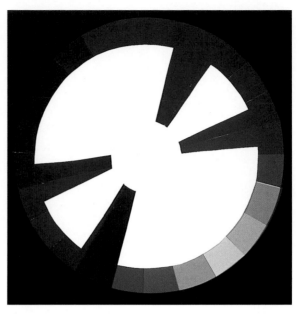

Figure 5.14   An overlay disk with a cut-out on one side and a pair of symmetrically placed cut-outs on the opposite side demonstrates the relationships of split-complementary colors.

Figure 5.15   Double-complementary relationships are shown by an overlay disk with two closely spaced cut-outs, symmetrically placed on each side of the disk.

Four hues are thus in use, two pairs of complementaries, positioned on the wheel in the form of a narrow letter X (see Figure 5.15). One complementary pair might be red and green, the other orange and blue. A more subtle double-complementary scheme could be made up of red-violet opposite yellow-green and violet opposite yellow. The hues that fall on one side of the wheel must be fairly close together (no more that one-fourth of the circumference of the wheel) if they are to avoid generating a *tetrad* or near tetrad relationship. Double-complementary schemes tend to be highly active and, unless carefully planned, can become chaotic or seemingly random with too many colors having no organized relationship.

TRIAD COLOR

Triad color schemes are based on three hues spaced approximately equally around the color wheel. This may mean the three primaries, red, yellow, and blue; the three secondaries, orange, green, and violet; or any three hues intermediate between primaries or secondaries (tertiaries or quatrenaries) equally spaced around the wheel. Triad schemes are among the most difficult to develop successfully because of their tendency to become glaring and harsh. Success depends or a careful choice of a particular hue to act as a dominant theme, used, perhaps, in limited areas, while the other two hues are used in more subdued forms, shades, or tints in larger areas adjusted to hold the scheme in balance. Triad color is inherently richly colorful and can produce remarkably satisfying results, but it requires great skill and care to avoid a sense of random scatter of diverse, unrelated color.

As with the color relationships previously discussed, a disk can be cut to form an overlay on a color wheel to aid in viewing the triad possibilities (see Figure 5.16). This disk will have three cutouts, each equal to about one-twelfth of the wheel's

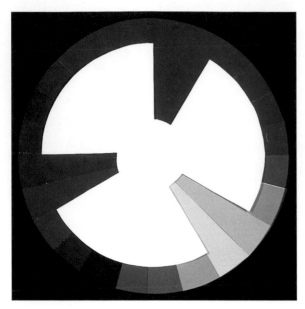

Figure 5.16   Triad color relationships are shown when an overlay disk with three cut-outs at the third points is placed over a full color wheel.

circumference, and spaced equidistant around the wheel. As the disk is moved about over a 12- or 24-hue color wheel, it will display the range of triad possibilities.

TETRAD COLOR

The remaining type of color relationship involves the use of four hues spaced about equally around the color wheel. This will lead to a scheme involving two sets of complementaries. If one pair is a primary and a secondary, the other pair will be two tertiaries. Such a scheme is similar to the double-complementary schemes previously discussed, but will differ in that the hues are more widely spaced at the quarter points of the full color circle. The effect of tetrad schemes is to bring into use hues from every part of the color circle with a resultant sense of extremely active, possibly over-varied color. Tetrad schemes are the least safe of all color relationships, the most likely to fall into chaotic or random patterns. As with triad schemes, it takes

great care to manage tetrad color in a way that avoids disorganization and a confusion of too much color. As with each of the other more difficult color relationships, success depends on selecting one hue as dominant and using it at a higher level of intensity, while the other hues are brought into the relationship by reducing their intensity and increasing the areas of their use.

A tetrad disk will have four cutouts equally spaced around the circumference of the wheel so as to display such groupings as blue, yellow-green, orange, and red-violet, for instance (see Figure 5.17). Notice that this range includes all three primaries and three secondaries, two alone and the other four in the combinations that form tertiaries. Any tetrad scheme will include a primary, a secondary, and two tertiaries made up of the other two primaries and two secondaries. A more subtle tetrad scheme will result if a 24-color wheel is used with the four hues shifted so as to all be quaternaries. Even in this situation, a tetrad scheme will tend to be difficult to develop without becoming disordered and random.

MODIFICATION OF COLOR HUES

Throughout the discussion of the hues arranged in a color wheel, hues have been treated as if they were in the pure or intense form in which they are displayed in the typical wheel chart. In practice, colors are sometimes used in such pure or intense form, but more often they are modified in ways that reduce their intensity without altering their hue. Given a particular hue in the most intense (saturated or chromatic) form that can be achieved, there are three ways of modifying it so as to create a vast range of color tones even within the confines of a particular hue designation. Each of these forms of modification is taken into account by the various color systems discussed in Chapter 3. Although the systems use slightly different terminology, all deal in some way with modifications that make colors lighter, darker, or closer to the neutrality of gray. Two types of modification make a color lighter or darker while a third modification neutralizes a hue without altering its lightness. Each of these modifications is explained in the following sections.

Tints

Any intense color can be modified by mixing it with white or light gray. When the proportion of white to intense color is high, a tint results that is often called *pale* or *pastel* (see Figure 5.18). When a small amount of white is mixed with a larger proportion of intense color, the result may still seem strong in a way that hardly suggests the term tint, but the resultant mixed color will still be both lighter and less intense (or less saturated) than the intense hue as displayed in the color wheel. Hues diluted with white to form tints are often given special names, such as pink, sea foam, or baby blue, but the exact meaning of these terms is always somewhat vague. The various color systems attempt to substitute a more consistent method of designation that makes use of a numerical scale to specify a particular sample in terms of its hue, its lightness as compared to a scale of grays ranging from white to black, and its saturation or intensity. While the addition of white to a hue will change both the saturation and lightness, these two characteristics are distinct although interdependent.

Shades

An intense color hue can also be modified by an admixture of black or dark gray creating a *shade.* Although that term is used with various meanings in general conversation (any color may be called a "shade of _____"), it has a more precise meaning in color theory, referring only to modification of hues by the addition of black or dark

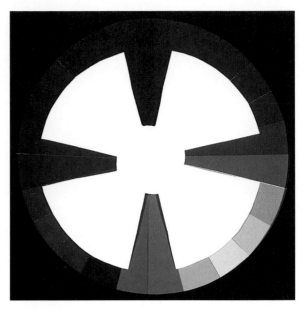

Figure 5.17   Tetrad color relationships are demonstrated by an overlay disk with four cut-outs at the quarter points placed on the full color wheel.

gray. As with tints, shades are often given special names, such as midnight blue or bottle green, but here again the exact meanings of such terms are uncertain and designation through the use of one of the established color systems is the only certain way of knowing what a particular color name means. As in the making of tints, darkening color by adding gray or black shifts both lightness and intensity or saturation. Some hues act differently from others

Figure 5.18   Tints result from dilution of saturated hues with addition of white. Here, red and blue become pink and pale-blue tints.

as black is added to form a shade. Dark blue or green are easily produced, but the addition of black to an intense yellow does not readily produce a dark yellow, a tone that can hardly be visualized. The darkening of yellows, oranges, and, to a lesser extent, yellow-greens tend to produce tones that are best described by other names such as tan or brown.

In the forming of both tints and shades, the modifier added to the intense hue may be a pure white or black, or a gray. A gray is made up of a mix of white and black so that a tint formed by adding a light gray is somewhat different from a tint formed by adding a lesser amount of pure white alone. Similarly, a shade formed by adding a dark gray which is made up of both black and white will produce a different tone from a mix of an intense hue with black alone. In general, the use of a gray in forming a tint or shade will make a greater reduction in intensity of color for a given shift in lightness than will result from the use of white or black alone.

Neutralization

Another way of altering an intense color hue involves the mixture of the hue in question with its complementary. In theory, an equal mix of a hue sample with its complementary will produce a neutral tone, a gray with a lightness equal to the average of the two samples mixed. In practice, such neutrals are usually described as *muddy,* that is, somewhat brownish or greenish rather than strictly neutral. Still, the addition of a complementary tone to a pure hue will shift it toward a neutral. Red mixed with green, blue with orange, or yellow with violet render neutral tones, each, it may be noticed, in effect a mixture of the three primaries. (See Figure 5.19.) When an intense color is mixed with a small amount of its complementary, the result retains the basic hue characteristics of the intense color while becoming less intense or saturated. The common terminology will refer to a hue modified in this way as somewhat *dull* as compared to the pure hue, usually called *bright.*

When using a complementary to dull or neutralize a color, it is of course possible to use a tint or shade of the appropriate complementary or to use a hue near, but not exactly in, the complementary position in the color wheel. When it is remembered that a tint or shade can be made up of a hue combined with both black and white in a gray, it becomes clear that an infinity of possibilities exist giving rise to the vast variety of colors theoretically available in any subtractive color medium. As a practical matter, it is possible to first mix complementaries in intense (pure) form and then alter the mix by adding black, white, or both to form a gray that will modify the mix of strong color, or, alternatively, to use tints or shades of complementary colors in mixing a neutral.

The difficulty and complexity of arriving at a desired color tone through the mixture of available pigments is familiar to anyone who has tried painting using such media as oil color, tempera, acrylics, or watercolors. It can be very helpful in understanding color phenomena to practice color mixing, using only the three primaries and black and white at first, and then adding other colors that are available in the medium being used. The colors sold as tempera, gouache, or designers' colors are ideal for such color experimentation since they dry quickly and can be thinned and cleaned with water. The ability to produce a small sample of any desired color by mixing paints and painting the resultant color onto a small sample card is a convenient skill for any designer. Further discussion of the use of such samples appears in Chapter 12.

COLOR WHEEL ANALYSIS

It is an interesting exercise to study the color of actual interiors in terms of a color wheel. It is possible to do such study in a real space, but it is more convenient to use color photographs as a basis of work at a studio worktable. Samples can be found or made up (colored papers or colors mixed and brushed onto cards) to match each important color of the interior being studied. Each sample can then be compared with a color wheel and placed in its appropriate position. The samples may, of course, be

Figure 5.19*b* Red plus green produces a neutral.

Figure 5.19*c* Blue plus orange produces a slightly different neutral.

Figure 5.19*d* Yellow plus violet produces a third neutral.

tints, shades, or neutralized versions of particular hues, but their position in relation to the color wheel can still be noted. It will then become clear that the scheme being studied is of one of the types previously discussed or, possibly, a slightly modified version of one of those types. If it is impossible to relate a scheme to any of the typical relationships discussed, it is probable that the color present is random and unplanned. It will usually be found that this is only the case with examples in which color relationships are unplanned and unsatisfactory.

Study of an existing unsatisfactory color situation can make good use of color wheel analysis. It may be found that certain colors fall outside of any organized relationship. By eliminating these colors, or by changing them into colors that relate to a planned scheme, an interior that is unsatisfactory or disappointing in color can be greatly improved. A decision about what to change can be based on color wheel analysis in combination with practical considerations. For example, an otherwise analogous scheme may be seen to include a single totally unrelated item. For example, a room using a wall of exposed brick, a tile floor, tan wall surfaces and draperies might include a rug or some cushions in a turquoise blue. Replacing such items with others in an orange-red could convert the discordant scheme to one that will be fully satisfactory.

Study of color schemes in relation to the concepts developed in this chapter using a color wheel as a tool are helpful in developing a sense of how colors work in relation to one another. As that sense develops, most designers find it unnecessary to refer to an actual wheel chart. Instead, a color scheme can be developed freely without thinking in a conscious way about the specific type of scheme and how its elements relate to color theory. The knowledge of theory becomes ingrained so as to make it possible to make good color choices (and avoid bad ones) using theoretical concepts without thinking about them in any specific way. An artist, in making a painting, usually works in this way— colors are chosen to work well together "by eye" without worrying about *why* a certain choice is right. A successful painting, when completed, can be analyzed in terms of color theory that was not in the artist's mind when the work was being done.

A comparison can be made with music theory, a subject that is studied by any serious musician so that the rules of harmony and of musical form become well known. Once known, the musician can compose or play with only occasional reference to the laws and rules of theory, possibly breaking those rules from time to time for special effect. The untrained but talented musician may be able to achieve good sounds without theoretical knowledge, but if the sounds *are* indeed good, it will be found that theoretical principles are at work even if they have not been consciously considered. In much the same way, successful color planning can often be accomplished simply by watching the results of placing various colors in relationship in a chart or in an actual space. A theoretical understanding will almost certainly make this informal way of working easier and more reliably successful.

A number of examples of actual interiors as shown in photographs together with charts illustrating the relation of the colors used to color wheel diagrams are shown in Chapter 10. Making similar studies of other interiors is a useful exercise in developing a sense of the application of color theory to real situations.

6
Color Charts

ABSTRACT CHARTS

The most useful technique for developing satisfactory color schemes is the making of color charts that are totally independent of the actual layout and general design of a particular space. Color charts can be made up from samples of actual materials to be used, but the difficulty of having on hand a full range of samples of every possible material in every possible color makes this impractical as a way to begin color planning. Instead, it is easiest to make up color charts from conveniently available colored materials such as colored papers or paint color sample chips. After a satisfactory abstract chart is arrived at, real materials can be searched out in colors that match (or almost match) the colors chosen for the chart. Chapter 9 is concerned with the steps involved in translating an abstract chart into actual material selections.

It is also sometimes convenient to make a hybrid form of color chart using actual material samples for items that have been preselected while using abstract samples for other elements. For example, if it is known that a space will have a wall or other surface of exposed brick, a sample of the actual brick can be used along with paper or other swatch samples in developing a complete scheme. In practice, a sample brick is a large and heavy object that may be inconvenient to work with or that may overemphasize the importance of that particular material color. It may be best to use a paper sample that matches the color of the brick or the other preselected material so that the chart developed will be consistently abstract in character.

CHART MATERIALS

The most convenient materials for color charting are colored papers. Paper has the advantage of being inexpensive, readily available, light in weight, and thin so that samples laid out to overlap in adjacent positions all lie in a single, flat plain. Colored papers can be acquired in several ways. There are a number of color paper systems available as commercial products in art supply stores (see Figure 6.1). Each system offers a sample book showing all of the available colors, and it is usually possible to obtain an assortment of all the available colors in fairly small sizes. Larger

Figure 6.1 A sample book showing the colored papers available from the Color-Aid system.

sheets of colored papers from color systems are more expensive, so that acquiring a large assortment can be costly, will call for suitable storage space, and may be less convenient to work with than smaller samples. Inexpensive colored papers, also available in assortments such as the construction paper offered for craft work, are generally not satisfactory as the primary medium for abstract charting because of the rough texture of such papers and the limited color choice.

To augment purchased colored papers, it is easy to collect papers in a wide range of colors from discarded materials such as advertising brochures, packaging materials, and similar scraps (see Figure 6.2). It is a helpful practice to make a habit of saving bits of colored paper from any source that comes to hand. Clipping solid color areas from printed materials, magazine pages, holiday wrappings, and any other sources can build up a fine file of color samples at no cost. Such found color samples will often be glossy rather than the flat of purchased color paper sheets—but this is not a serious disadvantage if care is taken to observe the papers under lighting that avoids reflection from glossy surfaces.

Found color samples may be collected in a scrap box, but, as a collection grows, it is useful to sort samples by color and make up file folders to hold related colors. A folder for each primary and secondary hue plus folders for black, whites and near whites, browns, and neutrals will keep samples sorted so that a search for a needed color will be relatively easy. It is useful to also collect samples of papers that are metallic and that have certain textures which relate to real materials (see Figure 6.3). Samples of paint colors, wood finishes, and plastic laminates are available from furniture manufacturers and are useful additions to a color sample collection (see Figure 6.4). Wood veneers are available in assortments of small-size pieces from various suppliers of wood products to craft users. Wood veneer without any finish can be somewhat misleading in that the actual finishing may shift color quite markedly. Applying some coating to veneer samples (wax or plastic spray, for example) will simulate finished wood. It is generally best to avoid papers where color

Figure 6.2 A variety of colored papers collected from many sources, such as advertising brochures, discarded bits of packaging materials, and even wrapping papers.

has been generated by halftone (four-color) process printing, which is easily identified by the tiny dots of color that can be seen under a magnifying glass. Solid ink colors are the most satisfactory color samples to collect. Sample charts supplied by paint manufacturers are also useful, although the samples provided are often very small and are, of course, restricted to the colors that a particular product line offers.

Mixing Color Chips

Color samples in an infinite variety of colors can, of course, be produced by mixing colors and painting the results onto slips of card. Three by five index cards or a somewhat heavier cardboard cut to that size are a good base. The designer then can use a favored color medium such as tempera, gouache, poster color, designers' color, or any other color medium—even house paint can be mixed and painted onto sample cards. In general, only opaque media are satisfactory. Watercolors can be used to modify the colors of another medium (such as tempera) while artists' oil colors or the pigments sold for mixing house paint can

be used to modify the colors of oil-based media. Many excellent basic colors are available in spray cans, and a vast range of colors can be found in regular liquid or in spray-can form for such special purposes as automobile touch-up or model making. The colors available for railroad, ship, and military models can be used in available tones or can be mixed. In mixing, it is, of course, necessary to be sure that the materials to be mixed are compatible. In general, water-based materials will mix with one another but materials with lacquer or other bases must be mixed only after some experimentation to be sure of good results. In any case, materials that are quick drying are best so that chips can be put to use almost immediately after mixing.

Mixing color becomes necessary when collections of available color samples do not include a desired tone. It is then appropriate to try for a new sample by mixing color according to the principles of theory learned in Chapters 4 and 5. Light colors are best mixed by starting with white and adding chromatic color a bit at a time, mixing hues as necessary to arrive at a desired tone. Moving a mix toward neutrality can

Figure 6.3 Decorative papers with marble patterns and metallic surfaces are useful materials for planning color relationships.

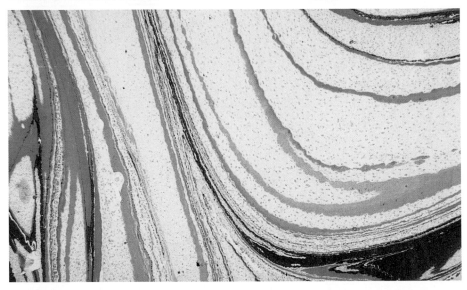

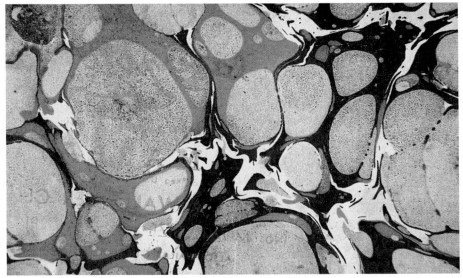

Figure 6.4 Wood finishes and laminates used in furniture production are shown in samples available from many furniture manufacturers.

involve adding gray or adding the complementary to the first hue used. Darkening involves adding black to the mix. If the desired tone is to be quite dark, no white should be used—only chromatic color, a complementary if needed, and black. Finally some gray or white can be added to the mix if it should become too dark.

Arriving at a desired color can take many steps of experimentation, so it is good practice to color a card as a sample at stages of mixing whenever a pleasant or useful tone is developed, even if it is not exactly the tone desired. Saving such trial samples helps to build up an extensive sample file that can be useful for future projects. It is not unusual to produce dozens of trials, perhaps to discard a mix and to start over several times in the process of mixing a particular desired tone. It should also be remembered that in most media, color shifts somewhat as a paint dries. This means that coloring a sample card and letting it dry is a necessary step at stages of mixing as a desired color is approached. Save the mix unchanged until a sample has dried so that further adjustment can be made to compensate for the shift that takes place during drying.

The larger the collection of available samples, the less necessary it will be to mix new samples, but every designer should be prepared to mix new color tones when needed. This will avoid any tendency to settle for a less than ideal color simply because no ideal sample is at hand.

MAKING A CHART

Before starting a color chart, it is necessary to have in mind a general idea of what is desired. The function of the space being planned, preferences of occupants or owners, geographic location and climate, and the intended atmosphere are matters dealt with in Chapters 9 and 10. These matters are an integral part of conceptualizing any interior design. It may be helpful to make some written notes on how these factors are to relate to color before creating a proposed color chart. Samples of color can now be selected to represent the colors of the various areas, objects, and details that will be present in the designed space.

Color samples can simply be tossed out in a cluster with no particular pattern (see Figure 6.5). It is best to start with col-

Figure 6.5 A cluster of color samples grouped to aid in building a color scheme.

Figure 6.6 Color samples arranged in an orderly collage arrangement.

ors that will occupy large areas (typically floors, walls, ceiling) or that will be intense and dominant even if occupying smaller areas. The scheme is built up by adding samples that relate well to those already chosen until there is a sample present for each significant color element in the planned space. How many color samples this may require needs to be considered. Several elements of a space may share one color, or each element may call for a color of its own. For a typical interior, a list of elements might be:

Floor

Walls (one or more colors)

Ceiling
Trim (moldings and baseboards)
Doors, paneling
Drapery
Furniture (frames and upholstery)
Details, accents, artwork

This will lead to anywhere from three or four to eight or ten color samples. It is easy to consider alternatives during this process—several possibilities can be viewed in sequence and possible alternatives may be put aside for further consideration later on.

It is not necessary to represent details of color pattern. Weaves of multiple color, woven or printed patterns such as stripes or checks, and more detailed designs in fabrics or wallpapers are simply represented by a single color sample that averages the tones present into a single color as it might appear from a distance. At this stage, patterns will usually not have been selected so that a solid tone sample can best stand for the general effect that will be the result of selections made at a later stage. Similarly, varied color in some materials, the veining of marble, tile in multiple colors, or the grain patterns of wood, for example, can be ignored with a color sample chosen to represent the total effect of such materials as seen from a distance.

Having collected the samples that seem to make a viable relationship in a cluster, it is best to make an orderly arrangement of them (see Figure 6.6). Some designers (and many students) like to make an abstract or collage arrangement that may be suggestive of an abstract painting. If color has been well chosen, such an arrangement may be aesthetically attractive as a design and will also confirm the validity of the colors chosen. There is always a danger that the forms of such a cluster arrangement may become an end in themselves and distract attention from the study of color per se.

Another possibility, perhaps less amusing but more disciplined, will be to arrange color samples in an orderly geometric pattern, in a band of parallel bars, for example, where the colors can be observed together without thought for the special pattern of the arrangement (see Figure 6.7). Such a color chart can be thought of as a spectrum band, somewhat similar to the spectrum generated by light passing through a prism, but made up of only the colors chosen for a particular scheme.

However arranged, it is best if the areas of color samples displayed are proportionate to the amount of each color that will be present in the completed space. Walls and floors will usually be large in area while the color of a particular cushion or accessory will usually be present in a small area. A color chart that shows large areas of colors actually in restricted use and small samples of colors that will actually occupy larger spaces can be sharply misleading. While it is not necessary to calculate exact areas of each color in mathematical terms, each color should be shown in a sample that corresponds to an estimate of the area of that color that will be present in the final realization of the scheme.

If colors are to be arranged in a spectrumlike band, the band can be laid out in a black and white line diagram and the color samples then placed on the layout, overlapping as necessary so that the area of each color showing is about proportional to the intended presence of that color. Such a chart simulates, in an abstract way, the color impression that the completed space will offer. A further subtlety in abstract chart making involves placing the chosen samples in an order that approximates the position relationships of the colors in the completed space. Logically, floor color will be placed at the bottom of such a chart; colors of walls, drapery, and furniture in its center; and ceiling color above. It is not usually possible to make placements that will reproduce the locations of each color

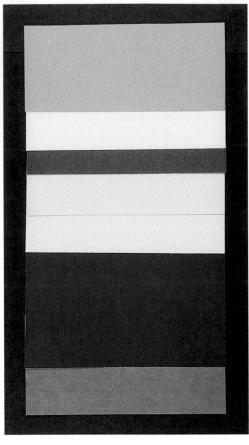

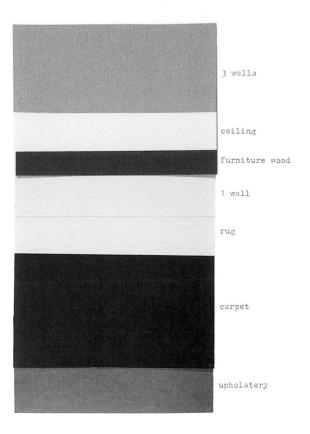

Figure 6.7   Color samples arranged in a neat band or bar chart with samples in order from top to bottom roughly matching their position in the space being planned.

Figure 6.8   Labels added to the bar chart to identify the location or use of each color.

element accurately, but an effort to come close to that ideal makes a chart more representative of the finished reality. A ceiling color holding a center position with floor color above and other colors below can distort the impression a chart conveys, even if the colors are well chosen and accurately proportioned. In arranging samples in a band, ideally each sample will be adjacent to, or at least close to, the colors that will be close or adjacent in the finished space. It is usually not possible to achieve an exact representation of every such relationship, but an effort in this direction will help to make the chart reveal some of the color interactions discussed in Chapter 7.

It is possible to make up a blank outline chart with bands designated in order from bottom to top to be used as a guide for making up spectrum band color charts. How many bands and the exact proportion of bands will have to be adjusted for each color chart, but a standard outline can be useful in guiding the makeup of the unique chart that will refer to a particular space. As a chart is made up or when it is completed, it is wise to make some notation of what each sample represents. This may be a separate listing or may be managed with labels placed adjacent to each color band (see Figure 6.8). Note that, although a sample chart will look well placed on a mat, the color of the mat may influence the way the color chart will look. Strongly colored mats are totally unsuitable but even white, black, or gray can alter the way a chart is perceived. A white mat, for example, will make a scheme that uses dark colors look even darker than it is. A black mat exaggerates the brightness of colors used. A neutral gray is often a good choice, but each sample chart should be given a background carefully chosen to both look well and avoid distorting the way the chart appears.

Ideally, color selection and chart making should take place under light that matches the light that will be ambient in the finished space. Many interiors are seen under various lighting conditions: daylight (which is itself varied with weather, season, and time of day) and artificial light that may be from mixed sources or mixed with daylight. Even when a particular light source is planned for an artificially lit space, there is no guarantee that future re-lamping of fixtures will not change the color balance of ambient light. There is no perfect solution to dealing with this problem. Fortunately, the human eye (or brain) tends to make adjustments so that light, as long as it is not strongly colored, does not cause extreme shifts in the way that colors are seen in relationship. Color charting is best done under daylight or a light source similar to daylight. Fluorescent light may distort some colors, so, if it is the lighting under which color charting is to be done, there should be a mix of daylight, incandescent light, or full-spectrum light also present to insure that choices made will be valid when applied to the elements present in the completed space.

Color charts are normally of a size that will be convenient at desktop level and for display in meetings and conferences. This means that the samples used will be relatively small as compared to the areas of color that will be present in a completed space. This presents a problem that has no simple solution. A tiny sample of a particular color can look very different from the same color in a large area. Colors of the sort that are called deep or dark are particularly misleading. A tiny sample of such a color may look almost black but be surprisingly colorful when seen in a large area. Such possibilities must be thought about and it may be wise to obtain large samples of certain colors before final decisions are made. The need to check large samples of color and the possibilities of on-site adjustments are discussed in more detail in Chapter 12. The samples in a chart are intended to stand for the way each color will *look* in its final placement. If the relationships in a chart are satisfactory, final relationships will also turn out well even if some adjustments must be made to allow for the shift from small sample to large area. The effects of textures and pattern in various materials can also be significant, but are dealt with in the translation of abstract charted color into charts using real materials as discussed in Chapter 9. Where a project will be made up of a number of spaces, separate or interconnected, it is useful to have color charts for each space made up in similar formats so that the charts can be looked at together to get a sense of the color progressions that will take place in moving from one space to another. Spaces that open into one another through wide doorways or openings need color schemes that relate well. A stairway connecting a lower and upper hall suggests that the color in each hall and in the stair area itself should be developed together so that a pleasant sequential relationship will be arrived at.

PLAN COLOR CHARTS

There are several alternative forms for color charts that are somewhat more troublesome to prepare, but that can be interesting and informative. Usually a simple, abstract color chart should be made before attempting such formats as a *plan color chart* or *color plan.* In a color plan, a floorplan layout is used as a base. A scale of ¼ inch = 1 foot is most often used, although a larger scale may be considered for a small space. On the plan, floor color is laid in for the full area, colored in any convenient medium or simulated by a colored paper cutout. Other elements, rugs, furniture, and so forth are then cut out in scale forms from appropriately colored paper or other sample materials. A plan with all color elements in place suggests a top view into the completed space. (See Figure 6.9.)

The obvious limitation of color plans is that wall and ceiling colors and colors of vertical elements such as drapery are missing. Adding one or more color elevations to the plan helps to provide a way of making the color plan representative of the complete color scheme for the finished space. It is not necessary for color plans and elevations to include the drawn detail of design or construction drawings; solid areas or blocks of color give the color plan an abstract quality which focuses attention on color relationships alone. One may think of a color plan and elevation as an abstract color chart similar to the spectrum charts previously discussed, but with the samples in an arrangement that reveals their size and placement in greater detail. (See Figure 6.10.)

COLOR MAQUETTES

A further extension of the color plan and elevation requires the making of a specialized form of chart related to the type of drawing called a *maquette.* This term refers to a way of showing an interior design that was often used in traditional decorating practice. The drawing for a maquette uses a carefully detailed plan (showing all furniture and other elements in top view) surrounded by four elevations that are each detailed drawings of one wall of the room

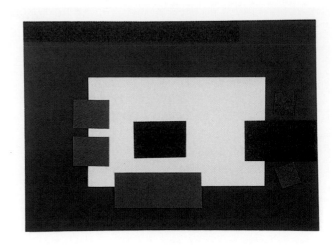

Figure 6.9   A plan chart with color samples placed in the locations where they will appear in the finished space.

Figure 6.10*a*   The addition of a diagrammatic elevation with color samples in place makes possible a more complete view of a proposed color scheme.

being shown. Furniture is shown in the elevations of the wall to which it will be closest. The elevations are placed in contact with the lines representing the wall in the plan so that each wall can be thought of as the vertical surface folded down onto the flat surface of the drawing. A maquette can then be cut out and the walls folded up into a vertical position so that a box is created

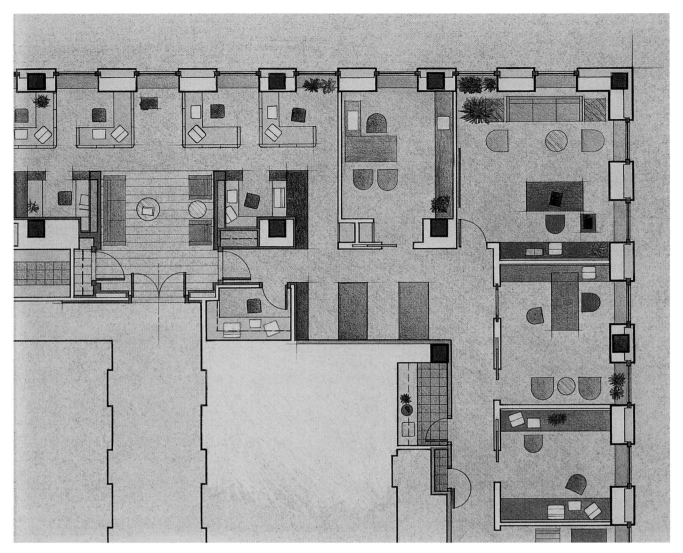

Figure 6.10b   A detailed floor plan with colors indicated in locations where they will finally appear. This is part of an office plan by Norman Diekman.

representing the completed room—a kind of simplified three-dimensional model. (See Figures 6.11 and 6.12.)

If a color plan and four-color elevations are put together in this way, a charted simulation of the room is created in three dimensions. The walls can be left movably hinged so that one or two can be folded flat while the others stand up and can be viewed with the maquette held up at eye level.

While this form of presentation works fairly well for a conventionally shaped room,

it can become difficult to make a color maquette for many complex or irregularly shaped spaces. A model, whether diagrammatic or realistically detailed, is the ultimate extension of the maquette idea and can be a helpful device for study of color placement in large and complex spaces. A simplified model that does not attempt to include realistic detail can be made up quite quickly. When colored paper and small clipped bits of fabrics and other materials are put in place, it is possible to look into the model at eye level to get a

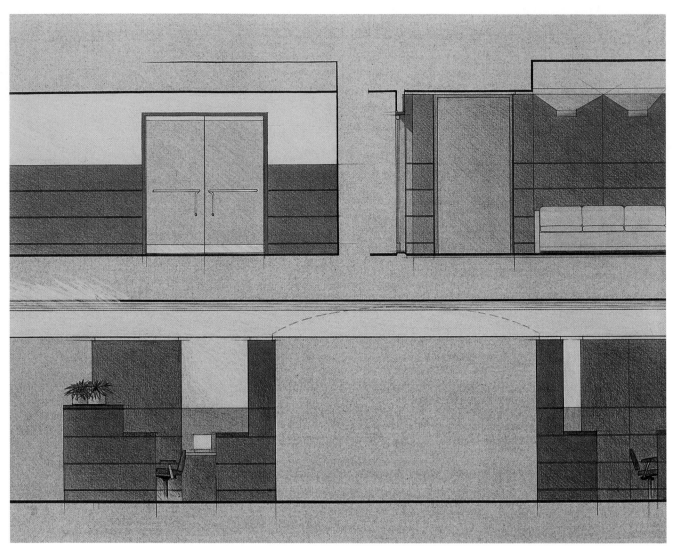

Figure 6.10c Color elevations for portions of the same office design project. (*Illustration courtesy of the designer, Norman Diekman.*)

sense of color relationships in space. A model of this type is particularly useful for large spaces such as open office interiors, larger showrooms, and spaces in large retail shops.

Color samples can also be applied to a perspective drawing, cut out to match areas of color as they appear in the perspective, and overlapped with near areas covering over part of more distant areas. This kind of perspective color chart is discussed more fully in Chapter 12 along with a discussion of color rendering.

USING COLOR CHARTS

A color chart, maquette, or other presentation of a color scheme is a unique assembly which is difficult to reproduce. It is usually wise to save extra samples of each color for use when searching out actual materials, for lending to a client, for showing others, or to serve any other purpose while the original chart is kept on file. If several copies are required, making up duplicate charts can become a significant chore, but may be a necessary step. Reproduction of charts

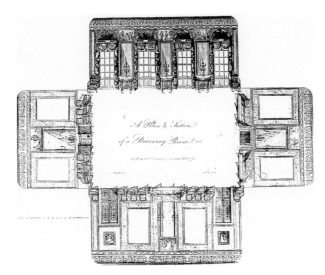

Figure 6.11a A maquette displayed on a flat page as it appears in Thomas Sheraton's 1793 *Cabinet-Maker and Upholsterer's Drawing-Book.*

Figure 6.11b When cut out, the walls of the room can be folded up to make a box arrangement that suggests a simplified model. The Sheraton maquette has been partly folded up in this way.

Figure 6.12 Another eighteenth-century maquette, this one by John Sanderson, a drawing in which the ceiling design is shown as reflected onto the floor. A photograph of the drawing has been reproduced and folded up to represent the room. Such a drawing may be colored with colored pencils or watercolors before cutting and folding to show a proposed scheme. (*Photo courtesy of the Metropolitan Museum of Art, New York.*)

through color photography for slides or prints or through duplication processes such as color Xerox will often distort color relationships, although such reproduction can be useful in some circumstances. In photographing any color materials, it is important that the selection of film, the lighting, and the use of any filters be carefully coordinated according to the recommendations of film manufacturers. Color slides or larger transparencies will give the most accurate reproduction of color, but when projected, the size of the image, the intensity of the projector light beam, and the level of light in the viewing room can all influence the way color will be seen. Projected slides are an ideal way of showing color materials to larger groups, but care must be taken that the projected image accurately represents the colors intended.

When color charts or samples are to be shown—in a meeting intended to obtain client approval, for example—it is important to be sure that the lighting and background colors of the room where the viewing will occur will not distort the colors shown. The fluorescent lighting in many offices and conference rooms, for example, or strong wall or ceiling colors that reflect colored light onto the viewing surface can distort color perception.

Clients of designers often take a strong interest in color planning and may enjoy having some role in the process. It can be helpful in such situations to present color schemes along with alternative samples so that a client can participate in the process of finalizing color, watching the interactions that take place as colors are placed in relationships, and thus coming to an understanding of how a certain scheme has been developed.

In working with a client, a designer may prefer not to discuss abstract color charts but rather to wait until the abstract charts have been translated into samples of actual materials. Changes may occur between abstract charts and charts of materials, and material charts offer information about color along with textures, patterns, and other details that may modify the way in which color is seen. Obtaining client approval of a materials chart gains acceptance of both color and material selection in one session, thus avoiding discussion of color issues twice. The making of color charts using real materials is the next logical step after abstract charts are complete. This is the subject of Chapter 9, but Chapters 7 and 8 first deal with issues involved in developing the color schemes that will be organized into abstract charts.

7
Color Schemes

COLOR HARMONY

It is widely recognized that when colors are used together, the results can be more or less successful, more or less disappointing. Random choices of color are likely to generate relationships that are unattractive or, at best, indifferent in the satisfaction felt by a viewer. When colors relate in a way that gives aesthetic satisfaction, it is customary to say the the colors are *harmonious. Color harmony* is a concept developed through a comparison with musical harmony. Music students study harmony to learn how to put together musical tones in ways that are satisfying to listeners. If piano keys are struck at random, a jangle results, while certain groupings of tones produce chords that are aesthetically pleasant. In music, *discords,* combinations of tones that are not harmonious, are also used at times for aesthetic effects that can contribute to emotional reactions. In a parallel way, colors can relate in ways that are harmonious, although harsh or clashing colors can also be used to create visual impact in certain circumstances. Study of color harmony is basic to the development of color schemes appropriate to interior spaces.

Color wheels such as those described in Chapter 5 are a basic tool for work in development of color schemes. An actual wheel chart may be used or the idea of the wheel simply kept in mind. In either case, discussion will constantly refer to the wheel and to the concepts of value and saturation. It is a useful basic exercise to look at color samples chosen at random and to mentally identify each in terms of hue, value, and saturation. This need not be done with the notation of a color system of the type described in Chapter 4; simply naming the hue and speaking of value and saturation as high, fairly high, medium, or low, for example, will serve to develop a habit of thinking of every color in these terms.

COLOR SCHEMES BY TYPE

Successful color schemes are generally one of several types that have come to be recognized and named. An experienced interior designer developing a color scheme

Figure 7.1 A bar chart showing a monotonal color scheme.

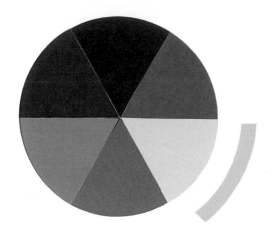

Figure 7.2 A color wheel with the location of the monotone basis in the preceding bar chart.

may not think about choosing a particular type of scheme, but, assuming it's successful, it will usually be found to fit into one of the recognized schematic types. Rigorous adherence to one or another type of scheme is not absolutely necessary—elements that do not relate to a particular scheme type can often be introduced as accents and variants—but a satisfactory scheme will rarely emerge if color choices are made in unrelated, random ways. Descriptions of the generally recognized color scheme types follow in order from least complex to most complex.

Monotonal Color

If only one color is used, a *clash,* or disharmony, becomes impossible. In a monotonal scheme, all colors are of the same hue and of same or near same value and saturation (see Figures 7.1 and 7.2). While a monotonal scheme is theoretically easy to create, it presents both practical and aesthetic difficulties that make its use fairly rare. The aesthetic problem is one of monotony. To step into a room where everything is white, or beige, or a particular tone of green or yellow can give rise to a strongly pleasant first reaction but, before long, vision and mind tire of the sameness of color and seek some variation.

The practical problem in monotonal color is that it is difficult to find a single color that will be suitable to every element in a space. An all-white living room, for example, will require a white floor covering and all white furniture. An all-white bathroom is not uncommon (although it may demonstrate the risk of monotony) but most other spaces call for a wider range of color tones for a number of reasons. Monotonal color is at least practical if the color chosen is in a middle range of value and of fairly low saturation. A living room or office, for example, could use a scheme of all beige, tan, light blue, or green. An all-pink room is possible, but is likely to seem forced and artificial as well as monotonous. The idea of a "red room" or "blue room" can seem attractive, but in practice the scheme of rooms with such names rarely is truly monotonal. The name refers to a dominant hue, but other color tones are usually introduced so that the scheme is actually of another type.

Figure 7.3 A mono-
chromatic scheme
shown in bar-chart
form.

A basically monotonal scheme is sometimes practical if there is provision for some
element that violates the requirement of
monotonality. For example, an all-white
bathroom can be made lively and interesting through the introduction of towels and
bath mat of strong color. Since these elements are readily changeable, this
becomes a means of introducing color
changes at little or no cost or trouble. The
white bathroom that uses orange towels
one week can become pleasantly different
with green or blue towels another week.
Similarly, changes of table linens, even
flowers, can introduce easily varied color
into a dining room using monotone color.

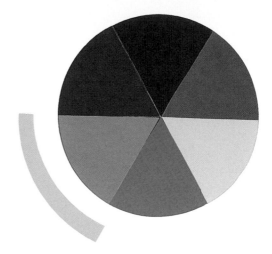

Figure 7.4 A wheel chart relating to the mono-
chrome bar chart.

Monochromatic Color

In a monochromatic color scheme, only
one hue is used, but it may be varied in
value and saturation. In practice the one
hue is not limited to a particular wavelength
of light, but is thought of as a narrow range
of hues close enough together to carry a
single color name (see Figures 7.3 and
7.4). In a red scheme, for example, the
reds used might vary, but all will be within a
segment of a color wheel no more than
one-twelfth its total circumference. Variation
in value could be within any part of the
range from pale pink to a deep red, with a
similar range of variation in saturation.
Notice that deep values of red with medium
to low saturation will usually be called
brown. Near white can be used in a monochromatic scheme, tinted slightly by the

dominant color hue. If all of the colors used
are desaturated, a monochromatic scheme
can be very subtle and quiet, particularly if
the range of value variation is also limited.
Strong contrast in value can make a monochromatic scheme more active and lively
while use of some intense (highly saturated)
tones can make such a scheme strongly
colorful. The typical "red room" or "green
room" makes use of a monochromatic
scheme with at least some strongly saturated color areas.

A special case of monochromatism
arises if white is selected as the key hue.
Variation in value then makes possible
schemes that are all white and gray, black
and gray, or white, black, and gray. As with
monotonal schemes, monochromatic

schemes virtually guarantee harmony but are subject to the risk of monotony. A space that is all red, all blue, or all gray will tend to make a strong first impression, but may become tiring or depressing over a period of time. This tends to suggest that monochromatic schemes are best used in spaces that are occupied only briefly such as bathrooms, vestibules, elevator cabs, or for spaces that form a suite of rooms that are used together or in sequence. The Red, Blue, and Green rooms of the White House in Washington, D.C., are of the latter sort—reception rooms that are used for formal events where occupants move from one space to another at short intervals.

Many people will say that they have a favorite color and will ask for its extensive use in an office or in rooms of a home. A monochromatic scheme based on such a favorite tone might seem logical, but is, in fact, questionable. Even a favorite color can become monotonous and either irritating or depressing when it dominates a space occupied for extended periods of time.

In practice, monochromatic schemes are often modified by inclusion of some element that is actually outside of the definition of monochromatism. As with monotone schemes, this sort of limited escape from the strict interpretation of the scheme's restrictions can be helpful even if it may, technically, lead to a scheme that can be classified as another type. An all-green room might be enlivened by some small element of bright, saturated red-orange. A space of soft blue tones can be relieved with some details in a suitably bright yellow. Accessories, flowers or plants, or a work of art can often serve to introduce this kind of variation into an otherwise overly limited scheme.

An all-white space can be brought to life with restricted areas of primary color. The use of white and neutral grays with very limited use of one, two, or all three primaries was a favorite approach of the modern movement of the 1920s and 1930s. De Stijl artists, including Mondrian in painting and Van Doesburg in sculpture, architecture, and interior design, made the use of monochromatism plus small areas of primary color a well-known approach subject to admiration, imitation (perhaps too much imitation), and often to harsh criticism as well.

Analogous Color

The next step into more complex color relationships is the development of schemes in which color hues are restricted to a limited group of tones that are adjacent on the color wheel. An analogous scheme uses at least two, usually three, hues that reach no more than one-fourth of the way around the color wheel (see Figures 7.5 and 7.6). Usually one hue is a dominant key color, and the hues on either side are included in the scheme. A scheme centered on yellow, for example, might include yellow-green and yellow-orange, the colors on either side. If using a color wheel of twelve hues, there are twelve possible analogous relationships for three hues each. While the central hue is usually dominant, an analogous scheme may use a dominant tone plus the next two adjacent hues on one side. Thus a scheme with blue as a theme color can become analogous through the addition of the tones blue-green and green, or tones of blue-violet and violet. Intermediate hues between the primary and secondary colors are also appropriate to an analogous scheme.

Value and saturation can vary freely within the hues that make up an analogous scheme. If all values are light, the scheme may be called *high key* while a scheme of all or mostly dark values will become *low key*. Saturation also can vary with saturated colors making a bright scheme, desaturated tones a muted scheme, and the use of both levels of saturation for a lively variation. Because the hues of an analogous scheme are closely related, harmony

Figure 7.5 A bar chart showing an analogous color scheme.

becomes virtually automatic while the range of available hues tends to make for more variety and freedom than characterized by monotonal and monochromatic schemes. Development of an analogous scheme often begins with a monochromatic basis that is then broadened to include the additional hues that create variety within a restricted range.

Analogous color is usually regarded as easy or safe, in that harsh, clashing, or discordant color is hardly likely to occur. As with monotone and monochromatic schemes, it is possible to introduce small areas of contrasting color to enliven an analogous scheme. Usually this will be complementary color—tones on the opposite side of the color wheel from the analogous group. The contrasting color will usually be of strong intensity but with a very limited variation of hue and used in a limited area. If the contrasting color becomes a major element in the scheme, it ceases to be truly analogous and will fall into one of the other schematic types.

Analogous schemes are often chosen where there is a desire to emphasize either warm or cool color without the limitations of monotone or monochromatic color. Warm color may be desired to offset the coldness of a certain climate, the cool of sunless northern light, or to create an atmosphere emphasizing a certain emotional tone of cheer and warmth. The following analogous groupings will produce warm color:

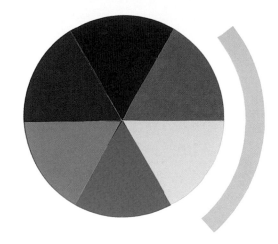

Figure 7.6 The colors of the analogous scheme as located on a color wheel.

yellow–yellow-orange–orange
yellow-orange–orange–red-orange
orange–red-orange–red
red-orange–red–red-violet
red–red-violet–violet

When a cool scheme is desired to offset the effects of a warm climate, strong sunlight from a southern or western orientation, or to emphasize a sense of calm, serenity, or contemplativeness, any of the following groupings can be considered:

violet–blue-violet–blue
blue-violet–blue–blue-green
blue–blue-green–green
blue-green–green–yellow green
green–yellow-green–yellow

Figure 7.7 A complementary color scheme in bar-chart form.

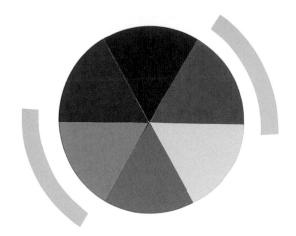

Figure 7.8 The location of the complementary hues on a color wheel.

The previous listings include ten of the possible twelve analogous schemes. The remaining two possibilities are as follows:

red-violet–violet–blue-violet
yellow-green–yellow–yellow-orange

These can be developed as either warm or cool schemes according to the intensity and quantity of warm or cool color used or may be planned as balanced schemes with neither warm nor cool colors predominating.

Analogous, monochromatic, and monotonal color schemes all run some risk of seeming forced or contrived. Many decorator color schemes fall into this trap—they are so planned that an occupant cannot forget the designer's excess of effort. At best, such schemes should seem simple and pleasant where they are used in spaces for normal work or living. More theatrical schemes can also be effective when they are used for spaces that are specialized in purpose or used for brief periods. Color that is theatrical can, of course, be particularly appropriate for stage design when dramatic intent can be heightened by carefully planned color and related lighting.

Complementary Color Schemes

Although somewhat more difficult to plan than the previously discussed schemes, complementary schemes are among the most often used and well liked of all schematic types. In a complementary scheme, colors are chosen from opposite sides of the color wheel and create a sense of liveliness and variety as they hold each other in balance (see Figures 7.7 and 7.8). The possible complements, made up of one primary and one secondary tone— red and green, blue and orange, yellow and violet—are each workable, with their popularity levels shown according to the declining order listed. A complementary scheme can also use the more subtle pairing of tertiaries—yellow-green with red-violet, yellow-orange with blue-violet, or red-orange with blue green. It is also possible to develop complementary schemes in which the colors on each side of the wheel are spread more broadly, with two or even three hues on one side balanced by the opposite two or three. Still another possibility uses three analogous hues on one side of the wheel with a single hue on the other side opposite the center hue of the first three. This scheme is demonstrated when analogous color is used with a complementary accent. It becomes a truly complementary scheme if the single hue is strong or extensive in area, asserting itself as a full balance to the colors opposite it on the wheel.

When the saturation of colors is high on both sides of a complementary scheme, the scene tends to become excessively active and possibly harsh. A space that is all blue and orange with both colors at high saturation and in large areas will tend to seem crude and possibly irritating. Such color is often used in flags, sporting colors, or in advertising displays, but will usually be unsuitable for most interiors. A more subtle complementary scheme results when the colors on one side of the wheel are of reduced saturation, shades or tints used in larger areas, while the complementary tone is stronger (leading to an active scheme) or also desaturated (to form a quiet scheme). Where all tones are desaturated and either very light or very dark, the scheme may become bland and uninteresting.

Examples of each of these complementary schematic types are in wide use. A room may have light, soft, green walls and a subdued green carpet with upholstery fabrics in a complementary red tone. Walls of cream color with trim painted in a related tan-yellow and floors of a darker natural wood color may work well with blue or blue-violet upholstery fabrics or window treatments. The tendency for complementary schemes to become harsh and inharmonious can be limited by the technique of slightly neutralizing the colors on each side of the wheel by the addition of a small amount of color from the opposite side. For instance, the green walls of the preceding example will be slightly grayed (softened) if the green contains a small amount of the opposite red and the red textiles are of a weave or pattern that contains a small share of green.

Several variations on complementary color are sufficiently different to deserve their own names. Discussion of these follows.

SPLIT-COMPLEMENTARY COLOR.   In split-complementary schemes, a single hue on one side of the color wheel is used with two separate hues from the other side of the wheel which are equidistant from a point directly opposite the single color (see Figures 7.9 and 7.10). For example, green on one side of the wheel might be used with red-orange and red-violet from the other side. The latter hues are on either side of red, which is the direct complementary of green. As with simple complementary schemes, the single hue may be somewhat spread to occupy more that one-twelfth of the circumference of the color wheel while the two balancing hues may be either spread or contracted. Each of the three hues can be used at varied levels of value and saturation, of course, so that a great range of possibilities exists with any split-complementary basis. In the preceding example, the green tones might be light and desaturated, while the two complementaries might be intense but used in small areas. In practice, such a scheme might be realized with the walls and floor in a soft green and textiles and accessories in bright red-oranges and red-violets. Alternatively, the twin complementaries might be of desaturated tones in large areas while the green might be an intense accent color.

In general, split-complementary schemes tend to be more muted than complementary schemes. The same technique of slightly neutralizing each color by the addition of a small amount of the other hues will tend to soften or mute the intensity of a split-complementary scheme.

DOUBLE-COMPLEMENTARY COLOR. This is a further extension of the use of

Figure 7.9 A split-complementary color scheme in chart form.

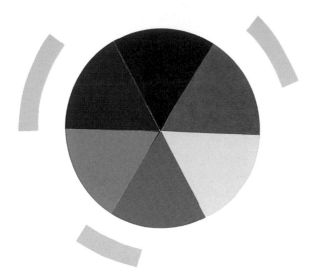

Figure 7.10 The color wheel with the split-complementary hue locations shown.

example, with blue and green on one side and orange and red on the other, a total of four hues, two primaries and two secondaries are in use with only one primary and one secondary omitted. When strong tones of the four hues of a double-complementary scheme are present, an intense and active color plan results that may readily become harsh and discordant. Double-complementary schemes are usually most workable when two or three of the hues in use are of low intensity—tints or shades rather than strong, bright tones.

The complexity of double-complementary color planning makes schemes of this type relatively difficult to develop successfully—more difficult than simple- or split-complementary schemes.

Triad Color

Any three hues spaced equally around the color wheel can form a triad (three-tone) color scheme (see Figures 7.13 and 7.14). In a 12-color wheel, the four possibilities are:

red–yellow–blue (the three primaries)
orange–green–violet (the three secondaries)
red-orange–blue-violet–yellow-green
red-violet–blue-green–yellow-orange

Each of these schemes suggests an intensely colorful result, but, in practice, lowered saturation and high or low values

complementary color. As the term suggests, a double-complementary scheme uses two pairs of complementaries. The two hues on each side of the wheel must be placed fairly close (within about one-fourth of the color wheel's circumference) or the scheme will become tetradic, which is another schematic type (see Figures 7.11 and 7.12). A typical double-complementary scheme might use red and its complement green along with violet and its complement yellow. A slightly more subtle scheme could use red-orange and yellow-orange on one side with their respective complementaries blue-green and blue-violet on the other side. If the hues are still more widely spread, for

Figure 7.11 A bar chart showing a double-complementary scheme.

for some or most of the hues makes such schemes workable although tending to be richly colorful. Red, yellow, and blue might, in practice, take the form of an oriental rug with strong red tones (as in an Afghan Bokara), pale cream walls, and a soft blue used in textiles. The balance between the hues in use, if carefully worked out, can make triad schemes very satisfying as can be seen in the paintings of such artists as Poussin, Turner, and Matisse.

A variant on triad color uses achromatic color (usually white) for major areas and then uses a set of triad hues in small areas and accents. A dining room with white walls and a neutral tone floor can be made very bright with textiles and accessories of orange, green, and violet, for example. Such tonality is often thought of as tropical as it appears in awnings, umbrellas, and apparel. The colors of cut flowers and flowering plants are a possible vehicle for introduction of triad color into a scheme that is otherwise largely achromatic.

Tetrad Color

When four hues equally spaced around the color wheel are used, a special type of split-complementary scheme results called *tetrad* (meaning four-color) leading to strongly colored schemes that need careful planning to avoid a seemingly chaotic and random effect (see Figures 7.15 and 7.16). Using a 12-color wheel, there are only three possible tetrad schemes:

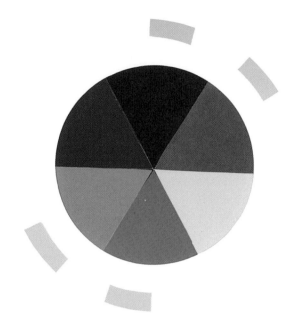

Figure 7.12 The double-complementary scheme located on a wheel chart.

red–yellow-orange–green–blue-violet
red-orange–yellow–blue-green–violet
orange–yellow-green–blue–red-violet

As with triad schemes, avoidance of harsh or garish results can be managed by using tones that are somewhat neutralized or are very light or very dark for most of the colors. Here, also, schemes that use white or near white as a major color can be made lively by introducing tetrad color in limited areas.

Figure 7.13   A triad color scheme in bar-chart form.

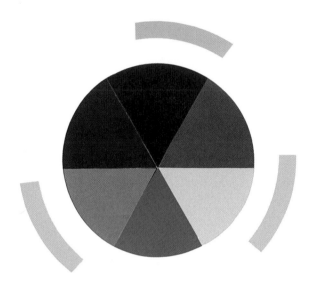

Figure 7.14   Triad scheme located on a color wheel.

USE OF COLOR HARMONY

A designer is under no fixed obligation to plan color according to the concepts of color harmony defined by the previously discussed scheme types. Putting together colors that simply look right on an intuitive basis is entirely possible as long as the final results are satisfactory. It is interesting to notice that schemes made in this way often turn out to fall into one of the schematic types listed—even if the designer was not thinking about such issues. The validity of the systematic approach to making color schemes lies in the fact that they explain the reasons why some relationships work better than others

and, while color planning is in progress, often give hints on how to proceed and how to adjust and improve a scheme while it is under development. With a partially developed scheme in work, it can be frustrating to search aimlessly through collections of samples and color swatches looking for an appropriate color to complete the scheme. By thinking of the scheme in terms of a particular type of harmony, it becomes possible to go more directly to a needed color—possibly one that is not in the collection of available samples but that must be searched out from manufacturers or custom prepared.

For example, suppose that wall and floor colors have been selected, and the designer must next choose textile colors. If the walls are pale blue and the floor a stronger blue, a number of possibilities will come to mind that can guide the next step. If fabrics are to be chosen for upholstery or window treatments, a range of alternatives can be considered. With two blues chosen, going to a similar blue will generate a monochromatic scheme with the virtues and limitations of that scheme type—the result will be safe, calm, and possibly a bit dull. If, instead, oranges are tried out, a complementary scheme will surface, probably lively but a bit harsh. Turning to greens will make the scheme analogous and accordingly harmonious, neither very active nor totally dull. A decision to use two or more colors of textile could lead to a split-complementary scheme or to a full color

Figure 7.15　A tetrad scheme in chart form.

triad. In each case, awareness of the characteristics of each schematic type will help in deciding what direction to take and, with a direction chosen, will make the selection of the needed elements more certain and easy.

With experience, most designers find that it becomes easy to put together successful color schemes without conscious thought of the color wheel and the terminology of color scheming. Searching through samples, one may think, "Too intense, something less saturated is needed" or "This is almost right, but something a bit more orange is needed." In such thinking, the theoretical concepts of color harmony are being used without their acting as a burdensome discipline.

While harmonious color is most often the goal of interior design practice, there may be situations where harsh or discordant color is acceptable or even desirable. Shocking color may attract attention to certain kinds of commercial facilities—a discount retail outlet, or a fast food shop, for example—where the aim is to gain notice and make a memorable impact within a short time. In art and in music, it is customary to study harmony, but painters and composers learn that disharmonious, even painful effects can be appropriate in communicating certain kinds of emotions with

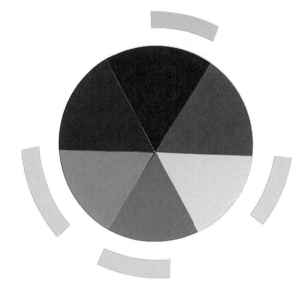

Figure 7.16　The color wheel showing tetrad color locations.

impact. These options are available to designers as well, but it requires an understanding of the concepts of color harmony in order to successfully break the rules with deliberate intent. Disappointing and unpleasant color is most often the result of unplanned and thoughtless color choices made without consideration of the relationships between colors. The value of theoretical color-scheme development lies in its helpfulness in leading to good choices and successful end results.

8
Color Schemes in Practice

THEORY AND PRACTICE

The previous chapter, devoted to the vast range of color relationships that can be developed theoretically, may suggest an intimidating complexity in the actual task of developing a particular color scheme. Students in design schools often seem to face a block when the moment to develop color for a project arrives. Planning and three-dimensional design are well advanced, perhaps furniture and other details have been chosen. Now it is time to establish color so that final selection of materials and finishes can proceed. Where to start when anything is possible? Perhaps it would have been best if color had been thought about at an earlier stage of design development, at least in a preliminary way. It is even possible to *begin* a design project with a color concept and refer to it mentally as planning and more detailed design proceed, but this is rarely done.

Some projects demand the development of color schemes virtually independently of other aspects of design. For example, in a hotel or motel, there may be dozens, even hundreds, of rooms, all alike except for color. In such circumstances, no one would suggest that dozens or hundreds of different schemes be developed, but it is quite usual to produce six, eight, or ten schemes so that identical rooms will be varied through color alone. Under these circumstances, the designer in charge of color must create, rather arbitrarily, a number of schemes that will each be of excellent quality, all equally applicable to a particular space. In a large office project, whole floors of a building may be planned in identical or near identical fashion, but monotony in the project can be countered by giving each floor a unique color scheme. Generating suitable, varied schemes becomes a challenge to the designer's skill and ease in working with color.

COLOR LOCATIONS

A useful first step involves drawing up a list of the places where color will be placed. Such a list might read as follows:

Floor
Walls (A)

Walls (B)
Ceiling
Trim
Furniture (frames)
Furniture (tops)
Upholstery material(s)
Window treatment
Art, accessories, miscellaneous

The realities of the space being planned might modify such a list with additional items or might omit items.

It might seem logical to now make a blank chart with spaces for each item, but, in practice, it is probably premature to do this. Available samples may be too small or too large to fit such a prototype chart and the effort to fit samples to the chart may distract from the work of actually choosing color. The list of locations may simply be kept at hand in memo form, or a sheet of background paper (usually white is best) might have the location terms listed along one edge.

DEVELOPING A SCHEME

The work now turns to placing a proposed sample color for each required location on display so as to form a grouping that can be viewed as a proposed scheme. At this stage, the samples will usually be in the form of colored papers or painted swatches as discussed in Chapter 6. Attempting to use samples of actual materials slows and complicates decision making and tends to be limiting in range of choices. It might seem that there would be no objection to using an actual material sample for an element already decided upon, but the introduction of real texture and mass may upset the visual evaluation of color alone. Even if it is known that a floor will be slate or a wall a particular stone, it is usually best to find a paper sample of matching color to stand in for the real material.

It is useful to make notes listing actual materials that may have been selected since such selections will often limit possible color choice. If a floor is to be slate or brick, for example, the colors available, while varied, fall within certain limits. Slate is always gray, even though the available grays range from warm to cool. Brick is available in various colors, but brick suitable as a floor material is not made in white or pale blue, for example. The available colors of many materials can be changed with paint, of course, but it would be foolish to paint many materials that are available in natural colors which may have been a major reason for their selection in the first place. Wood paneling for walls can be painted any color, but if a wood has been selected for its appearance (walnut, for example, or mahogany) the natural color, modified by a finish and possibly by staining, will fall within a limited range.

Painted surfaces and textiles are available in a color range that is virtually unlimited and many other materials are produced in an extensive range of color—tile and plastic laminate, for example—but availability may limit color choice to some degree. Similarly, some practical issues may need to be taken into account in a way that somewhat restricts color choice. Very light colors may not be practical in locations subject to heavy wear, such as the flooring in traffic paths. All such situations should be noted before beginning actual color selection.

The process of assembling a scheme involves choosing a first color, then adding additional colors in sequence, constantly trying for satisfying relationships. For each color selection, it is appropriate to consider a number of possibilities and, as each additional color is put in place, colors selected earlier may need to be modified or totally changed. Several alternatives may be laid out for a particular color with final selection being delayed until the total scheme is at least tentatively complete.

Ideally, samples of colors that will occupy large areas should be large, while colors that will be present in limited areas should be represented by proportionally smaller samples. As a practical matter, this kind of proportioning will usually be only partly successful, but it is helpful in evaluating a scheme to avoid having large samples of color that, in reality, will be only a minor element. Scheme development should take place under lighting similar to that which will exist in the completed space—daylight is usually satisfactory, and fluorescent light should be avoided except where it will be the light of the finished space. For a check, review color selected under daylight or under some other continuous-spectrum light source.

It is also helpful to remember that colors seem to shift with position—a color sample laid flat on a desktop will seem to change somewhat if it is stood up vertically. Wall colors, for example, should be looked at in an upright position, at least at the moment of selection, even if they are then laid flat as the scheme is assembled. Designers often make a point of trying to group samples in positions that relate to final positioning and area in a completed space, a process that will be no more than makeshift but still helpful in making sound decisions.

COLOR CHOICES

The foregoing discussion of method does nothing to help with the central questions of *what* color to choose in general concept or in detail. There are a number of approaches that have served designers well, individually or in combination. It is often suggested that a scheme begin with a *key* or *theme* color, selected for some logical reason. A key color will usually be important in a finished scheme either because it occupies a large area or because it will be dominant for some other reason. There are a variety of reasons for selecting a particular color tone as a key. These may be as follows:

A *given* color that will be important may have been preestablished. A fixed architectural element, a brick or marble wall, or a stone floor or chimney, for example, may be of a color that cannot be changed. A major work of art, a colorful painting or mural, or some favorite possession—a rug, tapestry, or piece of furniture—may inject a key color that must be used as a starting point. The color preference of a client may lead to a requirement that a favorite color be used as a key, leading to a "red room" or "green room" scheme.

Given circumstances of the space being designed, such as climate orientation, may, while not fixing a key color, lead to color preferences that narrow the choice.

Desired mood or emotional impact (discussed in more detail in Chapter 9) may suggest an appropriate key color.

Use of color determined by a corporate identity program (IBM blue, Cunard red, or BP green and yellow, for example) may suggest a key color choice.

Traditional expectation about what is appropriate for various functions may be a helpful guide in key color selection, even if it leaves a wide range for individual judgment.

An alternative to key color selection as a starting point can be the development of what is often called a *color concept*. This can be expressed in words that may or may not use actual color names. A color concept might be as follows:

Lots of green with many details in gold

or

Rich, warm tones with some spots of
contrasting bright color

or

Everything pink and white

As with key color, such concepts can be
developed in response to a client's preferences, to given circumstance, to traditions
or customs, or any number of other stimuli
which can act as a starting point for color
decisions.

A search for a basis for developing a
color scheme can turn to various possible
sources. Any color image can become a
guide to a scheme if it presents color in a
way that is both pleasant and appropriate
to the project in hand. A painting, for example, a color photograph with any kind of
subject—nature, a scientific study, a landscape or portrait—can be a starting point
for development of a color proposal. Color
illustrations of completed projects in which
color has been used in successful ways
can suggest a beginning from which new
and different relationships can be developed. Even banal images, calendar pictures, color postcards, brochures, or
advertisements can offer a set of color
selections that may be used as a basis for
a color proposal. It can be helpful to save
such images; build up a file of color materials that are appealing and that may turn
into guides toward color planning for totally
unrelated projects.

For most designers, the route to a color
concept is most often a kind of introspec-
tion in which all of the known realities of the
project are allowed to simmer in the mind
until they bring about a sense of a direction
in color that will be appropriate and satisfying for the particular character of the space
under consideration. This can lead to a key
or dominant color theme or to a vaguely
imagined scheme that will have qualities
that can be translated into more specifics
in a following step.

With a theme or key color or color
concept in mind, it becomes possible to
make a selection of a first color sample,
usually a tone that will be dominant in the
final space. While this often means a large
area (floor color is often suggested), it may
also be a small area with strong impact as
might occur when a colorful work of art
acts as key in a space where even large
areas of color will be selected so as to
avoid conflict with this strong element.

As additional colors are selected in
relation to the key color, it may be helpful to
think of the schematic types discussed in
Chapter 7. If the key color is blue, adding
tones of blue will tend to produce a monochromatic scheme. If the key color is red,
selecting greens will begin to build a complementary scheme. If the key color is subdued, it might suggest a strong color,
whether the intensification of similar hue or
of a contrasting hue as suitable to small
areas of accent. By shifting a few proposed
sample tones, a scheme can be made to
move, for example, from complementary to
split complementary or to triad so that the
effect of such varied schemes may be
evaluated as they appear on the desktop.

FAVORED APPROACHES

Many designers, in an effort to place some
limitation on the vast range of color scheme
possibilities always available, choose to
work within one or another approach that
has been found to be an effective guide to
satisfactory results. Some designers have
adopted one of these approaches—even
a particular form of one approach—as
a personal formula. Others turn to one or
several of these approaches at times,
and use them as a starting point before
moving out into other schemes, or use variations of such schemes. It is interesting to
notice that schemes developed on some

Figure 8.1 A neutral color scheme suggests calmness and dignity in this executive lounge area of the Chase Manhattan Bank headquarters building in New York. The architects were Skidmore, Owings and Merrill with Ward Bennett as consultant interior designer. (*Photo by John Pile.*)

other basis will often fall into one of these schematic types, and that schemes developed in one of these limited ways can usually be classified as fitting one of the scheme types discussed in the previous chapter.

Neutral Schemes

The use of neutral or, as it is sometimes called, *all-neutral,* color may sound drab and colorless, but it is a proven route to highly successful schemes that can appear richly colorful. (See Figure 8.1.) A variant on the all-neutral scheme may be called *neutral-plus,* a scheme that is in the main limited to neutral tones but that introduces one or more strongly chromatic hues in lim-

ited areas. An all-neutral scheme may be monochromatic or may be one of the other schematic types, such as complementary. It is characterized by using tones of very low saturation that may be all light (for high-key color), all dark (low key), or may run through a range of value. A favorite neutral scheme uses white as a key tone and may use grays and black in addition. The neutral-plus approach based on this neutral range has had important and extensive acceptance in the modern movement as it developed in the 1920s with the De Stijl movement and the influence of the Bauhaus. Many modern architects have come to regard white as an ideal color for its ability to display three-dimensional form

Figure 8.2   The neutral colors of concrete and wood set off the bright, primary paint colors used here by Le Corbusier in the hostel adjacent to the famous chapel at Ronchamp, France. (*Photo by John Pile.*)

unaltered by coloristic effects. With the addition of bright primary colors for use in small areas, a typical modern scheme emerges in which walls and ceilings are white while certain small wall areas, doors, furniture elements, and similar details are red, blue, or yellow. When the primary colors are used well, such schemes generate effects that are strongly colorful. (See Figure 8.2.)

All-white (or near-white) schemes without any primary accents are favorites for spaces where strong color is expected from other elements outside of the designers control. Galleries and museum interiors where strongly colorful artwork in varied colors will be displayed are often given white interiors in order to avoid color conflicts with displayed materials and to permit viewing of works without color distraction

from the setting (see Figure 8.3). Artists often paint the interiors of their studios all white for similar reasons. A practical problem arises in truly all-white interiors in the choice of floor color. White floors show dirt and wear and present problems of upkeep. In an artist's studio, a white painted floor is often used in spite of such issues. In more public spaces, some compromise in floor color is usual—perhaps a light gray with patterns or texture that makes for easier maintenance.

So much use of white has come under criticism in recent years with increasing challenge to the ideas of the modern movement. It is said that white is "empty," "boring," and monotonous, and an unpopular color to a major percentage of the population. Mahnke and Mahnke in their book *Color and Light in Man-Made Environments*

Figure 8.3 All-white or near-white color used for a galley space, the second floor of the Hammer Galleries in New York. Paul Heyer was the architect. (*Photo by Norman McGrath, courtesy of Paul Heyer.*)

Figure 8.4 An interior in white and neutral tones with small accents in bright red, generating a scheme that can be called neutral-plus. This is the French Government Tourist Office in New York. Berger-Rait were the designers. (*Photo © Derrick & Love.*)

devote a whole chapter to "The Case Against White" but leave open the question of whether the negative examples sited may not have been examples of poor color planning quite aside from the role of white.

A neutral scheme can be built on the gray scale that runs from white to black with a key color a medium or darker gray or black, and such a scheme can also be modified to neutral-plus by the addition of some limited chromatic color. Aside from the white-plus-primary schemes, most neutral schemes are based on chromatic color fairly close to neutral. A scheme of beiges, for example, or very soft, grayed greens or

blues, for example, falls into the all-neutral grouping and can also be made neutral-plus with the addition of small areas of strong color (see Figure 8.4). Neutrals close to gray but with a tint or shade of chromatic color can also be assembled into any one of the scheme types discussed in Chapter 7. Such schemes are very subtle but can be highly effective—they may seem all gray until it is noticed that some grays are warm and some cold in a carefully adjusted relationship.

Neutral color schemes are often thought of as being easy or safe. It is true that it is difficult to make a major coloristic error in a scheme that is all white or all near white unless it may be the error of monotony or dullness—errors usually easy to correct by the addition of the strong color that will make the scheme an example of neutral-plus. A neutral or near-neutral scheme is often spontaneously created through the use of the approach discussed next.

Natural Color

An idea that comes from the widely accepted view that the colors of nature are, in the main, beautiful, harmonious, and satisfying is that use of only the natural colors of materials will guarantee successful color in architecture and interior design. This is an idea that can be traced back to the Arts and Crafts movement of the nineteenth Century with its abhorrence of the use of harsh and ill-considered artificial coloring and its respect for the integrity of natural materials unfinished or finished so as to display their natural coloring. The concept of honesty in design, advanced as basic to excellence in most design theory, leads to a sense that hiding or altering the qualities of materials is a mistake. Since color is a characteristic quality of a material, the idea that only its natural color is acceptable becomes logical. Frank Lloyd Wright took up the cause of the all-natural approach to color, arguing that the choice of a material should take account of its color as well as all of its other characteristics (see Figure 8.5). Wright's followers have generally accepted his view, and many other architects and designers have followed this lead, perhaps in somewhat modified form, as well.

The natural colors of materials tend to fall into a somewhat limited range of tones so that a typical all-natural scheme will turn out to include off-white, beiges, tans, browns, dull reds, and possibly a bluish gray. The tones are generally of low to moderate saturation without intense or bright colors. As a result, an all-natural color scheme is generally quiet and subdued.

The colors harmonize because they are in a restricted range much as in a monochromatic scheme, although a natural scheme will not usually be monochromatic. It can be noticed that the colors of the most generally used materials fall within quite a restricted grouping. A list will run as follows:

Material	Typical color
Plaster	Off-white to beige
Wood	Light tan to medium brown
Brick	Tones of red or tan
Stone:	
fieldstone	Grays from warm to cool
travertine	Cream
marble	White, beiges
granite	Warm grays, brown
limestone	Light to medium gray
Tile	Dull red, tan, brown, gray
Metals:	
steel, painted	Red lead, zinc chromate, or aluminum
stainless steel	Metallic
chrome plate	Metallic
CorTen steel	Rust brown
aluminum	Dull metallic
copper	Copper color
Textiles	Off-white, beige, tan, (undyed) warm and cool grays, black
Leather	Tans, light to medium brown

It is, of course, assumed that all the materials listed will be left in their natural color, unpainted or undyed. Wood finishes will be clear, that is, wax, oil, lacquer, or varnish, so that they darken or shift color somewhat, but stains and colored paints are omitted. Metals such as steel that need protection are painted only with utilitarian primers such as red lead (dull red-orange) or zinc chromate (dull greenish-yellow) or aluminum paint. Textiles (including those

Figure 8.5 The living room of the Francis W. Little house of 1913 designed by Frank Lloyd Wright, as originally built in Wayzata, Minnesota, and now installed in the Metropolitan Museum of Art in New York. As in most of Wright's interiors, the colors are the natural hues of the materials used. (*Photo by John Pile.*)

used for floor covering) are in the natural colors of their fibers. A question may be raised as to whether dyed textiles might not be accepted provided the dyes are natural (as opposed to chemically manufactured) in origin. Natural dyes generally provide soft and harmonious tones that, as they appear in woven rugs or blankets, can add variety to a natural color interior. When living plants are present, they, inevitably, introduce the chromatic color green and, possibly, flower colors as well—indisputably natural colors.

Some confusing problems arise in modern practice when materials are chosen that are synthetic and may be said not to have any truly natural color. Plastics are a typical example. When plastic is made, some colorants are added to avoid an unattractive, streaked, or mottled appearance. Plastic laminates are of whatever color the top layer of lamination may be. Floor tiles of vinyl plastic can be of any color—is the color of slate or clay the only allowable choice? Glazed tiles may be glazed in any color as naturally as the color of the clay from which they are made. How to deal with such materials becomes a matter of choice. A color may be chosen from the palette of natural colors or another neutral (white, black, or a beige or gray) may be chosen to avoid breaking out of the typical natural color range. If a material must be painted to protect it from dirt, weather, or wear, the designer confronts a similar problem. Is it only permissible to paint plaster white or near white? What color is natural to iron and steel—primer color, black, aluminum or chrome plate?

In working with a natural color scheme, the designer is free to decide when to make exceptions—to use other colors in limited locations converting the color plan to a natural-plus scheme. The colors of a painting, a tapestry, or woven rug or blanket, if it relates well to the natural colors in use otherwise, can enliven a natural scheme. This may develop without the designer's intent in any case as occupants introduce accessories, artwork, books on shelves, or other elements with colors that are by no means natural. It is interesting to notice that in color photographs of interiors using natural color, the photographer has often chosen to introduce some small detail, perhaps a magazine or book cover or a vase of flowers, that adds an accent of chromatic color to an otherwise natural scheme.

Functional Color

Another basis for building a color scheme, or at least for making a start at color selection, involves basing color choices on function. Not surprisingly, this approach fits well into the theoretical position of the kind of modern design described as *functionalism.* In functionalist design, every decision is based on the purpose of the particular element being dealt with. Functional color makes every color choice on the basis of the function (purpose) of the element under consideration. Functional color often overlaps natural-color planning since the natural color of a material, if it is totally suitable to its purposeful role, does not need to be changed.

Difference with natural-color scheming arises when the natural color is not ideal for the purpose of the element in question. For

example, if the natural color of a wood floor is so light as to show dirt and wear to a troublesome degree, the functional approach would be to color the wood with a finish—perhaps paint or stain—of a more practical color. In addition to such strictly practical color decisions, functional-color planning opens up the use of color to a wide variety of other purposeful applications. Color may be used, for example, to draw attention to or minimize attention on some element. Trim, for example, might be painted in a color strongly contrasting with its surround to give emphasis to the elements it accents, or it may be painted to match the surround as to make it unobtrusive. A doorway can, in this way, be given importance or made relatively unnoticeable.

The overall purpose of a space can be made a basic factor in functional color choice, with colors chosen to promote calm and relaxation or to suggest activity and excitement. Chapter 11 is concerned with such emotional implications of color. A decision to emphasize warm or cool colors may be based on realities of climate or orientation. Color may be used to modify and improve aspects of size and shape of spaces as advancing and receding colors are chosen to alter spatial perception. Other functional uses of color include the introduction of colors that may have a specific meaning in a certain context (see Figure 8.6). Safety markings, for example, commonly use black and orange or black and yellow stripes (chosen for high visibility) while bright red makes exit signs and firefighting equipment readily visible. There is an established code for color marking pipe in industrial facilities to aid workers in identifying the various piping systems that may be combined in complex tangles. Such strictly utilitarian color uses can also be visually interesting and attractive and suggest possibilities for similar coded color use in other contexts.

The use of a strong theme color for each floor of a multilevel project can help to

Figure 8.6   Functional color: the interior of a Cornell University fieldhouse in Ithaca, New York, designed by Gwathmey Siegel & Associates: architects. The bright red of the bleacher seat area and the court markings have clear purpose beyond decoration. (*Photo © Jeff Goldberg/ESTO; courtesy of Gwathmey Siegel & Associates.*)

give each level an identity readily recognized and individual to that floor. School and college buildings, hotels and motels, and medical facilities can make good use of this type of coding. The colors developed as part of a corporate identity project can also be turned to functional use in certain types of interiors. The counters of various airlines or car rental firms at an airport terminal, for example, can be readily identified if each firm has a unique corporate color marking. National colors often serve the same function in such situations. The use of well-known national colors can be an identifying theme in the design of a restaurant serving a particular national cuisine. Good design judgment must be a factor in introducing such functional signal colors. Not every Italian restaurant needs to be red, white, and green, and the combination of red, white, and blue is so widely used as to reduce its meaning—does it

Figure 8.7   A reception area in the New York offices of Manufacturers Hanover Trust Company as designed by Swanke Hayden Connell Architects. A color scheme that combines natural and functional color approaches. (*Photo by Jaime Ardiles-Arce, courtesy of Swanke Hayden Connell Architects.*)

stand for France, England, the United States, Exxon Oil, or American Airlines? Overuse of a particular color coding still does not preclude discrete use in appropriate contexts.

COMBINED SCHEMES

While it is convenient to discuss the various ways of developing a color scheme sepa-

rately, there is nothing to prevent combining several approaches (see Figure 8.7). A decision to develop an all-natural scheme might, for example, become a starting point. If the natural colors of the materials chosen happen to fall in a neutral or near-neutral range (as often happens with natural tones), the scheme may be both neutral and natural. Addition of some enlivening chromatic colors that are not part of the neutral scheme might occur when some elements are added that introduce contrast converting the scheme to either neutral-plus, natural-plus, or both. A desire to use warm or cool colors, intense or subdued colors for functional reasons can further modify a scheme under development so that it is quite possible to find that all of the approaches have been used in combination. Whatever combination of approach has been used in developing a scheme, the final result can fall into any one of the theoretical color scheme types discussed in Chapter 7. A scheme may thus be monochromatic, neutral, natural, and functional all at once. The point of considering these various schematic types is not to suggest that the designer should insist on one particular theoretical scheme or one practical approach, but rather to offer various starting points and various ways of thinking as a scheme is being developed which offer logical suggestions for how to proceed within the vast range of possibilities that color choice offers.

ACCENT COLOR

In the discussion of color system development in Chapter 7 and in this chapter, mention of accent color frequently appears. This is a concept familiar in many everyday contexts. In fashion, for example, a colorful scarf or necktie is a favorite way to introduce an accent color to enliven an otherwise unexceptional outfit. A color accent is typically some element that is relatively small in size but sufficiently intense in color to draw attention. It is also most often easily changed so that it can shift the totality of a color scheme with minimal difficulty. In the discussions above, it is pointed out that easy or safe color schemes are most often those that use monotone, monochromatic, neutral, or analogous color, but that such schemes run the risk of being monotonous or dull. The typical route to brightening such schemes is the introduction of accent

color in small or limited areas. Usually, accent color is chosen to contrast with the dominant colors of a scheme in one way or another. Where the basic scheme is close to neutral, any strongly chromatic color can become appropriate as accent. In a scheme that emphasizes cream, white, and beige, an accent could be a red, a green, or a blue, for example—or any other chromatic tone. Similarly, in a scheme that uses white and grays as basic color, any chromatic tone will act as an accent if it is sufficiently saturated. The contrast in each of these cases is a matter of color saturation. With the basic colors desaturated, any saturated tone is appropriate as accent.

Since basic color in these situations is restrained, the accent color is often important in giving the total scheme its character. In a largely neutral scheme, a warm accent color moves the entire effect of the space toward warmth, while a cool accent will have the opposite impact. Since accent color is usually easy to change, this effect can be exploited as a means of altering the color impact of a space with seasonal change or simply to give variety. A largely neutral bedroom, for instance, can change from a summer to a winter ambience with a change of bed cover from blue-green to orange-red. A restaurant can be shifted in color effect by a change in the color of table linens and other minor accessories. It is interesting to note that in traditional liturgical church practice, each season of the church year has identifying colors that are used in vestments worn by clergy and used as altar covers to give to the white or gray church interior a color tonality suited to the season (see Figure 8.8).

Where the basic color of a scheme is an analogous grouping, accent color can either be a highly saturated version of one of the colors used, or it can be a complementary color. A blue and green analogous scheme might be accented with an intense, saturated blue, or with a strong red or red-orange. In a complementary

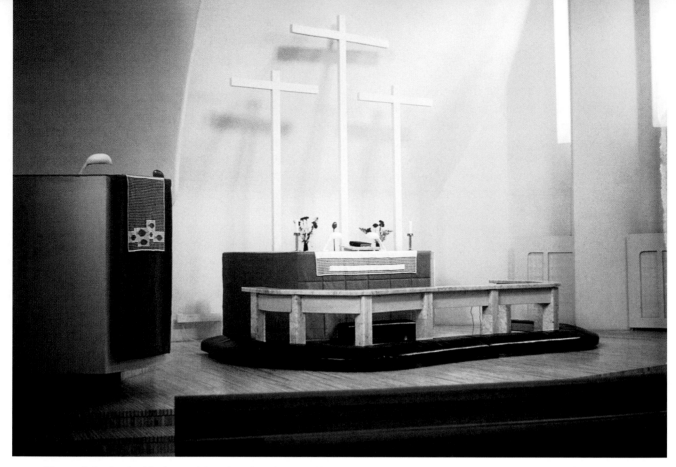

Figure 8.8   In the Vuoksenniska church at Imatra, Finland, Alvar Aalto used white and the color of natural wood, but strong color is introduced in the color of liturgical vestments, also designed by Aalto. The colors are changed with the succession of seasons of the church year; the green visible here is the color of the Trinity season. (*Photo by John Pile.*)

scheme, the tones on one side of the color circle will usually be less intense, but larger in extent than those on the other side. An accent can be found by introducing small areas of intense color on the side of the circle that is generally less saturated. For example, a complementary scheme might be based on large areas of beige or tan—basically red-orange tones in light and desaturated form—while, on the other side of the circle, smaller areas of blue-green would appear. An accent of intense red-orange would be possible. An alternative approach finds accent color in the form of a particularly intense area of tone from the complements to the tones that have major roles. In the example cited, this would mean an accent of intense blue-green.

DOMINANT AND SUBDOMINANT TONES

A concept borrowed from musical theory may be helpful in planning a color scheme of any one of the types already discussed. This is the idea of choosing a color tone or closely related group of tones to be considered as *dominant,* that is, thematic or important. The dominant tones are then brought into a relationship with a *subdominant* tone or group of tones, establishing a play of alternatives which gives life to the total scheme. The dominant tones may achieve dominance through intensity, through extent, or both, while the subdominant role is established through reduction of these elements. For example, in a monochromatic scheme, the dominant tones might be large areas of a light beige or tan while a subdominant could be established through the use of browns in smaller areas. In an analogous scheme, dominant tones of yellow and orange might be related to subdominant yellow-greens. In a complementary scheme, the tones that occupy larger areas will usually be dominant while the smaller areas of complementary color provide the subdominant tones. Note that accent color may occur among either dominant or subdominant tones, but will not ordinarily be present among both groups.

The concept of dominant and subdominant relationships may be helpful in working toward a degree of balance among the colors present in a scheme which offers interaction and life while still achieving a desired aesthetic effect—most often an effect that can be called harmonious.

ADAPTATION

In developing color schemes, choosing a type of scheme, and proceeding to the specifics of a scheme under development, it is helpful to remember the aspect of visual perception that relates to the adaptive function of the human organism. The senses and the brain functions that relate to the senses are organized to aid in adaptation to any situation—to any environment. It can be assumed that such adaptation serves to protect the individual from an excess of sensory reaction to a given situation. It can be noticed, for example, on entering an overheated room, that the heat will seem noticeably excessive for a time, but will gradually come to seem normal or at least nearly normal, and quite bearable. When moving from a heated space to a cooler out-of-doors, a similar reaction occurs in reverse, with the cool area soon seeming normal. This effect is familiar in warm weather when it is the outside air that is excessively warm and stepping into an

air-conditioned space seems, at first, remarkably (probably pleasantly) cool. Within a few minutes, the cooler air seems normal or even quite warm.

A comparable example of adaptation at work occurs when stepping from a brightly lit environment to one that is dim. At first it seems hard to see (as in a dim movie theater), but quite soon, adaptation takes place and vision becomes easy. On leaving the dim interior and moving to bright outdoor light, intense glare is sensed until adaptation makes the brighter light acceptable. In each of these examples—adaptation to heat and cold or to bright or dim light—there are limits to the possibility of adaptation established by physical and physiological realities. One cannot be comfortable in heat beyond a level the body can tolerate or in cold that is physically dangerous. Adaptation to bright light reaches a limit when glare demands shielding the eyes; dim light becomes inadequate for seeing to accomplish certain tasks, but some vision remains possible until near total darkness is reached.

The significance of adaptation in relation to color has been noted earlier in the discussion of the effects known as color constancy and in the formation of complementary reactions in simultaneous color. In each of these effects, adaptation is at work. Under warm-colored light (candle flame or an incandescent lamp) adaptation brings about a correction so that the viewer soon adapts to the color shift brought about by the light and sees all colors in a normal relationship. This effect is readily demonstrated by noting that sunglasses with a strong color tone (such as green, for example) will, when first put on, seem to shift all color to the tint of the lenses. Quite quickly, however, the eye and brain make an adaptive correction and colors are seen as normal. When the glasses are removed, a reverse shift takes place, and the normal scene appears tinted with color complementary to that of the glasses—upon removing green glasses, the world appears pink or orange for a short time, but then reverts to normal. Here, also, there is a limit to what adaptation can achieve. When looking through an intense blue glass, one that filters out all but blue light, all color will appear blue no matter how long viewing is continued, but it is evident that the adaptive mechanism is at work when the glass in removed and the world appears orange in tone for a few minutes until the attempted adaptation ceases.

After staring at an intense red color sample for a short time, a complementary green tone will be seen if vision is shifted to a white surface. The eye even selects small areas of the visual field for such adaptation so that a bright red shape seen against a black background will then appear as a green shape with a white surround when vision is shifted to a blank white surface.

It may be assumed that the purpose of all such adaptive reactions is to protect the organism against an excess of sensory intake—to introduce what might be regarded as a psychological defense against too much heat or cold, too much brightness or darkness, too much red, or too much green. In the making of color schemes, an understanding of the ways in which adaptation works can be helpful in explaining some common reactions and in working toward color that will be appropriate for intended functions. When strong color is present, the adaptive mechanism seeks complementary (opposite) color to reduce the impact of the color seen. Within a space, the provision of such alternative color offers the viewer relief from excess sensory input without requiring so much of the adaptive mechanism. The use of green or blue-green in hospital operating rooms—even for the clothing of personnel—is well known. The purpose is to provide relief from the intensely lit red tissue as viewed by the surgeon and assistants. In more ordinary environmental circumstances, the same needs for aid to the adaptive functions can be observed.

The problems of potential monotony in monochromatic and analogous color schemes has been discussed earlier. It can be suggested that the sense of monotony and the negative reactions that result are caused by the way in which the eye and brain call for adaptive relief from the overload of a particular color sensation. The excessive use of green, often called "institutional green," that was widely accepted some time ago is an example of the way in which unrelieved use of a particular color, however unobjectionable that color may be in itself, can lead to unpleasant reaction based on excessive demand for adaptation.

The popularity of complementary color schemes and the value of accent colors in hues that contrast with the dominant colors in monochromatic and analogous schemes can be explained as demonstrating the need for colors that provide relief from a dominant color and so reduce the need for maintaining an adaptive, defensive color shift through mental adjustment. Amid green leaves and grass, red flowers provide a relief that leads to a favorable aesthetic reaction. In general, neutral tones demand less color correction from the adaptive mechanisms, but their very lack of chromatic color stimulation can lead to negative reactions. White may seem blank, empty, and monotonous, grays and black may be monotonous and depressive. Small areas of color within neutral settings can be understood as relieving the mental strain of adapting to too much white, black, or other neutrals.

9

From Charts to Realization

SAMPLE CHARTS

Once a color scheme is developed in terms of abstract color swatches, the usual next step is to translate those swatches into samples of real materials suitable to the elements that will make up a completed space. In accomplishing this step, the designer must make some decisions (or obtain decisions from others) that involve material selections in terms other than color. For example, if a floor color is represented by a particular color swatch, it is also necessary to determine what the floor material will be before beginning a search for the actual floor material sample. There is an obvious interaction here between abstract color selection and real material choice since many materials are only available in a limited range of color. This issue should have been faced when making the abstract color chart, as discussed in Chapter 6, in order to avoid facing impossible problems at this stage. If a certain element is to be marble, the abstract color proposed must be one available in marble.

The task of locating appropriately colored materials will be made easier if a collection of material samples is readily available. Building up such a collection is a worthwhile effort for every interior designer. Most practicing designers and virtually all larger design firms establish a sample cabinet, even a sample room or library, and make an effort to have on hand files of paint color samples, fabric and carpet samples, samples of plastic laminates and tiles from the manufacturers whose products are most often specified. Most design schools provide material sample libraries for the use of their students, holding a number of samples of each item and replacing items as they are withdrawn by students for use in making color charts. Keeping such collections up-to-date can present a problem since manufacturers regularly discontinue older designs and colors and introduce new items in response to fashion and sales trends. It is a common experience to select a particular item that seems ideal only to discover that it is no longer available. A substitute must then be found.

Large firms in major cities often ask suppliers to make regular office visits to update sample collections, removing discontinued items and providing the latest samples. The individual designer or small firm will usually have to settle for making frequent visits to product showrooms to collect and request samples of items that seem to be likely candidates for future use. It is, of course, pointless to acquire samples of materials that are, by the standards of the particular designer, unattractive and unlikely to ever be desired.

While paint colors, textiles, and some floor materials are relatively easy to keep on file, some materials are bulky, inconvenient to store, costly, or difficult to acquire. Masonry materials, for example, various stones, bricks, and structural tile are inconvenient to store. Wood can be represented by small samples or even by veneers, but, since its appearance can be drastically changed by differing finish techniques, a collection of many woods each in several finishes can also be problematic. A possible strategy involves collecting and storing a small accumulation of favorite materials even if inconvenient to store, to collect color illustrations of a wider range of such materials, and to plan on obtaining actual samples of particular items only as they are actually needed. Alternative samples that are not actually used can be stored away for possible future use.

For the independent, individual designer and for smaller firms with specialized areas of practice, the choice of material samples to keep on hand can be influenced by the preferences and needs of that particular design practice. A residential practice, for example, will have little need for a great variety of metal samples, but may want to emphasize decorative printed textiles and patterned rugs, carpets, and wallpaper that would have little applicability in office design. In contrast, an office design firm or one specializing in other contract interiors such as transportation design, may need a fuller representation of materials known for good durability, soil resistance, and fire safety.

Some designers develop a personal color palette or limited range of preferred colors and so can assemble a small selection of samples that defines their favored color vocabulary. Frank Lloyd Wright, for example, because of his preference for natural-color emphasis, generally confined his color choices to natural tones of red to brown brick and tile, the warm tones of naturally finished woods, and textiles in neutral tones except for limited used of a bright scarlet red as an accent tone. Many designers working in the vocabulary of the International Style have restricted color choice to black, white, neutral gray, and the three primaries in strongly saturated form. Other designers have become known for certain favorite colors and so could restrict their sample collections to the colors and finishes that they particularly favor.

Sample storage

Insofar as possible, it is convenient to standardize the size of samples so that they may be stored in standard cabinets. The three by five dimension of standard index cards is convenient and many samples are provided in this size. Larger samples can be cut down to fit, smaller samples mounted on three by five cards. Textile swatches provided by fabric houses are of varied sizes and shapes, but often can be fitted to the three by five standard (see Figure 9.1). When each supplier's samples are kept together, it is not difficult to accept whatever swatch size is provided. However samples are kept, it is important to make certain that the relevant information is firmly attached to the sample. It is frustrating to find a sample that is of ideal color or pattern that has become separated from its identifying data as to maker and style number.

As a material sample collection increases, it is helpful to devise an orderly filing and storage system. Basic classification by types of material is customary. Classifications might include the following:

Masonry materials
Wood, plywood, and veneer
Ceramic and quarry tile

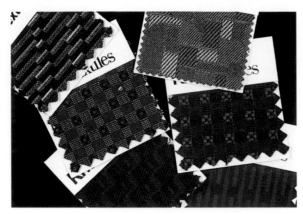

Figure 9.1 Textile sample swatches as they are usually provided by manufacturers and showrooms.

Resilient tile
Carpet and rugs
Glass and transparent plastic
Metal
Plastic laminates
Textiles
Wallpaper
Plastic wall covering
Paint and other finishes
Hardware

Within such general classifications, several ways of developing subclassifications are possible. Samples may be grouped by manufacturers or suppliers. Since samples are provided grouped in this way (a box of tiles or a book of wallpaper samples, for example), it is easy to retain this arrangement and it will be found convenient when moving from chart to ordering information. An alternative classification sorts samples by color, grouping all samples within a given category by hue and value. This makes locating a desired color sample easier but may require more organizational effort. Grouping by color is more useful for such products as carpets and textiles than for masonry, wood, or metal where grouping by type may be more convenient, such as brick, slate, marble, for masonry; wood by species; metals by type.

Certain materials present special problems in sample use. Wherever a pattern exists—whether a natural pattern such as wood grain or marble veining, a manufactured pattern such as striped, checked, or printed textiles, or patterned floor coverings—a sample does not accurately represent the material unless it includes the full variety of color present in the actual material. A fabric swatch from a print, for example, must be carefully chosen to include all the colors of the print. A particular small sample of a marble may not reveal the full color impact of its veining. Other materials may be used to create patterns from units of uniform color. Tiles, for example, may be laid to create borders, patterns of squares, or other designs. Single tiles of each color used can be misleading. White tile with a blue border, for example, if represented by only two tiles showing the two colors, gives an impression of more border color than will actually be present in the finished space. In making a material color chart, such issues must be recognized and some means found to make the chart representative of the reality of the materials as they will be used.

MATERIALS CHARTS

The most obvious way to proceed with material chart making is to make a blank chart that matches the abstract color chart in size and spacing of samples and to insert each material sample in the space that corresponds to the color swatch of the abstract chart. Doing this can present some difficulties in certain cases. Available samples may be too small or too large and in a form not easily cut to size. Some materials are thick or bulky in a way that does not fit a small chart. A brick, for example, or a slab sample of stone or terrazzo is not readily fitted into a small chart. It may be possible to substitute a paper illustration clipped from a brochure (for terrazzo, for

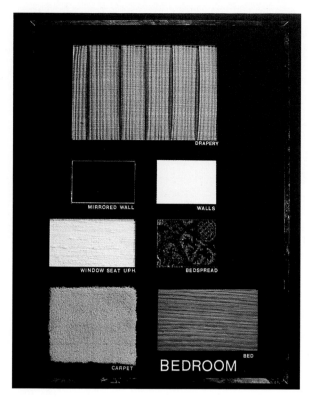

Figure 9.2 A sample board made up by a design student as part of an interior design project presentation.

Figure 9.3 A presentation of samples made orderly by adjusting thicknesses so that all samples are flush. The thinner items (textiles and color chips) are mounted on a thick backing so as to match the thickness of a thick carpet sample.

example) or to use a simple retail paper color sample. A matte paper of appropriate color will represent brick quite well if a careful color match is selected.

A compact sample chart is usually made by gluing the samples, cut to the desired size, to a sheet of mat board. A slightly more perfect sample board will result if the varied thicknesses of material samples are adjusted to bring all samples to a common surface level. This can be managed by cutting a mat to create an opening the size and shape of the complete chart and attaching the samples from the rear with thinner samples mounted on backing to bring their thickness up to a level common with the thickest sample. Sample charts of small size are most easily transported and stored, but large sample

boards are often made up to match the size of mounted renderings or drawings that make up part of a visual presentation. (See Figures 9.2 through 9.4.)

A large sample board presents some special problems. Samples must be large enough to show up well but should still be sized in proportion to the area of each material that will be present in the finished space. Ideally, the position of samples should come close to matching their position in the finished space. This means placing sample floor material and covering at the bottom of the sample grouping, ceiling color at the top, and the materials of walls, furniture, and other items in between in some logical arrangement. It is best to resist the temptation to make all samples the same size and place them in a geomet-

Figure 9.4   A sample board from a large and complex project, the Porto Vita apartment complex in Florida, designed by Judith Stockman.

ric arrangement since this may give a misleading impression of the relative importance of various materials in the completed project. The color of the mat surrounding a sample chart forming a sample board must be carefully chosen to avoid any influence on the samples shown. Neutral white, gray, or black are common choices, but the lightness or darkness of the mat surround can also influence color perception.

In all cases, samples need to be placed adjacent to one another with no mat showing in between. Ideally, samples should be placed so that their adjacency corresponds to the positions of the various materials as they will be placed in the completed space.

It is rarely possible to achieve placement as a perfect representation of material adjacencies, but a close approximation is desirable. Some designers prefer to assemble material samples on a sample board in various shapes overlapping in a way that creates a kind of collage (see Figure 9.5). While such a sample board may be attractive, it tends to distract attention from the information it contains and may appear overly decorative. It is usualy best to use a simple arrangement of neatly shaped samples.

An alternative method of converting color charts into material selections involves assembling samples of real materi-

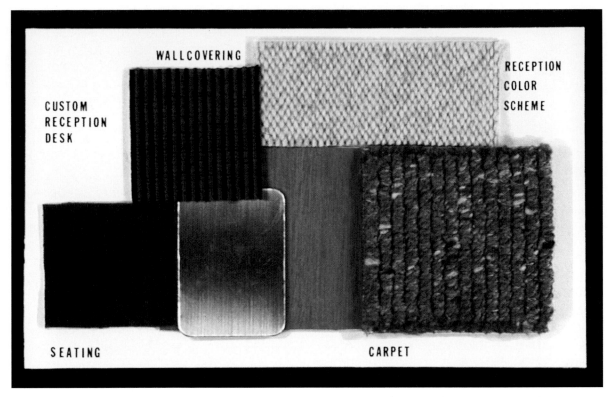

Figure 9.5 A collage arrangement of material and color samples from a student interior design project.

als of various, often quite large, sizes without any attempt to attach the samples to a chart or board. Typically, the samples relating to a particular space are grouped in a folder, envelope, or box ready to be spread out on a desk or tabletop for viewing (see Figure 9.6). This approach has the advantage of permitting easy inclusion of larger samples that may give a better impression of how the real materials will relate. Some designers insist on assembling large samples of carpet to be laid down on a floor, large samples of textiles that can be stretched over a piece of furniture or draped to simulate hanging curtains.

MATERIAL SAMPLES

Manufacturers of fabrics usually have available *memo squares,* samples a yard square which can be bought or borrowed

to make it possible to evaluate choices on the basis of a sizable sample. Preliminary selection is normally made from small swatches with the memo square sample requested only for the prime selection or, perhaps, one or two alternatives. Carpet manufacturers also have larger samples (three by five or five by eight feet) on hand in showrooms or, for larger projects, available on loan. Furniture manufacturers usually have large panels available in standard wood finishes that can be viewed at a showroom or borrowed. Custom cabinet makers will, on request, make up panels in one or more finishes under consideration. A large sample of paint color can be created easily by simply painting a panel of wallboard with paint from a small can of the mixed color specified.

For large projects, the selection of a particular material may involve large expenditures, making it seem prudent to view

Figure 9.6   A group of samples relating to a particular space ready to be kept together in a folder or envelope.

large samples before making decisions that, if they prove disappointing, could be major embarrassments to the designer and client alike. When samples are collected in this loosely assembled way, it is easy to arrange for consideration of substitution of various alternatives so that designer or designer and client together can observe the effect of alternative materials or alternative colors as part of a scheme. When working with clients, it is best to limit the number of alternatives offered since confusion may arise if many alternates for several elements are offered at one time.

MOCK-UP SPACES

This most extreme way of viewing samples arises when, in connection with a large project, a sample space or *mock-up* that simulates the final project is built. This is most often done for projects where there will be a large number of identical spaces, hotel rooms, for example, or private offices in a large office project. Actual samples of furniture, lamps, and lighting fixtures can be introduced (purchased or borrowed) to make the sample room a true prototype for the space as designed. Constructing one room makes it possible to evaluate color and material selections (and all other aspects of the space design) in a totally

realistic setting. Preparation for setting up such a mock-up space will follow the steps involved in designing a single room and will usually include the making of color scheme charts and material sample charts or sample boards.

COLOR PLANS

While color and material charts are being prepared or immediately after they have been approved, it is usually best to make up color plans. These are not presentation materials, but are project documents recording the locations of each material and color. Much material information will appear in working drawings, and some or all color information may be included in written specifications or finish charts included as part of a set of construction drawings. There is usually additional data that does not appear in these documents. Walls may be shown as "paint finish" without specifying color. When many paint colors are to be used in various spaces within a project, it is often most convenient to mark up a black and white (B&W) print of a plan with colored pencil or marker lines coded to a paint color list or set of samples. A furniture location plan can be convenient for indicating wall colors and can also be used to give data on furniture finishes, cover fabrics, and locations of drapery fabrics of various colors or patterns.

Many interior projects that do not involve construction work but are limited to color and material choices call for a special color and finish plan to give information on locations of various colors and finishes as well as furniture locations in relation to finish and color. A B&W line print of a floor plan that will have been made as part of the basic planning process is an ideal basis for such a color plan (see Figure 9.7). Small-size color plans can be reproduced by color Xerox, but, unfortunately, large architectural plans carrying color data are

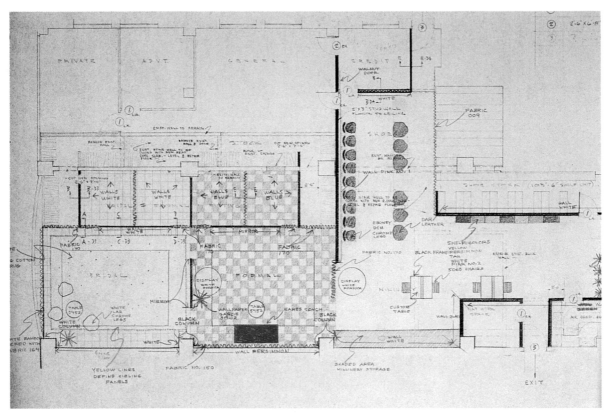

Figure 9.7   A color plan for use in completing a project on-site. A black and white print is marked with colored pencil to show the location of each material and color.

not readily reproduced by mechanical means. Making one or two copies (for filing and use on site) by hand is usually not overly laborious since it is only a matter of adding color lines and shading to an available plan print.

Once a selection of color and material has been arrived at for a particular space, it is important to record the decisions with written data identifying the products selected including the maker or source for each item and color and finish identifications. These notes can be attached to material charts or boards but should also be filed in duplicate to be used when the time comes for preparation of specifications and issuance of purchase orders.

The many materials that can be part of an interior space vary greatly in color character and variety of color available. The fol-

lowing summaries can serve as reminders of the ranges of color that particular materials can offer.

STONE.   Most often, stone is quite neutral in color with grays, tans, and browns most common. Limestone, sandstone, slate, and flagstone are of fairly uniform color within a particular block, but can vary somewhat from one stone to another. Flagstone, for example, can be selected to be of consistent color or can be in a variety of tones ranging through geenish, bluish, and neutral tones of gray. Granite has a more varied surface with a granular texture and is available in tones from a reddish brown to dark gray, almost black. Travertine is a porous stone with a warm, cream color tone overall. The pores, if left as open fissures, darken the overall color through the

Figure 9.8 Stone, most often appearing brown or gray in color, may be complex in color and pattern on close inspection. Granite can vary in color from almost black to shades of rose and pink.

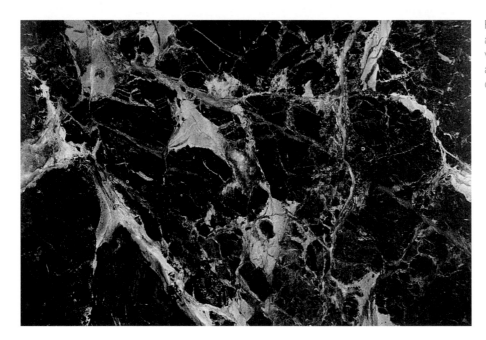

Figure 9.9 Marbles are available in many varied colors, often with a rich, irregular pattern of veining.

effects of light and shadow. If the pores are filled, the color of the filling can lighten or darken the overall color effect. The varieties of Marble are among the most colorful of masonry materials, available in a wide range of colors from near white, cream, and light gray to greens, blacks, and warm tones of red and orange. The veining of marble can be unobtrusive or strongly contrasting with overall color. Individual blocks of marble vary greatly in color and are often selected carefully to provide a desired tone and pattern of veining. Terrazzo is made by imbedding marble chips in cement and grinding the surface to a smooth finish. Great variety of color is available through

Figure 9.10 The varied colors of marbles were used in 1631 to form this elaborately patterned floor in the Venice Church of Santa Maria della Salute by Longhena. (*Photo by John Pile.*)

Figure 9.11 Travertine is a soft, light, cream-colored stone remarkable for its open texture of holes. Travertine is often filled with a cement mixture to close the open holes and provide a smooth surface.

the selection of the chip color (or colors) and the coloring of the cement binder. (See Figures 9.8 through 9.12.)

BRICK. Usually, bricks come in the clay colors of the familiar red or in tones of yellow, brown, or intermediates (see Figure 9.13). The color of the mortar influences the overall effect of brickwork color. Glazed brick is available in a wider range of colors similar to that of ceramic tile.

CONCRETE BLOCK AND EXPOSED MASS CONCRETE. Usually, these come in neutral tones of gray and tan often considered unattractive. Concrete can be

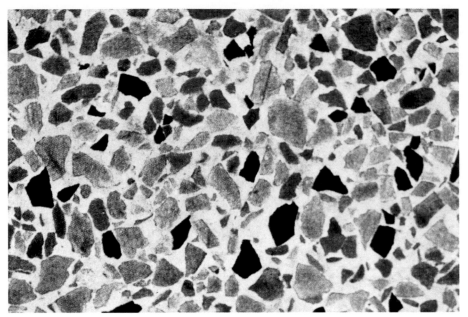

Figure 9.12 Terrazzo, a favorite floor material, uses marble chips imbedded in cement and polished off to a smooth surface. A vast variety of color and texture effects are possible through choice of color and size of the marble chips and the color of the surrounding cement.

Figure 9.13 Brick, most often thought of as red, is actually available in many shades of red, brown, and yellow. Glazed brick can be white or many other colors. The mortar of brick joints can also be colored to create additional variety in the effect of a brick surface. A brick wall can also be painted in almost any color.

painted to arrive at any desired color (see Figure 9.14).

TERRA-COTTA BLOCK.   Usually this is of the natural red-brown color or it can be had with glazed surfaces of varied color. Although not now in wide use, glazed terra-cotta was once extensively used in strongly colored decorative patterns.

TILE.   This material is available in a great variety of colors and sizes permitting surfaces of uniform color or of color patterning (see Figure 9.15). Individual tiles may also carry decorative patterns or images in one color (as with the blue on white of Dutch tile) or in varied colors. Quarry tile is a hard, unglazed tile available in tones of red, red-brown, and tan.

Figure 9.14 Concrete, usually gray or tan, varies considerably in color according to the color of the aggregate and sand used in the mix.

Figure 9.15 Tile is made in many sizes and in a variety of compositions that generate a range of natural colors in tans, browns, and reds. Glazed tile can be of any color. This tile floor in the monastery of Santa Creus in Spain uses medieval tiles in a warm, clay color. (*Photo by John Pile.*)

PLASTER.   This is a common wall and ceiling surface material, most often with a natural white surface, although admixture of sand can result in tints of warm cream or beige. Plaster surfaces are commonly painted and so can be of any color. Drywall materials (wallboard or Sheetrock) are widely used alternatives to plaster and are normally painted in any desired color.

WOOD.   Hard and soft woods are available in a wide variety of natural colors that correspond to various species. The color range is from the near white, beiges, and yellows of pine, birch, and maple to the darker tans of oak, the brown of walnut, and the various reddish-browns of such woods as mahogany, cherry, rosewood, and the very dark tones of ebony. Wood

Figure 9.16   Woods are of varied natural colors and can be altered in color through staining, bleaching, and other finishing processes including painting.

can be stained to darken and alter natural color or to totally shift color (see Figure 9.16). Bleaching can make wood tones lighter, making possible, for some lighter woods such as maple, near-white color. The grain patterns of wood vary from unobtrusive to quite marked and, with strongly grained species, become a factor in overall color tone. Open grain can be filled with a filler of similar, lighter, or darker tone shifting overall color to some extent. The level of gloss of a final natural finish also affects perceived color. Wood can, of course, also be painted in any desired color. Plywood color is determined by the visible layer of surface. Utility-grade plywood and the vari-

ous forms of particle- or chipboard used as utility alternatives to plywood are usually painted to cover their unappealing surfaces.

RESILIENT TILE.   Resilient sheet materials, as well as resilient tiles, are widely used for floor covering. Vinyl flooring in either sheet or tile form is made in a variety of bright and subdued colors. Many surface patterns are available in varied textures as are surface patterns that imitate (with limited success), marble, brick, stone, slate, and wood. (See Figure 9.17.) Reinforced vinyl tile (a replacement for the formerly used vinyl-asbestos products) use fillers with vinyl to produce a hard, inexpen-

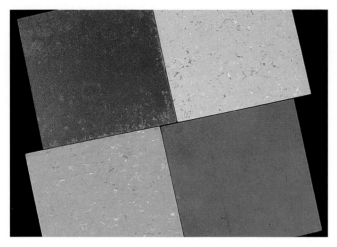 

Figure 9.17   Resilient tiles of plastic (vinyl) or other compositions are a popular floor covering material made in a wide range of colors and textures.

sive alternative to pure vinyl. Rubber tile is a more resilient alternative to vinyl which is also made in a wide range of colors. Cork tile is a highly resilient floor surface material available in the tans and browns, which are the natural colors of cork.

CARPETS AND RUGS.   These are floor materials available in a vast variety of colors, textures, and patterns (see Figure 9.18). Color may come from natural fibers in natural color or (more often) from dye. Weaves may be of uniform (solid) color or may result from interweaving two or more colored yarns. Patterns can be the result of weaving or may be printed onto a woven carpet. Many traditional methods of rug and carpet weaving can produce varied and intricate patterns ranging from simple stripes to the complex designs of traditional oriental rugs.

GLASS.   Most commonly, glass is used in clear, virtually colorless form but it can also be tinted or strongly colored. Mirror, also most often colorless, can be obtained in tinted or veined forms with strong color characteristics. Glass rich in color intensity can be used to make up decorative stained glass that, with the transmission of light,

projects color onto other surfaces. Acrylic plastic, available in clear and a variety of colors, is sometimes used as an alternative to glass.

METALS.   These materials can be used in their natural colors but are more often given a surface finish or plating for protection and for appearance. Steel is usually painted for rust protection or plated with another metal such as chromium with its highly reflective, virtually colorless surface. Stainless steel is used in its natural, silvery metallic tone. Aluminum is also usually finished to protect against corrosion either by the process of anodizing, which allows it to retain its natural soft, silvery tone or introduces some other color, or by an enamel or plastic coating, which may be of any color. Copper, brass, and bronze each have characteristic natural colors in reddish, golden yellow, or brown tones. Left unprotected, these metals develop a blue-green oxide surface that can be an attractive color. Metals used for the manufacture of plumbing fixtures, appliances, and furniture are usually finished with paint or enamel, which can be of a variety of colors. White finishes are common for fixtures and appliances.

PLASTIC LAMINATES.   These are made in a great variety of both strong and muted colors and in patterns that may be abstract or imitative of other materials, such as marble or wood, or in metallic colors. Laminates are now available with uniform color through the sheet thickness so that cut edges match surface color.

LEATHER.   This material and its alternative substitutes are often used for upholstery and more rarely for wall covering. The natural and near-natural colors of leather are in a tan to brown range. Black and many more chromatic colors are available in leathers which have been dyed or otherwise finished. Sheet materials using plastic coated onto a textile backing are available to simulate leather or for nonimitative use in a wide range of colors.

PLASTICS.   These are synthetic materials that can be made or finished in almost any color. Their uses for floor covering, leather substitutes, as alternatives to glass, and in the form of laminates have already been mentioned. Plastics are also used for parts of furniture, such as drawers and chair seats and backs. Fiberglass plastic has a small-scale random surface pattern formed by the glass fibers embedded in resin. The resin color, modified by this textural pattern, is typical of fiberglass objects except where a coating of uniform, solid color has been applied. Moldings of other plastics are usually of solid color in a full range of tones.

TEXTILES.   Usable for drapery, upholstery, and (sometimes) for wall covering, textiles are among the most varied sources for interior color. Fabrics may be made of yarn of natural color or dyed. A single color or several colors may be woven into a cloth of overall color or may be woven into patterns such as stripes, checks, or more complex designs. (See Figures 9.19 and 9.20.) Cloth may be piece-dyed in a single color or may be printed with patterns of almost any sort. Custom colors can be ordered, dyed, or printed in tones chosen by the designer, but textile firms offer a vast variety of colors and patterns from stock.

WALL COVERINGS.   These may include textiles (as previously mentioned, but now seldom used); woven materials such as grass cloth; or sheet materials of plasticized materials made in many textures and colors, some simulating other materials such as grass cloth or actual textiles. Wallpaper, simply paper printed in colors and designs, is another widely used wall covering (see Figure 9.21). Patterns include unobtrusive stripes and figures, strong colors and patterns, and imagery ranging from tiny flowers to large images of objects, ornamental motifs, and even architectural or landscape subjects. Gold leaf and silver leaf are extremely thin foils of actual metal that can be applied to surfaces (such as walls or ceilings) in a manner similar to wallpaper.

PAINT.   This is the most versatile of all color materials, readily available or mixed to order in any color or gloss. It is usable to give color to any material otherwise colorless or of unsatisfactory color, and, with successive coatings, it can change the existing color of many objects and surfaces with great ease. It is a key color material for all interior design work.

OBJECTS.   Of course, objects are made up of various materials, but may deserve consideration in terms of their color characteristics. Furniture, for example, may be of a particular wood, but may also be of painted metal (office furniture is often of this sort) or may incorporate a number of materials. Chairs and upholstered furniture can introduce color in wood or metal components as well as their more obvious areas of fabric or other covering material. A drawer chest may have a painted metal frame and panels painted in contrasting colors (see Figure 9.22). Appliances, often painted white, are also available in other colors that can relate to kitchen cabinets. Smaller objects may also contribute color to an interior. The role of accessories in residential spaces, of equipment (computer terminals, printers, and copy machines) in offices, and technical equipment in laboratories and hospitals may be a factor in color planning. Even such small objects as telephones, audio and TV equipment, and lamps often contribute color that needs to be considered in making up complete schemes.

Choice of materials in natural color, of materials in available standard colors, and selection of custom colors for materials that can be dyed or painted bring about the conversion of abstract color schemes developed in charts into reality-based decisions that can become the basis for ordering and specification of all the elements that give a completed interior its color.

Figure 9.18   Carpet is made in many colors and patterns and is a favorite material for floor surfaces. Special carpet is also made for use as a wall covering.

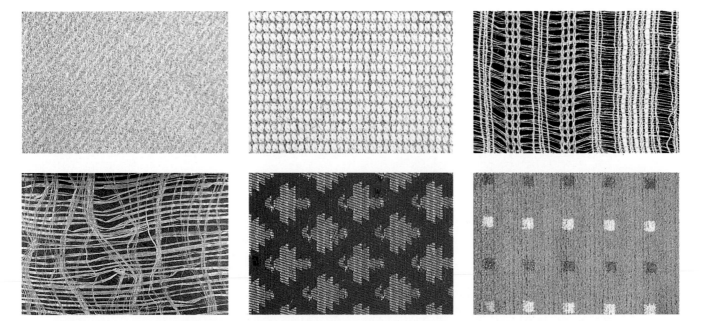

Figure 9.19   Textiles used for window treatments and for upholstered furniture covering are available in innummerable colors, textures, and patterns. Fabrics are also sometimes used as wall coverings. Leathers and plastic materials that simulate leather are also colorful alternatives for upholstery and for surfaces such as table- and desktops.

Figure 9.20 Handwoven textiles from many parts of the world are often made in rich colors and patterns. This is the West African weaving known as Kente cloth.

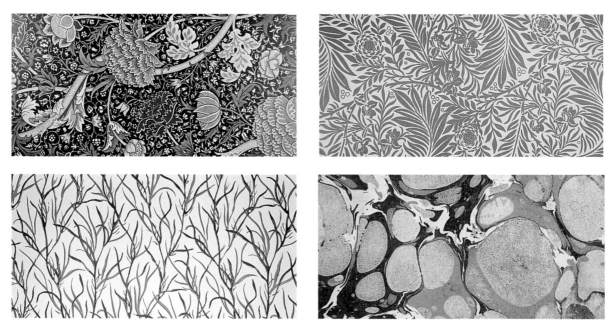

Figure 9.21 Wallpaper has been a favorite material for introducing color and pattern to wall surfaces. It is available in great variety at varied levels of quality.

Figure 9.22 Objects such as furniture and accessories in interiors can introduce color ranging from the natural tones of the woods of built-in or movable furniture to the strong colors of paint or plastic laminates. This drawer chest from the group called Steelframe by its maker, Herman Miller, was made with fronts and sides in bright paint colors.

10
Analysis of Color Schemes

This chapter is devoted to a demonstration of the way in which color charts relate to accomplished projects. For each of the project photographs provided here, two charts have been developed. One is a *ribbon,* or *band chart,* in which samples of the colors used are shown with widths proportionate to the amount of each color present in the actual space. The second chart is a color wheel showing the positions of the colors present on the color circle. By noting these positions, the color scheme can be identified as an example of one of the schematic types discussed in Chapters 7 and 8.

It should be mentioned that, although the photographs show spaces that are generally close to one of the named schematic types, there are often minor variations—elements that do not exactly fit the abstract concept of a particular type of color harmony. Reality invariably introduces minor elements that fall outside of any theoretical plan. These may be small accessories, elements that are not a permanent part of the space, or irregularities in the color of some particular material. Textile weaves often are made up of several bright colors that blend into a single color tone when seen from a distance. Some materials have variations within any given sample, as with the grain of wood, the veining of marble, and the small patterns or textures typical of many materials such as tile or plastic laminates. Here, also, for the purposes of analysis, these variations are ignored and the overall tonality of the material is represented by a single color tone.

It should also be noted that when using color photographs as a basis for analysis, the effects of lighting and the photographer's choice of film and filtration may alter the actual appearance. For the purposes of this study, however, the given photograph is accepted as a true picture of the actual colors present. The changing effects of sunlight at various times of day and in various seasons, the effects of weather on daylight, and the shifts that result when artificial light is introduced are well known, but it is assumed here that the effect of color constancy (discussed in Chapter 4) makes it possible to analyze color as it appears in a photograph in a way that will closely parallel the effects of color in the actual space under any lighting conditions.

An effort has been made to select interiors of a high level of design quality in overall terms and in aesthetic quality of color planning as well as those that serve as examples of a particular approach to color planning. Each project is identified with the name of the designer or designers involved.

Figure 10.1 In its own offices, the design firm of Interior Spaces has used strong, chromatic colors in limited areas to enliven the otherwise restrained setting of black floors, and white and neutral surfaces. (*Photo by Steve Hall/Hedrich Blessing.*)

Figure 10.2   In a bar chart, the bright colors are
seen to dominate the black, white, and neutral tones.

Figure 10.3   On a color wheel, the chromatic colors
are located in positions at each of the primary and
secondary colors, except for violet.

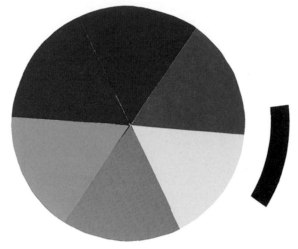

Figure 10.6   Such a near-monochromatic scheme has all color tones grouped at one location on the color wheel although there is considerable variation in value and saturation.

Figure 10.5   The bar chart demonstrates a scheme of great subtlety.

Figure 10.4   In this New York retail shop for the Ebel jewelry firm, Andrée Putman, the designer, has used a limited range of beige and tan tones that form a quiet background for the products on display. (Also see illustration in Chapter 12.) (*Photo © Peter Mauss/ESTO.*)

Figure 10.8   In a bar chart, the chromatic colors are seen surrounded by neutrals.

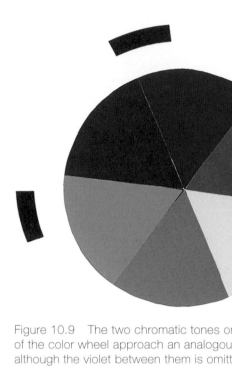

Figure 10.9   The two chromatic tones on one side of the color wheel approach an analogous scheme, although the violet between them is omitted.

Figure 10.7   A dining room in a New York corporate apartment provided by the Sony Corporation for its top management. In a generally white and neutral setting, the red-brown of a mahogany wall panel and the soft blue of the chair upholstery work together to give a sense of quiet color tonality. Interior design by Berger Rait Design Associates. (*Photo by © Derrick & Love.*)

Figure 10.10 An eighteenth-century American colonial room using a strong blue-green for painted paneling and a Chinese import wallpaper, along with warm tones in wood furniture and upholstery, appears warm and comfortable. The room was at one time installed in the American Wing of the Metropolitan Museum of Art in New York. (*Photo by John Pile.*)

Figure 10.11   In a bar chart, the yellow, green, and blue tones are close to analogous, but the reds and browns present in furniture make the total effect that of a tetrad or complementary scheme.

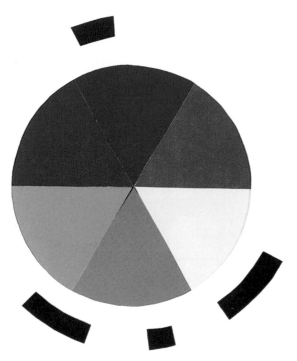

Figure 10.12   On a color circle, the complementary relationship of the colors present is clear and obvious.

Figure 10.13   A dignified seating area in the Boston building of the American Academy of Arts and Letters uses warm tones of beige, tan, and brown with limited areas of rose and soft blue to add a more chromatic relief. I.S.D. was the interior designer, working with Kallmann, McKinnell & Wood, architects. (*Photo by Jaime Ardiles-Arce, courtesy of Louis Beal, I.S.D.*)

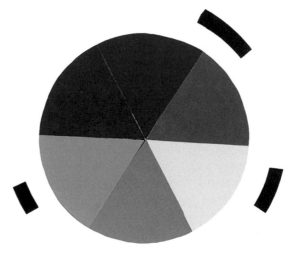

Figure 10.15 The nearly equal-spaced locations of the color tones on a color wheel is typical of a triad scheme with its comfortable balance of tones.

Figure 10.14 In a bar chart, the red, yellow, and blue bases of the soft tones makes the triad basis of the scheme apparent.

11
Psychological Impact of Color

It is widely recognized that color has strong psychological significance and can even, to some degree, influence physical reactions in human beings. There has been extensive research in this area in an attempt to reduce various beliefs and random observations to some reliable findings that can be put to practical use. Studies fall into a number of different types with findings that only relate to a limited degree. Color is experienced in widely varied contexts, so that what may seem a clear finding in one set of circumstances has little applicability under different conditions. The studies that are brought to the attention of designers fall into a number of different groups. The best known include the following:

Studies of aesthetic preference. Which colors are "liked" most; what combinations of colors are found most pleasing to a panel of informants in various contexts.

Physiological studies. These attempt to relate color experience to physical reactions such as pulse rate, blood pressure, and body temperature.

Studies of environmental color and emotions. These include efforts to relate environmental color to states of mind and emotional reactions such as stimulation, calm, or depression.

Studies relating environmental color to health effects. These include research on the incidence of various illnesses, levels of energy or exhaustion, and the role of color in treatment of physical and mental illness.

Studies relating to commercial purposes. These studies are concerned with color reactions such as attraction to a commercial facility (such as a store or restaurant), possible impact on inclination to make purchases, or level of satisfaction with services provided within a particular facility.

Work making use of color reactions or preferences as an element in psychological testing. The role of color cards in the Rorschach personality test is well known. In the Lowenfeld Mosaic test, the subject is asked to make an arrangement of small, colorful tiles in a frame. The choice and use of color is a major factor in the test interpretation. The

Luscher Color Test is based on a theory that color preferences can be the basis for a full understanding of personality traits.

Aside from such scientifically based investigation, there is extensive literature of theory having no basis other than opinion on observation and widely expressed thoughts about color. From all such material, it is possible to extract some information that seems to be trustworthy and that has some practical use. This chapter is devoted to a summary of such information. Chapter 12 discusses ways in which this data can be applied in planning various types of functional interior spaces.

WARM, COOL, AND NEUTRAL COLORS

Before moving to discussion of the impact of specific color hues, some more general observations can be noted that are so widely accepted as to seem fully factual in their content. If colors are considered as falling into the general families of *warm, cool,* and *neutral,* it is possible to summarize the implications of each group in a way that seems virtually obvious.

Warm colors.　These are generally associated with the impact that is suggested by the use of the word *warm* with other meanings. We speak of a warm greeting, a warm friendship, or a warm atmosphere. In color terms, the hues on the warm side of the color circle (red, orange, and yellow) and their related tints and shades are generally understood as comfortable, cozy, homelike, and pleasant. There is an association with physical warmth and the resultant sense of contentment. Experiments have shown that interiors with primarily warm color schemes will prove comfortable to occupants with actual air temperatures lower than required to achieve similar comfort in identical spaces using cooler colors (see Figure 11.1).

Cool colors.　These colors fall on the green-blue-violet side of the color circle. They are, not surprisingly, associated with calm, relaxation, and more contemplative experience (see Figure 11.2). Cool colors tend to lower the sense of actual air temperature and so are often preferred in situations where excessive heat (climatic or artificial) can be anticipated. At an extreme, cool colors may become depressive and negative in psychological impact.

Neutral colors.　White, black, gray, and chromatic colors desaturated with a high content of neutrals are in this category. They fall between warm and cool, having a less intense psychological impact, which, in its extreme form, may be thought of as bland or boring. In its more positive uses, neutral color may suggest businesslike, practical, and utilitarian atmospheres with a minimum of emotional content (see Figure 11.3).

Combinations of tones from the three main color families.　These are regularly used to put together a mix of emotional color reactions leading to a balance of sensation appropriate to a particular context (see Figure 11.4). The various types of color schemes discussed in Chapter 7 offer a range of possibilities in which, for example, a cool scheme can be made more comfortable by the introduction of some contrasting warmth, a warm scheme made more calm by introduction of cool color elements, a neutral scheme enlivened by appropriate warm or cool elements.

Figure 11.1　Warm color in a dining room where a variety of older and more modern themes are mixed. A residential space in the home of Robert Venturi and Denise Scott Brown. (*Photo by Paul Warchol, courtesy of Venturi and Scott Brown and Associates.*)

Figure 11.2   Cool colors offer a sense of calm and order in this conference room in the office of the American National Bank in Rockford, Illinois. I.S.D. was the interior designer with Larson & Darby, architects. (*Photo by Hedrich-Blessing; courtesy of Louis Beal, I.S.D.*)

Figure 11.3 Generally neutral color tones dominate the lobby of The Archive, a New York apartment building converted from a federal post office and archive building. The interior design was by Judith Stockman. (*Photo by Landon Clay, courtesy of Judith Stockman.*)

Advancing and receding color. A generally observable effect comes from a combination of optical and psychological effects. Warm colors tend to appear closer to an observer than their actual distance, while cool colors tend to appear farther away than they actually are. These effects of advancing and receding vary in intensity in propor-

tion to the intensity of the color in question. Similarly, dark colors will usually appear closer than light tones of similar hues. Spaces can be made to seem larger or smaller than they actually are through choice of color, and shapes of spaces can, to some degree, be modified by color choices. A long, narrow space, for example, can

Figure 11.4 Warm, cool, and neutral tones are all present in the living and dining area of a Chicago apartment. Interior design is by Powell/Kleinschmidt. (*Photo by © Don DuBroff.*)

be made to seem less long and less narrow through the use of warm color tones on the distant ends together with light and/or cool tones on the surfaces of the too-close sides. A high ceiling will appear lower in a dark tone, while a low ceiling will appear less oppressive in a light, cool tone. Designers can make practical use of these effects in obvious ways.

IMPACT OF SPECIFIC HUES

Such generalizations can be supplemented by the most accepted findings about the implications of specific color hues. Each of the six spectrum hues and several neutrals and other named colors deserve mention. A summary of the associations most often thought of as relating to each major color follows.

• *RED*   As the color of fire and blood, red has a primary implication of excitement, heat, intensity, and force. It is in a sense the strongest of colors. The association with fire leads to an association with danger and warnings against danger. When reduced to a tint, red become pink and loses some of its psychological intensity. Pink is commonly associated with femininity, with milder warmth, with charm, and delicacy. When reduced to a shade, red becomes a warm brown. (See Figure 11.5.)

Figure 11.5   Red and hues close to red dominate the interior of this office complex at the General Motors Saturn plant in Springhill, Tennessee. Design was by GM Argonaut. (*Photo by Balthazar Korab.*)

Figure 11.6 A strongly warm color tonality is established by the use of orange carpeting in open-plan offices for Montgomery Ward in Chicago; it establishes a color tonality dominating the space. The orange tone is reflected onto the white ceiling. Rogers Associates was the interior designer. (*Photo by John Pile.*)

- *ORANGE.* This color is a secondary, resulting from the mixture of red and yellow, and shares some of the qualities of its neighbors in the color circle. The intensity of excitement implied by red is somewhat reduced but is still present. The sense of cheer associated with yellow emerges so that orange becomes a color with happy commercial implications (see Figure 11.6). Its tints are among the tones of beige and tan that are favored as background colors, pleasant but not intrusive. Its shades are browns, discussed later.

- *YELLOW.* This is the warm color with the least problematic implications. It is less aggressive in impact than red and is generally seen as having a happy implication that may have a relationship with the reality that its most saturated form is still light with a high level of reflectivity. Yellow seems open and expansive, the color of sunlight and of the more attractive artificial lighting sources. Yellow has a strong place in interior design as the color of cheer, activity, and mild stimulation. Its tints, creams, beiges, and light tans, are popular background colors—warm but not overbearing. Shades of yellow become tans, lighter browns, and dark brown, all useful colors that retain some of the sense of lightness that characterizes the pure hue. (See Figure 11.7.)

- *GREEN.* This is a secondary falling between yellow and blue and is the warmest

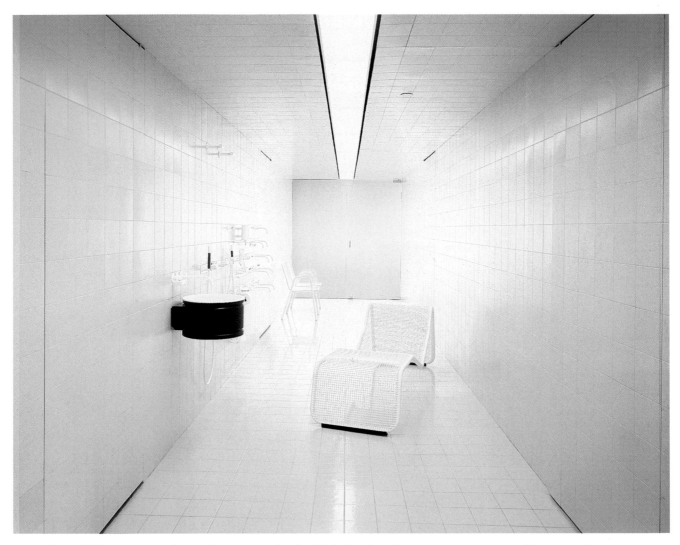

Figure 11.7   Intense yellow, a theme color for the Kroin furniture firm, is used as a dominating hue in the showroom and offices for that company. Vignelli Associates was responsible for the overall corporate identity program and advertising for Kroin and was the interior designer for this space. (*Photo courtesy of Vignelli Associates.*)

of the cool colors. Its content of yellow gives it some of the pleasant characteristics associated with yellow, while its blue content makes it seem more calm. At its best, green seems to combine the cheerfulness of yellow with a greater sense of stability. There has been a tendency to regard green as an ideal color offering some of the virtues of all other colors (see Figure 11.8). This tendency may have led to its overuse, especially as the infamous "institutional green"

that was a norm of office and institutional color schemes, giving it the designation of drab and dull. Green has associations with the natural colors of grass, trees, and other vegetation and so is thought of as the most natural color, calming and restful to the eyes. Associations with health and well-being connect to green. It is the color of the *go* signal, opposite to the danger implication of red. All of these qualities, in somewhat reduced intensity, survive in tints of green

Figure 11.8 In this New York gallery space by Paul Heyer, architect, green wall covering forms a suitable background for historic paintings. White is dominant in the stair area and gallery space beyond. (*Photo by Norman McGrath, courtesy of Paul Heyer.*)

Figure 11.9 American Shaker colonies often used a particular paint color that they called *heavenly blue* for elements in a meeting house. This example is in the Shaker Village at Sabbathday Lake, Maine. (*Photo by John Pile.*)

while shades move down to increasing levels of dignity and solidity.

• *BLUE.* This is the coolest of the cool colors having no content of warmer tones. It has associations with calm that can border on depression, but also with simplicity, purity, truth, and dignity. Blue is said to encourage thought, contemplation, and meditation and so is the color of intellectual activity (see Figure 11.9). Bright blue can be a lively color, but it lacks the tension of red and orange. It can lower body temperature, pulse rate, and blood pressure and thus stands as a full opposite to red in its physical effects. As the color of the sky and ocean, blue suggests openness and spaciousness. It is a color often associated with officialdom and authority. Its coolness may move toward coldness with negative implications. Tints of blue share the qualities of bright blue in somewhat reduced degree. Shades of blue, as they move downward toward black, become increasingly heavy, dignified, and, in excess, potentially depressive.

• *VIOLET.* This color and purple are commonly thought of as somewhat problematic. Violet, falling between red and blue in the color circle, incorporates the conflicting values of warmth and coolness, of liveliness and calm. In the spectrum, it does not stand between two neighbors (as the other secondaries, orange and green, do) but it falls, rather, at the end farthest from red. This reality may contribute to its reputation as a color of tension and ambiguity. In many contexts, it is suggested that violet and purple are best avoided altogether as too disturbing to many people. At the same time, violet is often viewed as the color of subtlety, sensitivity, and artistic expression (see Figure 11.10). Pale tints of violet or lavender are thought of as being light, playful, magical. Deeper violets and purples are dignified, mystical, and, in many contexts, threatening. Use of violets and purples must be approached with caution because of their possibly disturbing or troubling connotations.

- *BROWN.* The deeper shades of red, orange, and yellow seem sufficiently different from the chromatic colors to justify their own name. Browns are more alike than the hues that relate to them. Browns are all warm colors and have implications related to their parent tones. They tend to appear as warm and comforting, but have an unfortunate relationship to thoughts of dirt and soil. The more positive implications relate to the comforts of the farm, of simple homes, and the basic honesty of wood, undyed textiles, and such materials as brick, tile, and stone (see Figure 11.11). Browns lack the energetic implications of red, orange, and yellow but retain some of their qualities of warmth and comfort. When used with other warm tones, browns are favorite colors for expression of a combination of dignity and subdued comfort. There is always concern that browns may become depressive and drab if not used with other tones that have a more chromatic and lively implication.

- *WHITE.* Often defined as a noncolor (actually a resultant of the combination of all colors), white has a controversial place among color tones. Its lack of chromaticism makes it pure and therefore symbolic of purity, cleanliness, simplicity, and clarity (see Figure 11.12). It can also suggest emptiness, blankness, and boredom. White is a highly effective foil to chromatic colors and can be quite successful as an

Figure 11.10   Violet, a color often regarded as risky, is confidently used here in a bathroom in a residence in Kalamazoo, Michigan, designed by George Nelson and Gordon Chadwick, architects, with Dolores Engle, interior designer.

empty surround to more aggressive tones. The implications of white as a norm for the expression of sanitation is well known. Although the color name *white* suggests only one possible tone, the term is used for a variety of so-called whites that are, in fact, slight tints of more chromatic colors—warm or cool whites that relate well to more chromatic colors and are favorite background tones. The extensive use of white in design of the modern movement has made it something of a symbol of modernism to be favored or attacked in accordance with opinion of the value of modernism's stated principles.

Figure 11.11   In the New York restaurant American Charcuterie, shades of brown establish an atmosphere of traditional comfort. Stockman and Manners were the interior designers. (*Photo by Norman McGrath.*)

- *BLACK.*   This is the noncolor opposite to white, by definition a total absence of all chromatic color, reflecting, in a perfect example, no light whatsoever. Black is a strong color with powerful implications of strength, seriousness, dignity, and formality (see Figure 11.13). Black can also project a sense of emptiness or blankness but with implications more heavy and gloomy than the comparable aspects of white tones. Black in its more threatening aspects also has associations of a negative nature relating to depression, fear, and death. Black and white together form an extreme contrast of nonchromatic color that can be powerful and sharp, but can also be stern and forbidding. The combination of black, white, and primary chromatic color tones was a key aspect of the expressive program of early modernism and continues to be forceful and suggestive of the basics of the modern movement in design. Blacks can be warm or cool through the addition of some small component of chromatic color, making them, in a strict sense, no longer pure black. Dark grays and very dark (midnight) blues can be so close to black as to be scarcely distinguishable, and, therefore, such tones share the expressive qualities of black.

• *GRAY.* Colors that result from the mixture of black and white or from mixtures of complementaries are neutrals that can range from light to dark and from totally neutral (nonchromatic) tones to warmer or cooler tones, which result from the mixture of chromatic tone with white and black, or from the balance between the complementaries that have been mixed to form the gray in question. Grays in lighter ranges do not project strong associative implications. In darker tones they share the characteristics of black to a degree in both its positive and negative aspects. Dark gray can be authoritative or ominous and depressive. Light grays, particularly in warm-toned versions, are useful background tones, bland in themselves, but serving as effective foils for more chromatic color tones.

MEANINGS FROM COLOR

The idea that color can transmit meaning, emotional or cognitive messages, has its foundation in two areas. One is the conviction that some reactions to color are inborn, intuitive, and universal to everyone. The other lies in the body of learned associations that are dependent, in part, on realities that are known to everyone and, in part, to meanings that are learned within a particular society in a particular time and place. It is not easy to sort which of these sources is basic to one or another color interpretation, but it is possible to guess at certain probabilities.

The excitement that is associated with intense color, particularly with intense red and related warm colors, seems to be an inborn reaction related to physical responses to such stimuli. The sense of blankness or emptiness generated by solid white, black, or gray similarly seems to come from the lack of physical stimulation that such tones provide. Learning and experience seem to not be involved in the development of such basic reactions.

In comparison, some other basic reactions seem to be the result of learning through experience of a very simple and basic nature. The associations with warm and cool, with red and blue, for example, seem to be basic to human experience with heat—the heat of fire, of the sun—and cool—the cool of water. The colors of nature, sky, sea, grass, leaves, fruits, and berries provide examples of color in relation to realities that are learned through direct experience or, in the modern world, perhaps through indirect experience of images provided by art, photography, television, and other graphic media.

At another, more artificial level still, implications of various colors are learned through the customs of a particular society. The meaning of red and green traffic lights, the awareness that fire engines are (usually) painted red, the observation of the white tones in sanitary facilities, the warm tone of living quarters, and the tans and greens of institutional settings build up sets of associations and corresponding expectations. Everyone has learned the significance of pink and blue for infants, the role of black in mourning and funerary customs, the significance of the colors of a national flag. Once such color associations are learned, it is difficult to separate them from the inborn intuitive meanings that some color experience may have. All color reactions come to seem inevitable and immutable. It is hard in a Western culture to imagine associating white with funerals, black with weddings, pink with male infants, blue with females. In fact, there is no firm basis for many of the color meanings that are taken for granted, but once they become part of

Figure 11.12 White is widely accepted as a suitable color for a kitchen. This example is in a New York townhouse; Paul Heyer was the architect. (*Photo by Peter Paige, courtesy of Paul Heyer.*)

Figure 11.13 Black marbles establish a tone of solemnity in the chapel called St. Sindone at the cathedral of Turin, Italy. This was a project of the baroque era (1667–1690) designed by Guarino Guarini. (*Photo by John Pile.*)

the culture of a particular population, they are largely unalterable and might as well be accepted as basic for effective color usage.

USE OF COLOR IMPLICATIONS IN PRACTICE

Making use of the emotional impact of various colors in practice can follow quite a simple and obvious course. The aim must be to establish an idea of the mood, atmosphere, or impression that a given space should project. It is helpful to make some written notes, choosing words that are descriptive of what is intended. When working for a client, it is often helpful to review such verbal description in an effort to reach agreement on what is intended. It may be helpful to use a list of words that might include (along with any others that come to mind) such terms as the following:

Cheerful
Merry
Playful
Bright
Gracious
Cozy
Restful
Bright
Dim
Light
Heavy
Comfortable
Soothing

Homelike
Soft
Quiet
Calm ✓
Dull
Spacious ✓
Compact
Warm ✓
Cool ✓
Impersonal
Efficient
Businesslike
Sanitary
Professional
Creative
Youthful
Mature
Childish
Artistic
Fashionable
Simple ✓
Luxurious
Rich
Masculine
Feminine
Exciting
Stimulating
Austere
Monumental
Formal ✓
Solemn
Dignified
Active
Busy
Contemplative
Studious
Meditative
Impressive
Leisurely
Forceful
Urban
Rural

Institutional
Mechanical
Systematic
Orderly
Organized

It is assumed that some other words that might characterize spaces have such negative impact as to be unwanted in such a list. Ominous, depressing, chaotic, and dull, for example, although all too often descriptive of actual spaces, are hardly suggestive of favorable design efforts.

It might be attractive to suggest that each term in the preceding list could be connected with particular color choices, but this is not, of course, the case. It is not difficult to couple red with *exciting* or green with *calm,* but the complex variations of color and color relationships make it impossible to arrive at more subtle relationships in terms of specific color selections. Instead, it is simply suggested that having a firm idea of what characteristics are appropriate to a given space will lead to choices of color, materials, and color relationships that will further the intended purposes.

It is an interesting exercise (sometimes given as a classroom problem in design schools) to create a color and material selection for a space with a given function quite aside from any other aspects of the space's design. With a suggested color and material scheme in hand, it is interesting to seek reaction from various viewers. Viewers might be asked, "Seeing this color and material selection, what kind of space does this suggest?" It would be hoped that a scheme planned for a nursery classroom would not be thought of as suited to a corporate law firm's library, or that a scheme developed to suit a fast-food restaurant suggests a stylish boutique.

Another useful exercise might be to plan color and material schemes for a number of spaces, in actual charts or just in thoughtful terms, for a variety of functions such as the following:

A family living room
A residential kitchen
A dentist's reception space
A brokerage office
A law library
A guest room in a hotel in the tropics
A day care center
A prison dayroom
A designer's drafting room
An undertaker's chapel
An airport terminal concourse

Any number of such place descriptions may be developed in order to consider what color and material choice would be most appropriate for each one. While many schemes could suit any one of these various spaces, it becomes clear that certain directions are appropriate while other approaches, suitable to other functions, will not do.

COLOR AND FORM

It has been suggested by some color theorists that emotional responses to color and to form are related in a predictable way. At the Bauhaus in Germany in the 1920s, while Johannes Itten was an influential teacher, a theory was developed that suggested there were connections between each primary color and the simple geometric forms of the square, triangle, and circle. This led to the related suggestion that when color and form of parallel meaning were used together, a reinforcement of meaning took place while, presumably, unrelated form and color had lesser impact. While this view has never been methodically validated, it can be interesting to consider its implications.

In Bauhaus theory, the following relationships were regarded as basic:

Square relates to red
Triangle relates to yellow
Circle relates to blue

The supporting theory argues that the square, with its use of horizontal and vertical lines, is related to gravity and matter and so to red, "the color of matter." The angularity of the triangle and its "weightlessness" is viewed as relating to yellow, "the symbol of thought." The circle, with its qualities of relaxation and motion, is then seen as relating to blue (see Figure 11.14). In an effort to move this theoretical approach further, Itten proposed that the secondary colors each had a relationship to a geometric figure that would mediate between the forms relating to the primaries that combine to form it (see Figure 11.15). Thus:

Trapezoid relates to orange
Spherical triangle relates to green
Ellipse relates to violet

These views were adopted to some extent by Kandinsky and Klee in their Bauhaus teaching, although with less insistence than in Itten's classes.

Kandinsky developed a further elaboration of such color theory by proposing that four major contrasts could be studied in colors. The most important to him was the contrast between yellow and blue, in which yellow was viewed as absolute warmth, blue as absolute cold, and red mediated between the two extremes. The yellow-blue contrast was seen as matching the contrasts of hot-cold, light-dark, and active-passive. Thus:

yellow = hot, light, active
blue = cold, dark, passive

The other three major contrasts were viewed as black-white, red-green, and

Figure 11.14   A theory developed at the Bauhaus in the 1920s suggested that colors and shapes had certain widely recognizable relationships. Of the three primaries, red is viewed as relating to the square, yellow to the equilateral triangle, and blue to the circle.

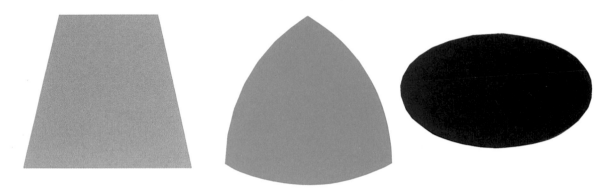

Figure 11.15   Some Bauhaus theorists extended the concept to relate each secondary color to a shape: orange to the trapezoid, green to the spherical triangle, and violet to the ellipse.

orange-violet. The contrast between black and white as being between the extremes of dark and light seems obvious. The contrast between red and green is understood as that of power and vitality (red) and calm and passivity (green). Orange and violet relate in their qualities to yellow and blue but with less force since the addition of red to the other primaries dilutes their force and mediates between them.

While such theoretical views may seem somewhat fanciful and of questionable practical use, they form an interesting territory for thoughtful exploration.

12
Use of Color in Various Functional Contexts

There are functional issues and well-accepted traditions that suggest certain color selections as appropriate to certain functional purposes while other color choices may be readily ruled out as totally inappropriate. This does not lead to standardization in which a certain purpose demands one and only one color scheme choice, but it does offer parameters—suggested directions and possible limitations that help to direct a designer toward color schemes that will prove satisfactory in practice.

A number of generalizations apply to color selection for many different functional situations. A decision to work toward a scheme dominated by warm, cool, or neutral tones can be influenced by several factors. These include the following:

Climate: Warm colors are generally more acceptable in cold climates, cool colors in warmer regions. Cool colors are also often preferred in situations where summer occupancy will be most usual (as in a beach house or summer cottage).

Orientation: Where windows will admit daylight, a southern orientation will suggest a cool to neutral color preference while a northern orientation suggests use of warmer color.

Activity: Warmer color tends to favor activity and stimulation, while neutral and cooler colors favor calm and contemplation. These effects increase in proportion to the intensity of the color used and permit a wide range of gradation through adjustment of color tones.

Preference: Spaces that will be used by a particular occupant can take account of individually expressed color preferences while spaces used by many occupants can best avoid overuse of any particular hue of strong intensity.

It is possible for these general influences to work in opposite directions. A south-facing space in a cold climate, for example, leads to opposing suggestions of cool and warm tones. Similarly, an expressed fondness for blue may be opposed by a desire for a lively and stimulating ambience. In such cases, it becomes a matter of judgment which consideration should be given priority or whether neutral or complementary color will serve best as a balance between opposite indications.

It is generally found best to arrange color selections to vary in value according to position within a space. Floor surfaces will normally be of the darkest tone level in a space, ceilings of light tones, while wall colors and tones used for furniture and window treatments fall at an intermediate level. This does not mean that floors should be dark; in a scheme where all values are light, the floor tone will still usually seem best if it is darker than walls or ceiling. Such a scheme can be called *high key* while a *low key* scheme may use all tones in a range from medium dark to dark, but the relative placement of tones will still be most agreeable when the gradation from darker below to lighter above is observed. Exceptions to this practice can be successful for some purposes but should be approached with caution. A black ceiling can be dramatic, but it may also be oppressive. A dark ceiling in a space with a light tone floor can be disturbing to many occupants.

Within the generalizations previously mentioned, there are a variety of factors that relate to specific functions which can be taken into consideration. This chapter attempts a survey of such directions and limitations but should not be regarded as a set of rules. Whatever may be usual and may seem appropriate can always be ignored if a better approach suited to a particular function and a particular situation comes to mind. Whether as a group of suggestions to be followed or as a set of rules to be broken when appropriate, the following survey suggests the most accepted views about color in relation to spatial function. Typical functions are grouped under headings descriptive of various categories of projects.

RESIDENTIAL INTERIORS

There is a widely felt preference for warm color tones in residential interiors that have associations with comfort and homelike ambience. Schemes that make extensive use of neutral or cool tones can often be given a sense of warmth through well-chosen, contrasting, warm accents. In a house or apartment with several rooms, it is often possible to choose certain spaces for color treatment that will avoid the possible monotony of warm color everywhere. Spaces that open into one another require consideration of how their colors will relate—either through unifying tones or through well-planned contrast. An entrance hall, living room, and dining room often form an interconnecting suite, for example, and call for a color plan in which the spaces are either treated as one or are given schemes that have a planned relationship.

Living Rooms and Dining Rooms

These rooms are usually most successful in color tones ranging from mildly warm to neutral, with stronger tones restricted to smaller areas or accents. Since these are rooms used by several people at various times and are often occupied for extended periods of time, intense color schemes are of questionable appropriateness (see Figure 12.1). The idea of a "red room," "blue room," or "green room" may seem attractive, but is best reserved for a situation where a number of living spaces will be available so that occupants can choose among alternative strong-color environments. Yellows, if not intense, are workable tones for living spaces in such pale or neutralized forms as cream, beige, or light tan. Where woodwork trim is present (in baseboards, window and door trim, and cornice moldings, for example), white or a more chromatic color can be used to contrast with wall color. Strong chromatic color can be introduced in furniture, window treatments, or in accessory items such as cushions or artwork. Floors are usually best kept in warm to neutral tones. Natural wood flooring and many carpets (such as warm-toned oriental rug designs)

Figure 12.1 A living room in a New York town house. A Victorian white marble mantel, a colorful modern painting, the natural colors of a maple chest, a woven rush settee, and an Eames molded-plywood chair fall into a relationship with light, warm-gray walls, white wood trim and ceiling. (*Photo by John Pile.*)

are satisfactory. Strong, solid colors of carpet are questionable as they tend to introduce an excessive domination of a particular hue.

Recreation or Family Rooms

These rooms can follow the suggestions for other living spaces, possibly with more emphasis on deeper tan or brown tones to suggest the traditional den atmosphere. If the recreation anticipated will be active (games or exercise, for example) cooler tones of green or blue can be considered. Avoid the knotty pine boarding that has become an overused cliché.

Bedrooms

These rooms can be approached in several ways. If thought of as alternative living or sitting rooms, color treatment can follow the previously mentioned suggestions. An alternative approach may use a stronger, more fully chromatic color scheme, chosen to suit the preferences of the occupant or simply as an opportunity to introduce varied color into a residence. Since bedroom color is only seen during waking hours, strong color tones have less chance of becoming a source of irritation to an occupant; still, it is best to avoid intense color on a ceiling or on large wall areas (see Fig-

Figure 12.2   A bedroom in a house on eastern Long Island. The blues of the bed cover and edges of the rug, together with the natural wood tones in furniture, work with the white walls and ceiling to generate a sense of cool tranquility. Alfredo De Vido was the architect and interior designer. (*Photo by William P. Steele.*)

ure 12.2). Bed coverings, pillows, and cushions can provide accent color which is easily changed with the seasons or simply for variety.

Children's Rooms

These rooms often make use of bright colors in a belief that children are particularly attracted to clear primaries. Infants have been found to respond to bright colors, which can be provided with toys and in other small areas, so that walls and floors may best be kept to more quiet color. Older children may enjoy some areas of bright color or may develop preferences similar to adults. Children often enjoy participating in preparing color schemes for their own

Figure 12.3 A kitchen in a New York apartment. Natural wood cabinets with red granite tops warm the tones of the white tile walls and white floor and ceiling. Gwathmey Siegel & Associates was the architect. (*Photo by Richard Bryant.*)

rooms, and there is no reason not to accept preferences even when they may seem inappropriate to adult observers.

Kitchens

As spaces occupied for limited periods of time, kitchens can make use of strong color for walls, cabinet fronts, and floors. Countertops are usually best kept in lighter tones to make visibility of food materials easy. All natural color, with its extensive use of natural wood tones, is also satisfactory in kitchens, and white remains satisfactory, especially if combined with some areas of chromatic color (see Figure 12.3). Tile, suitable for flooring and areas of wall, is available in a wide range of colors and patterns. Stainless steel, often used for sinks, is also suitable for countertops and fronts of appliances and counters—its neutral metallic tone can be relieved of any sense of coldness by introduction of strong color in flooring or other surfaces.

Bathrooms

Frequently, bathrooms make use of white for tiling and fixtures, probably chosen for its association with cleanliness and sanitation, but other colors can be helpful in increasing a sense of comfort. Strong color (pink, green, or blue, for example), popular at one time, is questionable because of its tendency to reflect onto skin color and alter the appearance of users. White, tan, or light, warm gray are preferred general color tones, with strong color in small accents such as bands of color tile. Towels in strong colors are readily changeable and offer a range of bright (as well as subdued) color tones.

Libraries, Studies, and Dens

These types of rooms suggest two alternative approaches. One possibility is to emphasize cooler colors, which are believed to promote calm, meditation, and similar contemplative activities. A more traditional view will emphasize the use of deeper, warm colors, such as the browns or tans of wood paneling which are commonly thought of as masculine in implication. Shelves of books will usually generate areas of suitable color in either approach. Tones of brown or red in upholstery and flooring work well in a warm color scheme. A middle group between the two common schemes might combine warm tones in paneling, shelving, and furniture with subdued green or blue for some wall areas or flooring.

NONRESIDENTIAL INTERIORS

Hotels and Motels

These buildings include a number of spaces with differing color possibilities. Entrance lobbies and front desk areas invite the use of strong color that will make a positive first impression. Traditional settings often make use of natural woods, brass, or other metallic elements and rich materials, such as marble possibly in strong color (see Figure 12.4a). Lobbies and lounges that may be occupied for longer time periods can use color similar to that of residential living room spaces. In general, warm color tones support a sense of comfort, although cooler color tones may be appropriate to warm climate locations. Color chosen to relate to location, climate, and local custom help to give a hotel character that contributes to guests' satisfaction. Hotel dining rooms can be viewed as restaurants. Guest rooms and baths can use varied color schemes similar to those of residential bedrooms and baths, but, since it is seldom possible to offer guests a choice among rooms with varied color schemes, all schemes should be planned to be agreeable to any guest and, insofar as possible, to express themes relating to the hotel's location and style (see Figure 12.4b). The usual guidelines relating to climate and orientation can serve to introduce some variety, although the management of some hotels prefers the simplicity of adopting one color scheme for all guest rooms and baths with a particular layout so that furniture, accessories, and linens are fully interchangeable between rooms.

Corridors leading to guest rooms call for especially lively color treatment to avoid the depressing effect of long, drab passages. Strong color at the ends of corridors and some treatment of side walls to introduce color variety can be helpful. Some multistory hotels make use of a key color theme for the corridors of each floor, making identification of individual floors easy. Elevator interiors can make use of strong color that might seem overbearing in spaces that are occupied for longer periods of time.

Restaurants

These spaces call for a particularly sensitive use of color. An inappropriate color scheme can cause a restaurant to fail even if it might

Figure 12.4*a* The lobby of the Paramount Hotel in New York. Phillipe Starck, the designer, used platinum leaf for a wall, marble for a floor, and a varied-color area rug. Furniture is in varied bright colors. (*Photo © by Peter Mauss/ESTO.*)

otherwise be successful. Appetite is very strongly affected by light and color, and the experience of eating can be made more pleasant or less through the choice of color in surroundings. Some color schemes that may appear attractive in the abstract can be objectionable when used as a setting for food service. Experience suggests that certain colors are best avoided entirely; these include black, darker or cold grays, strong tones of blue and violet, and yellow-greens. Red is believed to be stimulating to the appetite and other warm tones tend to generate a comfortable atmosphere, but must be used with restraint along with stronger accent colors (see Figure 12.5). It is customary to choose floor coverings and covering materials for seating (where used) in tones and patterns that will conceal spots and soiling, but this should not lead to color so close to that of food spotting as to be itself unattractive. Colors of tabletops or linens, dishes, glassware, and menus occupy major areas of a diner's field of vision and should be considered along with the colors of the interior space.

Style of food service should influence restaurant color choice. In general, bright colors and strong contrasts relate best to the qualities of fast-food outlets, cafeterias, and other restaurants where a rapid pace of service is anticipated (see Figure 12.6). Restaurants of more traditional style, possibly serving better cuisine at a more leisurely pace (and probably at higher prices) are better served by softer, warmer tones seen under a lower level of lighting. Natural wood tones, metallic elements, and mirrors are traditional elements in bar areas. Dining rooms of traditional clubs are commonly developed in tones of brown and tan suggesting a masculine atmosphere, while lighter tones of cream, beige, and yellow relate well to a more varied clientele.

Certain types of food service have developed traditions of style of setting. Seafood restaurants commonly use natural wood for tabletops and floors along with areas of off-white, tan, or brown in other elements. Blue is a favored accent color (supposedly associated with the sea) but should be used with care to avoid a cold and unappetizing implication. Certain national styles of cuisine can be emphasized through use of color, such as white and red in Danish, blue and yellow in Swedish, or red, green, and white in Italian restaurants. Bright and strong warm tones relate to Spanish and Mexican cookery, but such relationships are not essential and always threaten to turn to cliché when overused.

Retail Outlets

These spaces have the attractive display of merchandise as their primary purpose. A further purpose is the establishment of an ambience that will suit the kind and cost of merchandise offered and the style of the sales technique involved. As with hotels and restaurants, color has a strong impact on the atmosphere of a shop and can influence its commercial success. General rules, always subject to modification, suggest bright colors for low-cost, rapid turnover shops and markets and more subtle and muted color where higher prices and more leisurely service are offered (see Figure 12.7). Supermarkets and discount stores can use colors that are bright and contrasting although the low-end plain-pipe-rack outlet may prefer white or off-white walls and gray flooring to express its utilitarian image.

Men's clothing shops have a tradition of clublike browns, tans, and other subdued color. Women's shops are better served with soft, warm tones and pastel colors thought to be feminine in implication. Bright accent colors used with white, gray, and black and metallics relate well to high-tech products such as electronic and photo-

Figure 12.4b   A bedroom in the Paramount Hotel. Phillipe Starck was the interior designer. (*Photo © by Peter Mauss/ESTO.*)

Figure 12.5 At La Potagerie, a New York restaurant, bright red accents add warm and comfortable color to the more neutral tones of natural materials. Judith Stockman was the interior designer with J. Stockman and Charles Mount for the firm of George Nelson and Company. (*Photo by Norman McGrath.*)

graphic equipment. Sport and exercise equipment is best shown off in a surround of bright colors. Expensive jewelry and small gift items are best seen amid restrained and conservative color.

In food stores, white is a preferred color where dairy and frozen products are displayed. Lighter blues or blue-greens along with white are said to emphasize the red color of meats. The variety of display packaging for canned and boxed goods and the bright natural colors of fruits and vegetables are best seen against neutral tones. Bright colors are often adopted in a particular combination to identify a particular supermarket or other food chain. Such theme colors can be used in entrance and check-out areas but can give way to more

merchandise-related color in product display areas. (See Figure 12.8.)

Showrooms

Similar to retail shops, these spaces exist to show off merchandise to its best advantage and call for similar consideration of what will best suit the products on display while conveying some message about the manufacturer. Traditional furniture, for example, will look best in a setting with warm color tones, suggestive of residential spaces.

Modern furniture will relate to more abstract color relationships, white, primary color accents, or tones of natural materials such as wood, slate, marble, or metallic

Figure 12.6   A staff cafeteria in an office building for a finance company in Des Moines, Iowa. A purple end wall, orange painted columns, blue tile for the floor area in front of vending machines, and blue and orange chairs establish a sense of casual and speedy activity. Interior design was by John Pile. (*Photo by Norman McGrath.*)

elements. Showrooms for textiles, carpets, and rugs, because they must show off a wide variety of color, are best kept in neutral tones tending toward warm rather than cool (see Figure 12.9). Showroom display of automobiles is an important means of exhibiting current models in the best possible setting. Dark gray or black flooring, white, and strong color accents tend to accentuate the glitter of chrome and gleaming body colors. Since cars may be displayed in varied colors, strong colors in large areas are best avoided.

Galleries

For the display of paintings and other artworks, galleries commonly avoid strong colors that may conflict with the work

displayed. Although white is much used (even for floors in some cases), it is not necessarily a best choice. Light grays or tans for walls and medium neutral tones for floors make a suitable setting for modern art, but it has been suggested that works in heavy, gilded frames are better seen against walls with deeper colors such as red or green, as often used in the galleries of older, traditional museums (see Figure 12.10). Similar suggestions apply to residential spaces where an extensive display of artwork is planned.

Office Interiors

Because they are occupied for long periods, office spaces present a particularly sensitive issue. Private offices, because

Figure 12.8   The busy clutter of a large chain supermarket is made cheerful and lively by the hanging banners in bright, warm colors. (*Photo by John Pile.*)

they serve only one person, can be approached much as home dens or studies, with color adjusted to the occupant's tastes and desires (see Figure 12.11). However, in many large office complexes, occupancy of private offices can change frequently so that color treatment which will be agreeable to many occupants is called for. This also applies to general or open office areas where many users will occupy a given space. Where daylight will be present, the usual rule is to favor cooler color where the orientation is to the south or west and warmer colors for northern ori-

Figure 12.7   Subdued tones of beige and tan in a monochromatic range set off the glitter of merchandise (jewelry) in the Ebel retail shop in New York. Andrée Putman was the interior designer. (*Photo by © Peter Mauss/Esto.*)

entations. In the increasingly common office spaces where only artificial light is available, color in a range from warm neutral to warm tends to be the expressed preference of a majority of office workers (see Figure 12.12). Brighter colors can appear as accents in secondary spaces such as corridors or service areas. Many modern furniture systems offer panels and doors to storage compartments in brighter colors, often through fabric coloring, that can create accents which reduce the monotony of too much neutral tone. Work surfaces and floors should be in medium values in order to limit brightness contrast between surfaces within the field of view of office workers.

It is generally believed that cool colors favor concentration while warmer colors relate best to activity. Since most office work involves a mixture of these forms of work, it

Figure 12.9   Showroom display for glassware in the SoHo area of New York. Gallery Nilsson was designed by Peter Valentini with Judith Stockman & Associates. (*Photo by Durston Saylor, courtesy of Judith Stockman & Associates.*)

Figure 12.10 Hammer Galleries in New York uses the white that is a favorite background for the display of art, but varies wall colors in a few areas with stronger color (red in this example) to provide some background suitable to traditional painting styles. Paul Heyer was the architect. (*Photo by Norman McGrath.*)

Figure 12.11   Warm colors plus contrasting blue in an executive office for the chairman of CIGNA corporation. The design was by Swanke Hayden Connell Architects. (*Photo by Wolfgang Hoyt.*)

is difficult to make much use of this generalization. Conference and meeting rooms will reasonably be planned to use warmer colors than general and private offices. The outmoded emphasis on dull tan or beige or on the greens thought to be "eye savers" should be avoided. In multistory office complexes, it is often helpful to adopt a key color for each floor, emphasizing it at access points, in circulation areas, and, possibly, in a floor covering with related accents used in working areas.

Schools and College Buildings

These may include a variety of special purpose spaces including offices, cafeterias, dormitories, and other facilities discussed elsewhere. Classrooms and lecture halls call for colors that will be comfortable for students as their attention moves from desktop to teacher, lecturer to chalkboard. In general, mild color for walls and floors will minimize any undesirable excessive brightness contrast between paperwork and surroundings. Tones may be warmer or cooler as climate and orientation may suggest. Stronger color may be used for the front wall with color related to or contrasting with the green or blue of the chalkboard. The traditional black chalkboard is less desirable than the other tones now available, although the strong

Figure 12.12 Work stations in an open office area designed by Swanke Hayden Connell Architects for American Express. Blue carpet and blue panels for the work stations set a cool tonality. (*Photo by Wolfgang Hoyt.*)

green often selected may also present an unpleasantly "institutional" implication.

Classrooms for young children may use stronger color, usually in warm tones, although the use of intense primaries, which is sometimes suggested for nursery-age rooms, is not considered desirable (see Figure 12.13). Gymnasiums, auditoriums, and large lunchrooms are best in lighter tones, warm to neutral, possibly with some bright color accents in small areas. Stairways and corridors can use some areas of bright color—ends of corridors and doors, for example—to provide variety and stimulation while passing between other spaces.

Health Care Facilities

These interiors present a wide range of color problems relating to the varied needs of patients, visitors, doctors, nurses, and other staff and the varied nature of specific spaces. The use of bland buff, tan, and green is not recommended, and white is found to be blank and depressing by many viewers. Patients' rooms may be occupied for some times

Figure 12.13 A nursery room interior by the famous French modern architect Le Corbusier—part of the Unité apartment building at Firminy-Vert in France. A largely white and neutral color interior is enlivened by a few walls of intense orange-red and structural members painted a deep blue. The space is full of color but avoids the clichés of too much primary color often imagined to be suitable for rooms used by young children. (*Photo by John Pile.*)

by patients who may be anxious at times or bored. Color that suggests comfort and a somewhat homelike atmosphere can ease the difficulties of a hospital stay, and some research suggests that it may contribute to a favorable rate of recovery (see Figure 12.14). Ceilings and walls opposite the foot of the bed occupy the patient's field of view, possibly for an extended time. White, green, and dull tans are undesirable for these areas. Although cool colors are considered to be calming, their possibly depressing tendency suggests that warm tones are preferable. Stronger greens and blues, if used at all, are best restricted to smaller accents within generally warm schemes. Bathrooms should use warm tones, possibly stronger than those of the adjacent rooms and selected to be flattering to skin color. Generally, color that will be comfortable for patients will be found pleasant by visitors and will be practical for medical staff when working in patients' rooms.

In intensive care units, cooler colors are suggested to present a calming atmosphere. Operating rooms usually make use of major areas of blue-green which offer relief from and contrast to the red tones that fill the field of vision of the surgeon and

Figure 12.14 A patient's room in a hospital in Stamford, Connecticut, designed by I.S.D., interior designers, with Perkins and Will, architects. Warm color tones work to reduce any sense of institutional chill. (*Photo courtesy of Louis Beal; I.S.D.*)

Figure 12.15 A bedroom in a nursing home. Color in pleasant variety helps to generate a tone of residential comfort. A room in the C.A.B.S. Nursing Home in the Bedford-Stuyvesant district of Brooklyn. William Breger Associates was the architect and Leeds Associates was the interior designer. (*Photo by Martha Carder; courtesy of Suzanne Sekey.*)

other medical personnel at work there. Examination and treatment rooms can use moderately cool colors, except in dermatology and obstetric areas, and all colors should be muted to avoid the possibility of reflected color interfering with patient diagnosis. Maternity patient rooms can use warm colors suggesting a residential ambience, but nurseries should avoid stronger chromatic colors which can distort the skin color of infants.

Hospital corridors are often very long and carry heavy traffic of many different kinds. Institutional buff or green or white are objectionable, but bright and active color schemes may add to the sense of clutter and confusion. In general, mild warm tones are best for side walls with brighter accent colors used for end walls, doors, and other limited areas. Public access areas, lobbies, and waiting areas can use brighter colored schemes, planned to suggest good organization and a maximum degree of comfort. Staff offices, laboratories, lounges, and cafeterias in hospitals can be treated in the same way as such areas in other facilities.

Mental hospitals and facilities for psychiatric care are often occupied by patients for long periods of time during which it is thought that behavior and rates of recovery can be strongly influenced by color. As in other hospitals, greens and buffs are depressing and undesirable. Attractive color suggesting residential surroundings is best, but overactive schemes using strong color are to be avoided. Strong blues may prove depressive and strong reds and oranges overly exciting to certain patients. Violet, purple, and black are not to be used. Glossy, reflective surfaces and finishes are disturbing to some patients and, so, are also to be avoided.

In nursing homes, many patients may be long-term occupants best served by warmer color schemes suggesting a homelike ambience (see Figures 12.15 and 12.16). Color preferences of elderly patients tend to be conservative so that warm paint colors, wood tones, and conservative patterns in carpet and drapery are generally best liked. Bed covers and chair upholstery are suitable locations for more lively color and pattern.

Medical and dental offices, group practice facilities, and clinics can follow suggestions for offices and for comparable hospital facilities. Waiting rooms are particularly sensitive areas where patients and visitors suffer from anxiety or boredom. Lively color used with good coordination and a degree of restraint can convey a sense of professionalism and efficiency.

Transportation Equipment and Facilities

These spaces call for use of lively color for ticketing, waiting, and other terminal areas, while more subdued color is most comfortable within vehicles. Airlines and other transportation companies can make good use of bright colors taken from their corporate color themes, although the use of strong red, white, and blue together is so common as to be both monotonous and unsuccessful in establishing identity. (See Figure 12.17). Because travel within vehicles can often be boring and occasionally unpleasant, color that is restrained and calming is appropriate, although tones in the neutral to warm range are generally preferred to cooler tones, which can be depressing. Strong greens are said to suggest illness. Stronger color can be introduced on end walls, in vestibules, rest rooms, and other spaces occupied only briefly. Bright colors, varied at each location, are useful in stations on rail and subway lines where they aid easy identification of a particular stop and offer pleasant variety and stimulation.

Oceangoing ships have many characteristics in common with hotels, where a snug and homelike sense is best in staterooms and where public areas can be varied in character, permitting passengers to move into areas they find most appealing at any particular time (see Figure 12.18).

Figure 12.16 Buildings for religious services, temples, and churches call for color that is at once serene and inspiring. In the 1940 Tabernacle Church of Christ in Columbus, Indiana, Eliel and Eero Saarinen limited color to pure white and the tones of natural wood. (*Photo by John Pile.*)

Figure 12.17   The USAir terminal at New York's LaGuardia airport uses an almost totally achromatic color scheme of white throughout. A sense of order and liveliness results, helping to control the feelings of anxiety and pressure too often associated with air travel. William Nicholas Bodouva & Associates was the architect. (*Photo by John Pile.*)

Figure 12.18   Public spaces aboard an oceanliner call for a balance between excitement and calm. The interior design produced by Dennis Lennon and Partners, design coordinators for the liner Queen Elizabeth II, set a high standard in this field. In the dining room, white, Cunard red, and accents of blue create a cheerful environment in which details of table service (see also page 249) combine to generate a pleasing environment. (*Photo by John Pile.*)

Green is traditionally avoided as suggestive of seasickness, although its use is probably satisfactory in some spaces on cruise ships operating in tropical climates.

Industrial Facilities

These spaces can be made more efficient, more comfortable for workers, and safer through appropriate use of color. As might be expected, color choice can influence perception of heat or cold. Work that must be done in areas subject to excess heat can be made more acceptable through use of areas of blue and green. Warm reds and oranges offer similar improvement for areas subject to intense cold. Light colors, particularly green, can reduce irritation created by high noise levels. In general, it is best to avoid strong brightness contrasts (dark floors, white walls) and to use medium-light values of close-to-neutral tones for larger areas while limiting bright accent colors to offer relief from eye strain in restricted areas. Where materials or equipment are strongly colored, accents in contrasting color tones are helpful.

The use of color to promote safety in industrial facilities usually follows recommendations developed by various researchers. Machinery and equipment is usually finished in tones of green, which form a strong contrast with other colors used for specific purposes. Bright yellow can be used as a caution marker to emphasize possible hazards at obstacles, level changes, and to improve visibility of moving equipment such as cranes and forklifts. Red is used for fire safety equipment, for containers of dangerous materials, and to indicate control switches and buttons on machines. Blue is used to mark electrical controls and repair areas, and white indicates trash containers, drinking fountains, and food service areas.

Black and white diagonal striping can be used to mark traffic paths and to call attention to steps, stairs, and other elements that need special attention. Piping is commonly painted according to a color code that uses bright colors to identify the various functions of pipes. This aids identification for repair or modification and, incidentally, introduces lively color into many industrial facilities and into the utility areas associated with other building types.

Although much research has been done in an effort to identify the best color for many different functions, results often seem inconclusive and even contradictory. It must be remembered that color is not seen in isolation but is always only one factor among many that give any interior space its particular ambience. Climate, temperature and humidity, orientation, and geographic location all influence the impact of perceived color. Lighting interacts with color very strongly with changes in daylight, with seasons and time of day and changes in intensity and type of artificial lighting all exerting influence on the success of any color application. Thoughtful observation of existing spaces noting their use of color and light in relation to their function is a helpful guide in making color decisions while using the guidelines discussed in this chapter as a general guide to reasonable starting points.

13
Color in Historic Interiors

The strong appeal of varied colors has meant that they have had a long history of extensive use since ancient times. The ways in which color has been used during successive historic periods is a significant part of modern understanding of past design practice. Until fairly recently, the practice of interior decorators has been focused on reproduction, more or less complete and accurate, of period, traditional design. Knowledge of the color preferences of bygone periods was, therefore, an important part of a decorator's training. With the coming of modernism and the abandonment of historic imitation as a basis for interior design, study of historic color tended to be put aside. Fortunately, a new interest in historic restoration and preservation has turned attention back to study of the lively and interesting use of color in the past.

Many older buildings now preserved for their historic or aesthetic value turn out to have been altered and damaged over the years with color, a particularly easy element to change, often modified again and again until the original color has virtually vanished. Other buildings and their interiors that preserve their original color quite

fully aid efforts to restore original color in preservation sites. Modern techniques of restoration include methods of study that analyze layers of paint and study paint and dye chemistry in an effort to recreate original color in historic examples. It is often discovered that old color schemes were more lively and daring than later refinishing and more recent imitation might suggest. Through study of the surfaces of historic buildings, their walls, floors, and ceilings and through study of preserved textiles and objects, it becomes possible to piece together some idea of the ways in which color was used in earlier times. Whether this is of importance as an aid to preservation and restoration, or if it is simply reviewed as a source of ideas and inspiration, it is useful to consider what is known about use of color in historic interiors.

In every period, color has been used in varied ways in different spaces so that it is impossible to suggest any single color treatment as characteristic of a particular period. Still, availability of materials and colorants has changed over time and preferences for certain colors and certain combinations have changed so that it is possible to point out typical uses of color

Figure 13.1 An ancient Egyptian house as it appears in a model placed in a tomb around 2000 B.C. The columns are painted with stripes and details in bright colors. Hangings are also brightly colored in contrast with the yellow-tan of the plastered mud brick walls. (*Photo by John Pile.*)

and to find preserved examples that give an idea of what the norms of color use have been in the past. The following is an attempt to summarize the ways in which color was most widely used in the generally recognized historical periods.

ANCIENT EGYPT

Information about Egyptian color usage is surprisingly complete because of the Egyptian burial customs that placed many objects in tombs—actual furniture as well as small models of houses and other objects—which have been preserved into modern times. The preserved color that can be studied on objects now in museums makes it clear that strong and bright

color was well liked and extensively used (see Figure 13.1). Furniture, usually of natural wood, often made use of ebony (almost black) and white ivory inlay to create strong patterns. Ivory inlay was often painted in bright colors such as red and blue. While the richness of such objects as the furniture recovered from the famous tomb of Tutankhamen was probably not equalled in houses of average people, a house model (now in the Metropolitan Museum of Art in New York City) from a tomb of about 2000 B.C. has yellow clay plastered walls, walls of a deep red, columns painted with stripes of white, blue, green, orange, and red, and hanging cloth panels striped in blue and white on an orange background. Mud brick walls were generally whitewashed and ceilings were often painted blue. It seems certain that very intense and varied color was the norm of Egyptian practice.

ANCIENT GREECE

Information about Greek use of color in interiors is limited to traces found in various ruins which suggest that strong color was widely used. In the prehistoric palace at Knossos on the island of Crete, wall paintings show columns painted in a strong red with black capitals and moldings. Many walls carry decorative paintings using deep red, white, and tones of blue and green. Even less information is available about the use of color in classical Greece. The famous temples, now nearly white or in the beige of natural stones, were, it is believed on the basis of traces remaining on the stone, originally painted in strong colors such as red and blue. Perhaps these colors were used to emphasize details rather than to cover whole surfaces. Many attempts to show such use of color in drawings and paintings including imagined interior views exist, but the accuracy of the color they show is a matter for conjecture.

ANCIENT ROME

Fairly extensive knowledge of Roman use of interior color comes from the ruins at Pompeii and Herculaneum where rooms, even whole houses, have been excavated from the towns buried by the eruption of Vesuvius in 79 A.D. Walls were frequently painted in designs that simulated views of

Figure 13.2 The interior of the Roman Pantheon (ca. 128 A.D.), the greatest of the ancient Roman temples, has an interior richly colorful with facings and flooring of marble—mostly replaced in post-Roman times but probably similar to the original detailing. (*Photo by John Pile.*)

the out-of-doors or that illustrated mythological figures and stories. Dominant colors were the strong red, often called *Pompeiian,* black, and, in smaller details a full range of naturalistic color. Backgrounds for figures are usually the typical Pompeiian red. Floors often used mosaic in a range of color. Gilding and actual gold were favorite elements for the display of wealth. The interior of the Pantheon in Rome, with its use of richly colorful marbles, bronze, and gilding suggest the strong color typical of temple interiors, with the warm tones of various marbles dominant (see Figure 13.2).

EARLY CHRISTIAN AND BYZANTINE ERA

Most of the surviving work of these eras is in churches. Ancient Roman practice survived to some extent with use of varicolored marbles for walls and columns. The most striking characteristic work of the years between the fall of Rome and the development of medieval society is the extensive use of mosaic within church interiors. The pictorial images were formed from tiny stones of varied colors with blue, green, and gold tones dominating the other colors that form more or less realistic figure images (see Figure 13.3). Floors are also made up in geometric patterns formed by marble and other stone blocks assembled to form abstract mosaic patterns.

MIDDLE AGES

Any surviving medieval interiors, those of churches, cathedrals, and remaining parts

Figure 13.3   St. Mark's in Venice (ca. 1063–1073) is richly lined with colorful pictorial mosaics typical of Byzantine practice. (*Photo by John Pile.*)

of castles are now dominated by the colors of stone—primarily gray and warm gray. Medieval paintings that show domestic interiors suggest an extensive use of strong color in a full range with reds, greens, and blues used at high levels of saturation. The natural colors of wood and stone, browns and grays, appear as background for the bright colors of textiles and painted surfaces. There is evidence that the stone of church and cathedral interiors was also often painted in strong colors which have faded or disappeared over the intervening years. The art of stained glass brought strong color into interiors of churches where windows made up of many colored-glass pieces introduced strong and bright reds and blues along with smaller areas in a full range of bright colors. (See Figures 13.4 and 13.5.)

RENAISSANCE

Medieval practice continued in the interiors of the early Renaissance in Italy with natural wood and stone tones of browns and grays forming a background for brighter colors in textiles. Plastered walls usually had the tan or ochre color of the sand used in the plaster. White plaster and paint were not used. Painted wall surfaces might be deep green or dull red. Medieval paintings and manuscript illuminations often show interiors with many areas of bright color, usually in textiles such as bed covers, curtains, or wall hangings using greens and reds and, to a lesser extent, oranges and blues, all at a high level of saturation (see Figure 13.6). Gilding was often used on ornamental details to show off the wealth and status of affluent owners. Oriental rugs appear, often used as table coverings rather than as floor carpet.

In Spain, Moorish influences introduced tile with white backgrounds and patterns in blue and yellow. The French Renaissance followed Italian patterns of using subdued

gray and brown color in architectural elements with strong, chromatic colors in textiles used on furniture, as curtains, and as wall hangings (see Figure 13.7). In Holland and Flanders, white walls and floors tiled in black and white form settings for the browns of furniture and the more chromatic colors of textiles.

The French Renaissance moved from the restrained color of Italian examples into increasingly elaborate use of colored marbles, gilding, and wall painting resulting in the richness of such palace interiors as those at Versailles. Later, in the rococo era, an increasingly subtle use of delicate color developed. Walls were often painted in pale rose color, in light yellows, or in soft grays tinted green, blue, or violet with details in white or gold. Parquet floors in natural wood tones were often partially covered with rugs of subtle, pastel colors. The Napoleonic period Empire style introduced color tones intended to suggest the empire of ancient Rome. Pompeiian red along with black and gold were favorite colors intended to flatter Napoleonic ambitions. (See Figures 13.8 and 13.9.) Percier and Fontaine, often described as the first professional decorators, were known for interiors in which a strong theme color such as a red or blue-green was consistently used along with the brown tones of natural wood.

English Renaissance color is based on the tones of natural wood and stone, the near white of plastered ceilings and walls, and the restrained colors of textiles. From the Elizabethan era through Georgian periods, English color retains an emphasis on the browns of wood, the white to tan of plaster, and the occasional bright color of

Figure 13.4 The interior of the medieval castle was dominated by the gray of stone and the brown tones of the wood ceiling structure. In this room in the French castle of Langais (1465–1469), tapestry and a colorful tile floor relieve the austerity. (*Photo by John Pile.*)

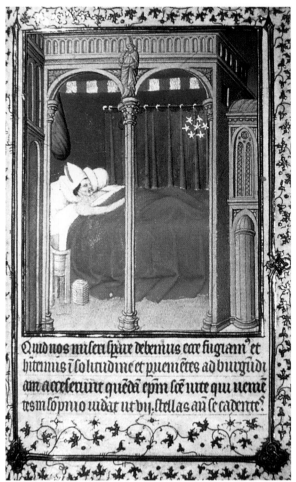

Figure 13.6   In this illustration from a medieval manuscript, a bishop (who can be recognized as such from the miter he is wearing) sleeps under a brilliant orange-red blanket with curtains of red and blue in the background.

Figure 13.5   The gray stone of the medieval cathedral interior was made colorful by the light passing through windows of stained glass. In the nave of Exeter Cathedral in England (ca. 1300), gray stone dominates the color. (*Photo by John Pile.*)

Figure 13.7   In the chateau Azay-le-Rideau (1518–1529) of the Early Renaissance in France, stone walls were hung with a covering of colorful fabric while bed coverings and hangings provided additional color.

Figure 13.8   The neoclassicism of the Petit Trianon at Versailles (1762–1768), designed by Ange-Jacques Gabriel, uses restrained color, soft pastels for wall paneling with ornamentation in white and gold. (*Photo by John Pile.*)

Figure 13.9   A room of the Palace of Fontainbleau outside of Paris, as reconstructed in the Empire style ca. 1805, used Pompeiian red, black, and gold to flatter Napoleon's imperial ambitions.

Figure 13.10   A room from Kirtlington Park, near Oxford, England (ca. 1748), has white plasterwork set off by the wood floor and furniture and the colors of furniture upholstery fabrics. The room is now installed in the Metropolitan Museum of Art in New York. (*Photo by John Pile.*)

bed curtains or tapestry wall hangings. In the mid- to late-eighteenth century, the Adam Brothers were responsible for introducing more adventurous color to English interiors. Some Adam rooms were all black and white and pale gray, but others used a variety of strong color—green marbles, gilt, and varied color marbles for floors, for example, or, in certain rooms, tapestries on all wall surfaces with dominant pink tones, or, in another room, Pompeiian tones of red, blue, and tan. Adam color schemes were very varied and suggested movement toward a modern approach of using color in a planned way unique to each individual space. (See Figures 13.10 through 13.12.)

Renaissance influences in England came to an end at the beginning of the nineteenth century with the English Regency period. Interior color tended to become rich and varied to the point of excess (see Figure 13.13). Strong reds and yellows, gilding, and colorful rugs were assembled to make up the lavish tonality of such spaces as the rooms of the Royal Pavilion at Brighton. The influence of French Empire style was intermixed with exotic concepts from real or imagined Indian and Chinese sources.

COLONIAL AMERICA

In the early settlements of colonial America, interior spaces were dominated by the natural color of the woods that made up floors, ceilings, and the paneling of most walls. Natural brick was the material of fireplaces and chimney breasts. Plaster was used occasionally, usually of the beige or tan tones of the sand in its makeup rather

Figure 13.11 The Adam Brothers used color in varied ways. In the entrance hall of Syon House, near London (1762–1769), color is achromatic near white except for the marble floor and dark sculpture. (*Photo by John Pile.*)

than white. Chromatic color sometimes appeared in the colors of the fabrics used in making braided rugs and quilts. With the increasing wealth and sophistication that developed in the eighteenth century, English influence and English design practice introduced more use of chromatic color. Wood paneling was sometimes painted in tones of gray, soft blue, or green, or, occasionally, in a red-brown. Wood trim, including moldings, trim around doors and windows, and doors themselves, were frequently painted in colors selected to relate to the textiles of upholstery or drapery. Floors were sometimes painted in solid colors or in patterns of varied colors. Colorful stenciled decoration was often used on plastered or wood-surfaced walls. Textiles and wallpapers with elaborate patterns came into use both as imports and, as domestic production developed, American made (see Figure 13.14). Chinese motifs became well known and popular, often using yellow as a dominant color or with the soft tones of Chinese landscape painting. Toward the end of the eighteenth century, the Federal period introduced a rising use of varied color drawn from the increasingly available colorful textiles for drapery and upholstery, which used bright greens, deeper blues, gold, and tones of red.

VICTORIAN ERA

The Federal period merges into the Greek revival in America with increasingly accurate reproduction of the details of ancient Greek design. Color is generally restrained, with tones of gray and tan for walls, ceilings and trim white or nearly white, gilt accents on frames of pictures and mirrors and on some details. Floors were often natural wood or, with increasing frequency, wall-to-wall carpet in floral or geometric patterns and varied, somewhat dense colors. Black marble fireplaces were popular, and uphol-

Figure 13.12   In contrast to the reserved color of the Syon entrance hall, the Adams at nearby Osterley Park (1763–1780) used lively color based on Pompeiian themes in this library. (*Photo by John Pile.*)

stery and drapery often used strong colors, reds, blues, and greens in stripes or figured patterns.

The Gothic revival replaced Greek-inspired design with either accurate or fanciful versions of medieval precedent. The romantic idea of the Middle Ages as a period of dramatic, violent, and often gloomy events was translated into a fondness for darker tones of deep colors, dense reds and greens in muted values. The Gothic revival slips imperceptibly into the typically Victorian patterns of elaborate and ornamental detail chosen from any and all historic or newly invented precedents (see Figure 13.15). Color became typically heavy, dark, and often, to modern viewers, gloomy. Walls were often covered with wallpapers in deep colors, stripes, and patterns. Embossed papers were popular in dark reds and browns. The term the *brown decades* is often given to the years after the Civil War, with reference to the fondness for such colors as mauve, deep olive green, and brown. Woodwork was often of oak or mahogany stained to darken its color to deep red-brown, and dark brown walnut was a favored wood for furniture. Upholstery was often covered in brown or black leather or in woven horsehair in dark gray or black.

A surprising contrast to the gloom and heaviness of the typical Victorian interior appears in the communities built by the religious sect known as American Shakers (see Figure 13.16). While having no stated artistic or aesthetic goal, the Shakers turned, out of moral conviction, to a vocabulary of simplicity and restraint. Shaker interiors were painted white, with natural wood or paint in light tan for floors and most furniture. Paint was used sparingly for some furniture and for woodwork details in a dull red or subdued blue. Window curtains were white, while chair seats sometimes used woven tapes of red, black, or tan. Bed covers were simple weaves, often using blue. The typical Shaker interior was bright and modestly colorful in a way that is generally appealing to modern viewers.

The craftsman movement, developed by Gustav Stickley on the basis of the ideas of the English reformer, William Morris, brought about a new respect for the natural colors of materials such as woven fibers, natural leather, and wood—particularly the darkened natural oak that gave the movement the popular name of "Golden Oak" design. The early work of Frank Lloyd Wright and some of his contemporaries took up a similar devotion to the natural colors of materials, with a resulting palette using the browns and tans of natural wood, the dull reds of brick and tile, and the beiges and tans of undyed textile fabrics to generate a soft and warm tonality (see Figure 13.17). To this, Wright added a characteristic sharp scarlet red, used only in small details, that remained typical of all of his work throughout his career.

ECLECTICISM

Beginning in the 1890s and continuing until the 1930s, interior design became dominated by a pursuit of accurate historic imitation. Every interior was decorated in accordance with a particular historic style, colonial, Louis XV or XVI, Georgian, Adam Brothers, or any other past period that appealed to the client or decorator. In this climate, color choice had no consistent theme but was rather based on knowledge, more or less accurate, of the color of the period being imitated. It is amusing to note that it was often in kitchens and bathrooms, spaces for which no clear historic

Figure 13.13 The Royal Pavilion at Brighton, England (1802–1823), designed by John Nash, is full of the rich and exotic color typical of the Regency period. Red and gold are dominant colors, with pink and green in carpets of this music room. (*Photo by John Pile.*)

Figure 13.14   An American Colonial room of 1765–1766 from the Powel house in Philadelphia, now in the American Wing of the Metropolitan Museum of Art in New York. The wallpaper is a painted import from China. (*Photo by Richard Cheek, courtesy of the Metropolitan Museum of Art, Rogers Fund, 1918.*)

Figure 13.15   In the London house of Thomas Carlyle, Victorian color typical of the mid- to late-nineteenth century. Tones of green and blue set off the gold frame of the painting. (*Photo by John Pile.*)

Figure 13.16   American Shaker interiors use white and a few paint colors to generate interiors of great dignity and simplicity. This room is at the community at Sabbathday Lake, Maine, and dates from the mid-nineteenth century. (*Photo by John Pile.*)

Figure 13.17   Frank Lloyd Wright's dependence on the soft natural colors of materials in the living space of Falling-water, the famous house in western Pennsylvania. Vermillion red in fabrics enlivens the otherwise near-neutral color. (*Photo by John Pile.*)

Figure 13.18 The art deco lobby of the Chrysler Building in New York (1928–1930) uses red-orange and black marbles to create a spectacular interior typical of the deco style. (*Photo by John Pile.*)

Figure 13.19 In his own drawing for the Schröder house at Utrecht, Holland (1924), Gerrit Rietveld uses achromatic color along with areas of primary colors in a way typical of the De Stijl movement.

precedents existed, that most creative color appeared. The idea of a bathroom with coordinated color in floors, walls, and fixtures is a development of the early twentieth century. Pinks, blues, and greens were favorite colors. Similarly, kitchen tile walls, linoleum floors, and the enameled trim of stoves appeared in the golden yellows and greens that were favorite tonalities.

ART DECO

After World War I, a search for a new vocabulary of design suited to the modern world began in Europe. In France, the exhibit titled "Les Arts Decoratif" attracted designs that turned away from historic precedents and introduced an emphasis on materials thought to be characteristically modern, such as aluminum or chrome, glass in black and other colors, and strong colors such as orange and olive green. The resulting interiors, now designated as *art deco,* came to be viewed as *modernistic,* that is, in a style comparable to earlier historic styles but with a relationship to the world of the twentieth century. Examples of art deco color can be found in England and America as well as in continental Europe (see figure 13.18). The use of black, metallics, particularly chrome and stainless steel, of opaque glass in such colors as black, dark green, and brown, along with mirrors—sometimes tinted blue or orange—of marble in strong tones of green and dark gray, and of wood veneers in natural tones or bleached to near white became stylish. Textiles and carpet appeared with sharp geometric patterns using black, greens, and dull reds as favorite color themes.

Art deco design tended to be most favored in theatrical contexts (film and stage sets and in theaters themselves), in exhibit buildings, and in the interiors of restaurants, hotels, oceanliners, and in the public spaces of skyscrapers, where the desire to assert modernity in a visible way was an important consideration. Residential interiors of the 1920s and 1930s tended to remain loyal to the eclectic urge toward historic imitation with the corresponding acceptance of color chosen with little consistent pattern.

MODERNISM

A more serious and thoughtful effort to find a design vocabulary for the twentieth century surfaced in several locations where influential movements, connected into the fine arts and with strong acceptance in the profession of architecture, developed. In Holland, the movement called De Stijl (the title of a magazine) accepted the abstract color theories of artists such as Mondrian and Van Doesburg and translated their approaches into interior design. This meant that only the achromatic tones of white, black, and gray could be used except for small areas and details in the pure primary tones of red, yellow, and blue (see Figure 13.19). The colors of light natural woods were also sometimes admitted, as in some of the furniture of Gerrit Rietveld.

In Germany, closely parallel use of color became part of the approach of the group of architects and designers connected with the famous design school, the Bauhaus. Bauhaus color theory is discussed in some detail in Chapter 11. The stylistic term *international style,* coined to describe the modern work of many European designers, came to be closely associated with the austere use of white along with small areas of pure primaries as a favored color theme. Green appeared in the generous use of living plants, and other colors are often present in works of modern art frequently on view in modernist interiors. Not all European modernist work was as limited in color as is often supposed. Perhaps familiarity through black and white photography

Figure 13.20   Mies van der Rohe's Barcelona Pavilion (1929) uses the natural colors of materials including richly colorful marbles along with curtains of scarlet red. (*Photo by Jim Morgan.*)

(before color photography became commonplace) has supported the myth that all modern interiors were colorless. The famous Barcelona Pavilion of 1929 by Mies van der Rohe, for example, used the warm tone of travertine marble along with screen walls of green onyx and orange onyx doree marbles (see Figure 13.20). The glass walls were tinted green while a drapery panel was of a brilliant scarlet red. Le Corbusier was an adventurous user of strong color, introducing walls painted in blue, turquoise, orange, and brown at high levels of saturation. Light from the sky was often colored by passing it through tubular skylights or from angled reflecting surfaces painted in bright colors. (See Figure 13.21.)

Modern design developed with great success in the Scandinavian countries, but a more varied use of color was characteristic of work there, which made extensive use of natural wood tones and various bright colors in textiles along with much white, a color that had long been favored in historic interiors in those regions (see Figure 13.22). The term *Danish Modern* became synonymous with the warm light brown of natural teak wood along with lively reds and blues in textiles, a color vocabulary with wide public acceptance in post–World War II America.

A sharp division developed in American interior design of the 1940s, which has extended to some degree until the present time. The profession of interior decoration carried forward the practice of historic imitation, but also often adopted the form vocabulary of modernism while using color schemes carefully developed to combine varied colors in rich and elaborate schemes that could range from appealing and comfortable to contrived and ostentatious. In contrast, designers who preferred the term *interior designer* tended to work in color more closely allied to the European modernists with a strong connection to Bauhaus color theory. Modern architects, increasingly active in interior design, tended

to relate to this second direction. White, neutrals, and chrome formed the basic color vocabulary of the work of interior designers, with natural colors of materials (wood, marble, brick, for example) and limited accents in strongly chromatic colors (with the primaries, particularly, much in evidence).

Scandinavian influence entered into the mainstream of modern American design through the role of the Finnish architect, Eliel Saarinen, who was in charge of design teaching at Cranbrook Academy from 1932 until his death in 1950. Many American designers were students at Cranbrook, including the architect Eero Saarinen (Eliel's son), Charles Eames, Florence Schust Knoll, Benjamin Baldwin, and Jack Lenor Larsen, each known for a lively and creative use of color in a full range of strong tones along with whites and the colors of natural wood.

The term *late modernism* has come into use to describe the work of designers who continue to follow the general design directions of the modernism of the 1920s through the 1960s. Late modern interiors, similar to those of the earlier modernists, tend to use white paint, the natural colors of wood, stone, and brick along with limited use of bright, chromatic color. The range of bright colors used as accent is somewhat more inclusive than the favorites of earlier modernism, possibly in response to the more daring practice of the postmodernists (see Figure 13.23).

POSTMODERNISM

Modernism in design has always had detractors who urge designers to cling to or return to earlier practice. A more serious challenge to modernism has emerged in the form of the direction now generally called postmodernism. In the 1960s, a combination of dissatisfaction with the concepts of modernism and a desire to move

Figure 13.21 The living room of the Villa Savoye at Poissy, France (1928–1930), uses tones of blue and red-brown along with white and neutrals in a way typical of the earlier work of Le Corbusier. (*Photo by Jin Bae Park.*)

Figure 13.22 Yellow in flooring and various details warms the white tones of the entrance area of the Paimio Sanatorium (1929–1933) in Finland by Alvar Aalto. (*Photo by John Pile.*)

Figure 13.23   In the East Wing of the National Gallery of Art in Washington, D.C., the late modern interior by I. M. Pei and Partners is almost entirely white except for the brilliant red accent provided by the Alexander Calder mobile. (*Photo by John Pile.*)

Figure 13.24 The colorful marbles in wall surfaces and floors suggest the postmodern movement toward strong color. Philip Johnson was the architect for this office building at 685 Third Avenue (often called "The Lipstick") building in New York. (*Photo by John Pile.*)

Figure 13.25 Postmodern color in the ground floor restaurant of the Asahi Building in Tokyo. Philippe Starck was the architect and interior designer. (*Photo by John Pile.*)

forward into something new and different led to a kind of rebellion against modernism and the growth of a stylistic direction inevitably called *postmodernism.* The characteristics of this direction were a turn away from the order and logic of modernism toward a freer acceptance of varied form, inclusion of references to historic design, and, reasonably enough, a willingness to turn to a varied and inclusive use of color. Secondary colors, pastels, and shades that would have appeared frivolous to modernists came into wide use. Favorite postmodern colors include tones of peach or apricot, olive green, turquoise, and violet. Colorful patterns are often used for tex-

tiles and even appear as wall decoration or on the surfaces of furniture. (See Figures 13.24 and 13.25.)

The Italian movement of the 1980s that called itself *Memphis,* a development closely allied with postmodernism, was particularly daring in the use of bright color and strong pattern in ways that often appeared shocking or tasteless. While the directions suggested by Memphis have not become a dominant force in contemporary design, they have joined with postmodern practice to open up a willingness to use color in free and varied ways that might have been rejected in the recent past.

14
Work with Color

Every interior calls for color planning and systematic steps to transfer the planned color treatment into realization. Several of the necessary steps have been the subjects of earlier chapters. In this chapter, these planning steps are discussed as integral to the process of project execution. When consideration of color should be taken up during the course of an interior project's development is open to discussion. It can be argued that color, at a conceptual level, should be thought about at the very earliest beginnings, the making of first sketches, or even in the mental images that precede first sketches. While some designers are able to think in color at the beginning of an interior project, it is probably much more common to work on design in terms of planning and three-dimensional form while color is left for later selection. The fact that most sketching is done in black and white makes it easy to carry design development forward while postponing color decisions.

It is probably a habit formed by students in design schools to work on planning and full development of design while leaving consideration of color to the end of a project when presentation drawings, ren-

derings, and color charts are required. Many practicing designers follow this pattern and larger design firms sometimes institutionalize this approach by forming a special department that works on color and material selection only after the other phases of design are well advanced—or even completed and approved. The common practice of allocating architectural design and interior design to separate designers or organizations makes this process inevitable in such situations. The interior designer may be presented with complete plans with all decisions set, including choices of materials, so that color is made into a matter quite apart from basic design. Interior work that deals with existing spaces confronts a similar situation where many aspects of the space in question are fixed while color remains a primary matter for fresh consideration.

PRELIMINARY COLOR PLANNING

Interior designers cannot escape some of these realities when they are imposed by

Figure 14.1 Samples scattered on a desktop as a first step in developing a color concept.

the way a design project is organized, but, when the interior designer has more complete control of a total project, it is highly desirable to think of color in a general way along with the development of the first conceptual sketches. Such thoughts can be recorded with notes in a notebook or notes made directly on sketches. It is even better to assemble actual color samples, small swatches, torn bits of colored paper, scraps of cloth, strands of yarn, or any other materials that will record actual color intentions (see Figure 14.1). Such materials can be grouped together in an envelope (transluscent glassine is ideal) for each space being considered. Later, larger color samples can be collected and grouped, ready to form the basis for the development of abstract charts as described in detail in Chapter 6.

While the preliminary design is being developed, it is also timely to collect color data on any elements that have been predetermined and that must be taken into

account in color planning. In an ideal situation there would be no such items, but many real projects must take account of one or more of the following:

1. Materials having color characteristics that cannot be changed, such as a wall or walls of brick, stone, or wood paneling in a natural finish; or floors of slate, tile, flagstone, natural wood boards, or parquet. While some of these materials could be painted or stained to change color, it may have been decided to retain natural color—whether already existing or planned as part of projected construction.
2. Objects to be retained and incorporated in the space to be designed. Valued older furniture or rugs, works of art, or collected objects may be owned by a client, and their use in the space desired. In this case also, some color change may be possi-

ble (reupholstering or refinishing furniture, for example) but a valued painting or rug with strong color character is a factor that must be taken into account.

3. Color themes may be required as part of a client's existing policy for color use. Colors that are part of a corporate identity program may be a required part of new color planning.

It is also wise to make note of any clear wishes expressed by a client, even if these seem of questionable value. A desire for "a blue room," for example, or a color prejudice such as "don't use any green" can best be noted for acceptance or for modification as a project moves ahead. With such notes in hand, work can proceed to the making of color charts.

ABSTRACT CHARTS

An abstract chart for each space can be produced at varied levels of formality. It may be sufficient to simply group swatches of colored paper in a random arrangement, or, if a more organized approach seems needed, such swatches can be trimmed to a desired size and shape and mounted on a backing to form a clear record of intentions (see Figure 14.2). As discussed in Chapter 6, such a chart may adjust the sizing of each sample to relate to the area of color that will be present in the final project—floors and ceilings, for example, which usually involve large areas, may be represented by large swatches, while areas of furniture materials, upholstery, drapery, or accent colors in accessories can be represented by smaller samples. It is also usual to place samples in an order that roughly corresponds to the location of the color in question in the real space. A typical chart will thus place floor cover at the bottom and ceiling color at the top of a vertical band, with other samples located in

Figure 14.2   Colors organized into an orderly band or spectrumlike color chart suitable for use as a basis in material sample selection.

between in positions that relate to actual intended location.

Some designers may prefer to make up a blank chart with areas indicated in black and white lines, with spaces for notations on location of each color and any data that may be available on the actual material that will be used in the finished space. In such a chart, the areas provided for each sample will be more or less arbitrary since a standard chart is intended for use for any space. The area of floor and ceiling assigned, for example, may not be appropriate for a small space (a bath or elevator cab, for instance) but a thoughtful designer can make needed adjustments or can use a nonstandard chart format.

It is in this first, abstract color charting that changes and adjustment can be most easily made. Alternative charts can be made up to show varied schemes, or alternative swatches may be selected for particular areas allowing for revisions that may be made in discussion with other designers or with a client representative.

MATERIALS SAMPLE CHARTS

The usual step following acceptance of abstract charting is the production of a color and materials sample chart or *board* for each space under development (see Figure 14.3). Chapter 9 is devoted to the making of such charts. Because actual materials must be selected and samples in desired colors must be obtained, the making of such charts can involve considerable time and trouble. Alternative colors or materials can still be considered at this stage, but providing the alternative samples can be troublesome and inconvenient. Ideally, final color and material charts should define the intended end result and should be available as the basis for specifications, ordering of products, and provision of information to contractors to direct the placement of paint colors and other elements that involve color.

COLOR DRAWINGS

For many projects, color drawings may be desired to show planned design in full color. Such drawings are often required for presentation to clients in order to obtain approval of all aspects of an interior design project. Color drawings can take a number of forms, varying in complexity and difficulty of production from quite simple to very elaborate. Among the types of color drawing that can be considered are the following:

1. *A color floor plan.* Such a plan makes use of the basic architectural plan of a space, usually with furniture drawn in its planned size and location (see Figure 14.4). Color is then applied to the plan with colored pencil, watercolor, or with cut bits of colored paper or fabric applied to the locations where the colors will occur. The limitation of such a color plan is, of course, that colors on horizontal surfaces (floor, tops of furniture items) are easily shown, but wall colors, colors of hanging drapery, and other items not visible in the plan are not visible or are understated. Wall colors can be suggested by color lines drawn on the plan but it is usually best to combine a color plan with some display of swatches to fill in information about walls and other vertical surfaces and ceiling color. To deal with these limitations, the following possibilities can be considered.

2. *Color elevations used with color floor plans.* These will show colors of walls and colors of objects adjacent to walls in front view. A set of four wall elevations in color and a color plan can be combined to form the following kind of color presentation.

3. *Color macquette.* This is a form of drawing that was widely used by designers during some historic periods and by more modern designers working in historic styles. A room is represented by a plan with each of the four wall elevations attached along the edge where wall and floor join. All of the drawings are colored by any desired medium (colored pencil or watercolor or a combination of media) and can be viewed laid flat or cut out and folded so that the walls are shown standing up surrounding the floor plan. Such a macquette makes an approach to a model— one or two walls can be folded down to permit viewing into the space at eye level with some degree of simulation of reality. (See Figures 14.5 and 14.6.) It may be noted that this form of presentation has a

Figure 14.3   Colors including some samples of actual materials organized into a chart or sample board ready for evaluation.

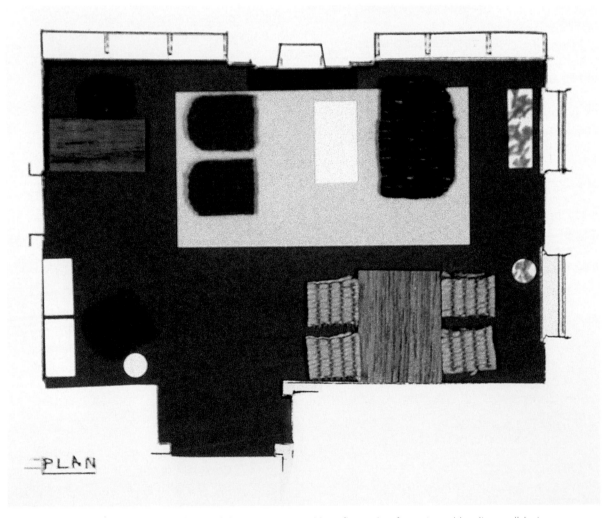

PLAN

Figure 14.4   The same color and material tones arranged in a floor-plan format, making it possible to see where each color will be used.

Figure 14.5   A maquette color presentation in which bits of color samples and materials have been placed in both floor plan and elevation locations. Folding up the wall elevations creates something approaching a three-dimensional model. The maquette was made by Jim Valkus in the office of George Nelson for Herman Miller.

certain charm, suggesting the dollhouselike qualities of a model in a way that is often appealing to clients. It is a technique that works best for rooms of moderate size and simple shape. For large open spaces or for spaces of complex shape, it can prove to be impractical.

An alternative way of making color plans, elevations, and, possibly, a macquette uses pasted slips of colored paper and sometimes bits of fabric in the shapes and locations of each area of color. In this form, the result will seem more abstract than the more realistic techniques of drawing used for conventional macquette presentation and so may seem more appropriate for modern work.

4. *Color renderings.*   These are probably the most widely used methods for realistic presentation of color schemes. A rendering is based on a perspective drawing to which is added areas of color using any desired art medium such as pastel, tempera, gouache, or watercolor. The making of a successful rendering requires considerable skill and practice. There is extensive literature, how-to books, offering instruction and advice on the making of perspectives and techniques of rendering. Good renderings can approach photographs in giving accurate and attractive images of planned interiors. However, many renderings are, unfortunately, misleading and exaggerated and less appropriate to modern design

Figure 14.6   A color and material chart showing the same scheme as previously shown, but organized conventionally in a flat sheet that could be used as a page in a presentation booklet.

work than more restrained means of representation. A good rendering has, among its advantages, the possibility of representing light and shade and, therefore, the effects of daylight at a particular time of day and the effects of planned artificial lighting. (See Figures 14.7 through 14.9.)

Many designers find that the specialized techniques of good rendering are too time-consuming and difficult to undertake and so turn to specialists who have highly developed skills in rendering when such presentation drawings are called for. A skilled renderer will need, of course, accurate plan and elevation drawings and full information about color and materials. The renderer may make the underlying perspective drawing or may make use of an accurate perspective provided by the designer.

ALTERNATIVE COLOR PRESENTATION

Several other means of color presentation are available to be used in combination

with drawing or as an alternative. These include the following:

1. *A full-color model.*   This is an alternative way to make color visible along with all other aspects of a planned design project. A simple model can be made by most designers using somewhat abstract representation of details of furniture. (See Figure 14.10.) Highly realistic model making, like rendering, calls for special skill, and it is, therefore, usually the work of experienced specialists who, like renderers, must be provided with full details of the project in drawings and color and material information. Models for larger projects are usually built in a scale of ¼ inch = 1 foot. This scale is ideal for showing larger spaces or projects involving a number of rooms. For a single room of moderate dimensions, larger scales can be used. The scale of 1 inch = 1 foot. is ideal for presenting a single room. It is the usual scale for dollhouse hobbyists, and, as a result, a wide range of materials and accessory objects are available in this scale. As with maquettes, the realistic qualities of models make

Figure 14.7   A simple rendering using a few color tones added to a print made from a line drawing. The subject is a proposed remodeling of a space in the Castello Sforzesco in Milan by the firm of Belgiojoso, Peressutti and Rogers (BBPR).

them particularly well suited for presentation to clients.

2. *Photographs of models.*   These are suitable for presentation to clients particularly when groups or committees need to view presentation material. Models made for photography can be prepared with a temporary assembly of materials and can have walls or ceilings made removable to give easy camera access at eye level. Models made at 1 inch = 1 foot scale can be highly realistic and make possible photographs that can hardly be distinguished from images of actual constructed spaces (see Figure 14.11). Model photography and lighting for model photography require suitable equipment and some special skill,

although many designers find it possible to develop the needed techniques. A modern 35 mm single lens reflex camera is well suited to model photography when equipped with a lens capable of very close focusing or with lens attachments that permit closeup photography. Flood lamps or daylight are preferable to flash illumination since the effects of lighting can be observed and adjusted to give desired effects.

3. *Computer imaging.*   Recently developed techniques can be used to show planned interiors in realistic perspective, in color, and, with sophisticated techniques that offer an approach to virtual reality, can simulate movement through a planned interior space

Figure 14.8   A color rendering using watercolor and tempera on tracing paper by Heather Blake Smith for Casson, Conder and Partners, architects. The space is a registrar's room for the General Dental Council of London, England.

in a way that is convincing and impressive. Suitable equipment and programming is required for these recently developed and constantly improving techniques. Subtleties of color and lighting make extensive demands on computer-based imaging systems, but on-going improvement may make computer imaging the most available and most useful of all ways of viewing color in advance of actual project completion.

RECORDING COLOR DATA

Once all color and material decisions have been made, it is important to establish good techniques for recording and preserv-

ing these decisions. Samples should be grouped by space and filed away in a suitable file folder or envelope. Information about decisions that involve catalog numbers, identification of sources, and all similar data need to be listed in an orderly way. Some designers make use of special forms to record this information. Project realization calls for transfer of color and material information into the media that will control the project's completion. These include the following:

1. *Drawings.*   These should include thorough notes and/or schedules, all identifications of materials and finishes that fall within the work of

Figure 14.9   A line drawing with color tones added to suggest the placement of color tones in a completed space. The drawing was prepared by John Pile for the firm of Sandgren and Murtha showing a public lobby space for the headquarters of Metropolitan Life Insurance Company in New York.

general contracting. A checklist of such items will include:

> Floor materials and finishes
> Wall materials and finishes
> Ceiling material and finish
> Hardware finishes
> Light-fixture finishes
> Electrical hardware (with plates, etc.) color and finish
> Plumbing fixtures
> Appliances
> Woodwork and trim finishes
> Paint colors and locations

The last item often calls for a special drawing, usually a print of an archi-tectural plan in which locations of paint colors are shown by colored pencil lines keyed to color specifica-tions or to sample swatches.

2. *Specifications.*   Simple projects often dispense with written specifi-cations substituting notes on draw-ings. Larger projects usually require a full set of written specifications that may include catalog numbers or other indications of color. Paint color may be specified by number relating to a particular manufac-turer's products or to a color sys-tem that provides color standards.

Specifications may include requirements for submission of

Figure 14.10   A color model viewed from above showing a proposed open office space for a bank project. The model was made by John Pile for the firm of JFN.

samples for checking and approval for such items as wood finish; materials of varied color, such as brick, tile, stone (such as slate), marbles, or terrazzo (which is made up of a mix of marble chips and cement); or any other elements in which color and finish may involve uncertainty about the visual result of elements described in words.

3. *Purchase orders.*   A number of items that fall outside a construction contract are usually the subject of written purchase orders. For some simple projects where no construction work is involved, most color information will be translated into realization through purchase orders.

The items to be ordered may include some or all of the following:

- Carpet and/or rugs
- Other floor covering
- Furniture
- Lamps and/or light fixtures
- Upholstery fabrics
- Drapery fabrics
- Window blinds or other window treatments
- Wallpaper or other wall covering
- Accessories
- Artwork (including mounting and framing)

Several matters require special attention when orders are being

Figure 14.11   A large-scale (1 inch = 1 foot) full-color, highly realistic model showing a proposed furniture display as developed in the office of George Nelson and Company for Herman Miller.

placed. Furniture orders may require care in specifying finishes; there may be several items involved: wood finish, top, hardware, cover fabric, and so on. When upholstery fabric is ordered from a fabric house, it is important to be sure that information is given correctly as to what cover goes on what item of furniture. Similarly, drapery fabrics and other window treatment items need to be given clear identification to establish correct location. Metal finishes for hardware, furniture elements, and lighting and electrical elements may need careful coordi-

nation to assure matching (where required) and proper location.

CUSTOM COLORS

Some purchased items may involve custom colors. Carpet may be dyed to order. Some textiles are available in special dye colors or in prints using custom-selected colors. Providing samples to be matched and assuring that the results will be satisfactory can involve some problems. The appearance of a woven material depends on texture as well as color, and the size of a sample may influence the perception of color. Samples of dyed yarn are better for indicating carpet color than colored paints or papers, but it is still best to see a large sample, particularly if a color mix is involved, before approving a custom color for a large area. Similarly, a large sample should be checked before approving custom weave, dye, or print color for textiles.

ON-SITE ADJUSTMENTS

On-site supervision of a project can include inspection and, if necessary, adjustment of paint colors. Since paint color is one of the few items that can be changed without great difficulty, it is possible to go on-site after other work is complete to bring to the site the largest available samples of carpet, fabrics, and other finish items, and to request a primer or second coat of paint in the color specified or requested to match a sample. By viewing a large area of paint in relation to the other samples, it is possible to decide on approval or, if necessary, to make an adjustment in the color of the final coat of paint. A large area of color may appear too light or too dark, dull or overly bright as compared to the small sample used for selection. A cooperative paint contractor will be ready to make minor adjustments in the paint mix used for the final coat.

On-site supervision also calls for careful checking for possible errors. It is, unfortunately, not unusual for furniture to be delivered with wrong finishes or wrong cover materials. Where items have simply been wrongly placed (the furniture for one room placed in another room, for example), correction is easy. If items have actually been manufactured in ways that include error, adjustment may be troublesome and slow; it should not be costly if the error is the responsibility of the supplier. Errors by contractors and suppliers are quite common and it is part of the interior designer's

responsibility to identify errors and arrange for corrections.

It is also possible that a client may be dissatisfied with the color choices seen in a completed space. It is part of good service by a designer to make an effort to deal with such problems if the demands of a client are not unreasonable. Costs of changes can become a matter for dispute. If approvals of all color choices have been obtained in some clear way before specification and ordering has taken place, the financial impact for requested changes is clearly the responsibility of the client.

APPROVALS

One way to test client satisfaction with color and design of costly items involves purchase on an approval basis. Dealers in expensive rugs, in antiques, and in fine art are often willing to sell or lend an item *on approval,* that is, on a trial basis for a period of time that may be agreed upon or may be open-ended. The client buyer-to-be is then able to live with the object in question in its intended final location for a long enough time to learn to like or dislike it, as the case may be. Dealers know from experience that, if an object is well enough liked to be requested on approval, the probability of giving it back after a period of time may become unthinkable, and the item will indeed be purchased. When a client expresses uncertainty about a designer's choice in terms of color (or any other aspect of design), arranging for an approval period is often a sound way of testing satisfaction at no risk. This is an approach that, obviously, can only be used with objects that are movable, and it is usually only available from sellers accustomed to dealing in costly objects.

Maintaining good records of color selections (including samples whenever possible) can be helpful when, as time goes by, refinishing of some elements may be necessary or changes are desired long after a project's original completion. Good relationships between designer and client are aided by a willingness and ability to provide a continuing service to insure that a project holds up well over an extended period of time.

STANDARD COLOR SCHEMES

In design firms that produce a significant volume of work, particularly work that involves frequent repetition of particular types of space, it may become reasonable to develop standard color schemes appropriate for repeated use. A situation in which this is a virtual necessity is the development of color for a prototype space intended to be reused as an aid to recognition of a particular firm or chain. Restaurants belonging to a chain and sharing a corporate name are an example of this need. While slight variations may be accepted, it is usually best if each shop uses color in a similar way that stamps the chain with its own character and aids identification by potential customers. Airlines, similarly, desire a color theme that will identify their ticket offices, check-in counters, and waiting lounges wherever they may be located. The same color theme may be tied into aircraft interior design and, possibly, to aircraft exterior graphics and other graphic materials, such as printed items and advertisements. Finding a unique color identity for any one firm that will distinguish it from competitors is often something of a challenge. Car rental firms, shipping and communication companies, and other organizations having many shops or offices may follow a similar pattern.

A slightly different possibility for the development of standardized color schemes arises in the design of large projects made up of many similar or identical units. Office buildings with many similar private offices, hotels and motels, or health care facilities with many similar rooms invite repeated color schemes. While treating each project and each space as new and unique is customary, it is obviously unnecessary and pointless to develop dozens, even hundreds of different schemes for the many rooms of a hotel, office building, or hospital. One scheme endlessly repeated throughout a project may become monotonous and boring, but also offers simplicity and some possible economies in purchasing and maintaining spaces. A small number of different schemes can offer sufficient variety to avoid total monotony, or a standard basic scheme may offer variety through the inclusion of one element that can be varied. A neutral scheme using bright accent color in upholstery or drapery, for example, can be varied by providing a number of differing choices of accent color.

Another possibility that some design firms may consider is the development of a variety of standard color schemes ready for use in any project. Schemes that have proven attractive and successful, for example, can be filed away and reused in later projects perhaps with minor variations or in virtually identical form. Assuming that the users of various projects rarely see more than one project, reuse of color has no significant drawbacks provided that the schemes used are fully suitable to the requirements in each situation. Some designers even go as far as developing a particular color approach as part of a personal design style, applying the same approach to every project. While this may sound limiting and uncreative, it has been the approach to color of many distinguished and successful designers. The color of the interiors of Frank Lloyd Wright's many projects, for example, is surprisingly consistent in its use of warm, natural wood, brick and stone tones along with occasional accent of scarlet red (see Figure 14.12). The interior decorative work of Elsie de Wolfe became known for schemes

Figure 14.12   The warm tones of natural materials as used by Frank Lloyd Wright in his own home at Taliesin near Spring Green, Wisconsin. *(Photo by Yatsuto Tanaka.)*

dominated by white, light grays, and beige. Where a designer has established an identification with such an established approach to color use, clients will usually be pleased to find that the color schemes proposed for their projects follow the anticipated pattern characteristic of that designer's work.

15
Problems with Color

Successful use of color is readily recognizable as an important element in outstanding interior design. Working with color is generally enjoyable and designers usually look forward to this aspect of their work. It is surprising, therefore, to observe how many interiors can be characterized as unsatisfactory—even disastrous—in color terms. It must be assumed that most such failures are the result of total indifference to color decisions or to decisions made at various times and places by people with little interest or ability in design-related matters.

While the students in design schools can hardly be indifferent to color issues, it is also a fact that some, perhaps even many, students experience difficulty in arriving at color schemes that are satisfactory—satisfactory to the students themselves and to their instructors. While it can be said that there is no such thing as a bad color, it is certainly obvious that unpleasant color relationships can readily occur as colors are put together in the various elements that make up a room or other interior space. This chapter is concerned with identifying some of the difficulties that may arise in interior color and with suggesting ways to minimize such problems.

Earlier chapters have dealt with the concepts of color harmony and have offered suggested methods for arriving at satisfying color schemes. In a very large proportion of the interiors encountered in everyday life, it seems clear that such concepts and methods have had no role. Perhaps there were no designers at all, no direction from thoughtful and skillful people, whether professional or amateur, to guide the selection of color. Color selection may also sometimes be guided by mistaken ideas about style or by ideas that assume that issues of practicality, economy, or easy maintenance make it difficult or impossible to arrive at satisfactory color use.

Probably the most common cause of unsatisfactory color in interiors occurs when color decisions are made without thought for relationships, at different times and places, so that colors that do not relate well come together more or less by accident. In residential spaces, the owners or occupants may make decisions or accept decisions by others without much thought for the reality that the comfort and quality of the interior they will occupy is strongly influenced by color relationships. It is commonplace to find, for example, that floor, wall, and ceiling colors have been predetermined by a builder, a landlord, or a previous occupant. *Decoration* is often thought of as being no more that directing a painter to paint walls and ceiling. The painter may produce a color card with a limited range of interior house paints and ask for a simple choice among pink, green, blue, or cream. The unthinking householder points to the least offensive of these samples or names a favorite color and so establishes a surround of pink, perhaps, or green of a tone and intensity that may well be a poor basis from which to proceed. Floor color may come from a preexisting carpet or tile or may be whatever tone results from the finishing of wood flooring. It is a matter of chance in such situations whether floor tone and wall tones relate well or set up an unpleasant discord.

Into such a space, occupants may move preexisting furniture from various sources, from a former home, from an inheritance, from secondhand shops, or from any other source that offers items which seem useful in practical terms regardless of their colors. If new things are to be purchased, decisions tend to be made at the time and place of purchase with only casual concern for color. A carpet or rug may be chosen at a floor-covering dealer's showroom. Drapery material may be chosen at another time and place—perhaps as suggested by the dealer in window treatments. Into the resultant mix will be added pictures on walls, various accessories such as lamps, cushions, and curios, each bringing its own input of color. It is hardly surprising that the everyday way of doing things almost inevitably brings about a total effect that ranges from indifferent to aggressively unpleasant. Because such unplanned color is selected over a period of time with each selection having a limited logic of its own, occupants become

accustomed to the chaotic color around them and are often quite unaware of the negative impact that such environmental circumstances can have.

When the approach to color is more systematic with color planning a thoughtfully considered matter, whether by professional or amateur designers, unsatisfactory results are still a possibility. In general, it can be suggested that most color failures fall into the categories of either too little or too much. The direction of too little is likely to lead to interior color that is dull, drab, and boring. It is surprising that professionally selected color can readily fall into this kind of error. The term *institutional* comes to mind as descriptive of the kind of color all too often associated with hospitals, schools, and industrial facilities where color choices have been made on the basis of economy, easy maintenance, and simplicity of specification. Floors, for instance, may be brown or black as a result of the questionable belief that such tones will not show dirt or wear. Walls may be painted in a tone of beige, often with a wainscoating of darker tan or buff, guaranteeing a total effect of grim institutionality.

In reaction against institutional buff, green is often selected, perhaps in response to advice often offered that green is an eye-saver color or to a conviction that its combination of yellow and blue components will make it neither warm nor cool and thus acceptable in every situation. Brown floor and institutional green walls assure a drab and depressing interior only equalled by green walls *and* green flooring. Green is not, of course, a bad color; it is only its thoughtless overuse that has made it a notorious color offender.

White, one of the most useful of all colors, can also be a source of dullness when overused for extensive wall surfaces without variety or relief. Some research into the color preferences of the occupants of spaces, office workers, for example, or hospital patients, has found that many people associate white with blankness, emptiness, boredom, and depression. Builders of apartment houses and suburban houses built speculatively in subdivisions often paint all wall surfaces white or off-white in the conviction that this color will offend no one. Occupants then accept the white box interiors without much thought and so start color selection with a major element that can begin a drift toward drabness as unrelated items are added into such spaces.

The problem of too much color is more likely to arise when color has been thought about, but thought about in careless and simplistic ways. The person with a favorite color is often tempted to try for a room entirely filled with that color. The idea of a "red room" or a "blue room" has a certain charm and fascination, and some well-known examples that are quite successful tempt the amateur designer into too much of a good thing. While the "blue room" of the popular song may invoke an image of cozy restfulness, and the Red, Blue, and Green rooms of the White House may make an attractive picture, these examples do not make ideal prototypes for typical living spaces, offices, or other practical interiors. The blue room of the song exists only in the imagination, and that of the White House is but one room in a series that are varied, used only briefly and in sequence. Examination of such one-color rooms that are professionally designed will also reveal that there is actually considerable variety of color present, not a single intense color for every element.

The other common case of too much color comes about when a variety of strong colors are used together. Although complementary and triad color schemes can be effective, they must be developed with great care to avoid the kind of strained color relationships that are often called *clashing*. It is highly unlikely that the use of the complementaries red and green, for example, will be successful if both are selected at high intensity for all the various elements of a room. A bright green rug, red wall coverings, red and green drapery and upholstery fabrics selected at various shops and showrooms are likely to produce a painful and strained interior however colorful it may seem. Red and green, if used with discretion, can produce a good complementary relationship because they *are* complementaries. Strong colors that are neither in opposite (complementary) nor adjacent (analogous) positions on the color wheel are even less likely to be successful when used together for all the elements of a space. The following relationships:

red and yellow
red and blue
orange and green
orange and violet
yellow and blue
green and violet

are each particularly problematic because they are neither complementary nor close together in the six-color wheel. The probability of such color relationships proving objectionable is closely related to the intensity of the color in use. Intensity is a matter of saturation or *brightness.* Tints and shades are inevitably less saturated than pure colors. The relationship of orange and violet, for example, will be most problematic if the tones in use are intense. If one tone is a pale tint, it may well be acceptable in relation to the other tone which is in more intense form. A delicate violet, a tint close to white or light gray, might, for example, be quite acceptable in relation to an orange closer to red than to yellow and quite strong in saturation.

The total areas of colors present are also important factors in creating color relationships that may be troublesome. Large areas of strong color are more likely to conflict than small areas placed within a more neutral surround. A room with all of the floor in purple and the walls in a strong orange tone is likely to be problematic. A small accent area of orange-red, however, may be quite effective in relation to larger areas of a violet that is near white. In general, the larger an area of strong color, the more aggressive it will seem and the more likely it will come into conflict with other colors. This leads to the suggestion that large areas of strong color be restricted to one hue within a given space. A floor of strong color will work best if other colors in the space are either large areas of related color at diminished intensity (tint or shade) or large areas of complementary color at diminished intensity. Small areas of either related color or complementary color can be satisfactory as accents.

Translating the above suggestions into typical examples might suggest the following:

> A strong blue-green floor covering with walls of a light tint of similar blue-green plus accents of intense blue or green (an analogous scheme)
> A strong blue-green floor covering with walls of a light tint of warm beige with accents in small areas of orange-red (a complementary scheme)
> A floor with a strong tone of brown (tile or natural wood) with walls of a related light tan or beige and accents of red or red-orange (an analogous scheme)
> A similar brown floor with walls of a pale, near-gray, blue-green tint and accents of red or red-orange (a complementary scheme)

An endless listing of similarly workable color relationships can readily be drawn up.

When major areas of color are less saturated, harsh clashes are less likely to occur, but the alternative problem of dullness or monotony may surface. While schemes using all neutral or near-neutral tones are generally safe, they are subject

to the problem of dullness. The solution to this problem is generally easy—it is simply a matter of adding one or more small areas of saturated color in either a related or contrasting hue. For example:

> Light-gray or pale-beige floor color and white walls can be made lively by the addition of small areas of red-orange or blue-green accent.
> Very light-gray walls with white trim and a near-neutral wood floor tone can be enhanced with small accent areas in any strong hue: red, yellow, blue-green, or violet.

There are a number of specific problems that can be associated with the various hues of the color wheel and several of the other named colors. While most of these problems have been discussed elsewhere in this and other chapters, a list of such problems may be useful with some suggestions about their avoidance.

- *Red* is an aggressive color that, when used in large areas at high intensity, can become irritating. Tints of red (pinks) diminish this abrasive impact. Small areas of intense red are well suited to accent color. Large areas of red are best reserved for space that will be occupied for brief periods of time, such as vestibules and elevator interiors.

- *Orange* shares many of the qualities of red and is similarly best reduced to tints (peach or apricot, for example) for use in large areas. Like red, orange is effective as accent or in areas for short-term occupancy.

- *Yellow,* well known to be both warm and cheerful, is useful in larger areas, but tends to become banal and boring when overused. Both strong, sharp yellow and the tints such as cream color are subject to the problems of banality. It is helpful to seek out subtle variants on yellow tones developed by some neutralization through content of a small component of complementary tones. Bright yellow is a useful accent color.

- *Green,* generally thought of as cheerful but calming, is also subject to problems of dullness, monotony, and a certain depressive quality when overused or used in tints or shades that can be seen as institutional. Greens seem to be colors that call for balancing values of complementary color, as in fully complementary schemes, or in strong accents in schemes that are otherwise monochromatic. Green is a color that generates a strong dislike among some small proportion of the population and so calls for some caution in many situations. It is traditionally associated with illness and is therefore often discouraged in transport design where it may have an association with motion sickness.

- *Blue* is a color that attracts strong feeling of either like or dislike. Its association with calm and contemplation can readily move toward depression—the phrase *feeling blue* is a reflection of this possibility. As the most cool of cool colors, the need for contrasting warm color is often felt where large areas of blue are present, even in the form of pale tints. Blue can also be quite dark while still being strongly chromatic. Such dark blues can be dignified and attractive, but must always be used with caution to avoid a sense of heaviness and depression. Blue is a questionable color for use in health care facilities and other institutions and should be used with care and with suitable balancing contrast in other contexts.

- *Violet* is the most problematic of the chromatic colors. There are strong prejudices against violets and purples among many people that stem from associations with death and sorrow. It is also noted that it stands between warm and cool and so takes on a certain ambiguity that may be disturbing. Violets, particularly in pale tints, can be very successful in some contexts but are to be used with caution. Purples are even more problematic, sometimes

leading to the suggestion that they are best avoided entirely in interior design. This view seems excessive, but it is certainly best to avoid strong violets or purples in any situation where a sense of depression or irritation may be a problem. Violets and purples are suitable accent colors for contrast with tones of yellow.

- *Brown* and the related tones of tan and buff are commonly viewed as dull, depressing colors. Deeper tones of brown are rarely used as paint colors in interiors, although desaturated tones of light tan or cream color are often useful. Brown becomes a highly acceptable color when it occurs as the natural color of various materials. Many woods appear as tones of brown, particularly when finished. Mahogany, walnut, and oak as used for flooring or paneling are shades of brown. Other woods of lighter color including birch, maple, and pine will appear with lighter tones of brown or tan or may be finished in a range of deeper brown tones. Leather is often of natural or artificially colored brown or tan tones. Many textiles are also available in natural or dyed shades of tan or brown. In these forms, brown is a useful color in development of schemes that are quiet, dignified, and often thought of as typically masculine. To avoid any tendency toward drabness, accent color in more chromatic tones such as warm reds or oranges (creating an analogous scheme), or in tones of blue or green (creating a complementary scheme) are useful. Use of brown tends to generate a low-key scheme, although brown tints such as tan or beige can be related to lighter, high-key color.

- *Grays* are usually thought of as neutral, nonchromatic colors although, in cool- or warm-tinted form, they can be useful elements in schemes that can be strongly colorful. Grays that are truly neutral with no content of chromatic color can become depressing, even grim in implication. Where chromatic color is present as an accent, light gray can be brought into a successful relationship through tinting with the chromatic color in use. Use of subtly tinted grays can be restful and pleasant when some elements of chromatic color are present to offset any sense of dullness.

• *Black,* in its most pure form as a total absence of all chromatic color, must be used with caution. In practice, most so-called black is actually a dark gray, often with a warm or cool component. Black granite or marble, for instance, actually has a component of warm color. Black paint, if glossy, is strongly reflective and so has mirrorlike characteristics in reflecting adjacent color tones. Flat or matte black tends to make a harsh contrast with other color tones and is also easily marred or damaged. Black, when used in sharp contrast to white or metallic tones such as brass or chrome, can be striking and dramatic, but can also be harsh and tiring when overused. The reputation of black as a stylish color has tended to its excessive use in contexts where overly glaring contrasts can seem pretentious and tasteless, as in the much used relationship of black and gold.

• *White,* the tone that combines reflectance of all chromatic colors, has become a favorite tonality in modern interior design with what may be thought of as overuse or thoughtless and excessive use. White rarely is truly pure, almost always having some tint of warm or cool chromatic color. Paint color charts often display many forms of white with varied names such as off-white, bone white, oyster white, or warm white. Because all whites are highly reflective, their use tends to produce a bright, high-key color environment. Because the human eye responds by closing down to admit less light, darker tones present in the field of view will appear even darker than they are. This explains why the use of white along with darker tones tends to produce highly contrasting color and brightness relationships. The use of white as a background for the display of art or other objects may not be ideal because, while the white surround avoids unpleasant color relationships, the brightness contrast between the surround and the objects on view may be excessive, causing the objects to appear dull or dark. This suggests that white is best used in situations where other colors present are of light or pale tones. It has also previously been mentioned that white, when used without relief, may appear blank, empty, and boring to many observers. Although white has become a favorite color in modern architecture and interior design because of its ability to reveal three-dimensional form, it is best used with other colors as accents or as major areas of tone. White can serve very well as an accent color where other tones are present as in the usually very successful use of white as a trim color in relation to either strong or delicate tones in larger areas.

In the discussion of yellow, a suggestion is included that can have applicability in setting up other color relationships. This is the suggestion that harmony can be aided if each color present in a particular environment contains a small component of the other colors present. This is most easily described in relation to placing two colors together. If red and green are being used together, a small amount of red added to the green and a small amount of green added to the red will tend to slightly neutralize the intensity of each color and reduce the harshness of contrast that may result in a clash. When mixing colors in order to produce samples, this kind of modification of color tone is easy to manage. In the past, when designers generally produced samples by mixing, this was a much-favored technique. In modern practice, when colors are generally selected from a chart or specified in some other way so that no mixing process is involved, using this principle becomes somewhat difficult.

To recognize a red that has been modified by addition of green—ideally a particular green—requires careful training of color observation. When a color is modified by the addition of a small component of another hue, the original color is, in effect, moved to a slightly different position on the color wheel. The only exception results when the second, added color is a complementary. In that case the original color is somewhat neutralized (reduced in saturation). The saturation of any color can be reduced in two ways: (1) by the addition of white, black, or gray, or (2) by the addition of a complementary color. It is the latter case, in which neutralization has resulted from the addition of a complementary, that can provide a color tone which will most readily harmonize with its complementary.

Primary colors will be shifted slightly by the addition of a small amount of another primary or by the addition of an adjacent secondary. Addition to a primary of a small amount of the complementary will cause some neutralization. Secondary colors will be shifted slightly by the addition of an adjacent primary but will be somewhat neutralized by the addition of either the complementary or another secondary. A listing of these effects follows with the basic color listed first, followed by the additive color used in small quantity.

Primaries:
    Red + yellow = shift toward orange
    Red + blue = shift toward violet
    Red + orange = slight shift toward orange
    Red + violet = slight shift toward violet
    Red + green = some neutralization
    Yellow + blue = shift toward green
    Yellow + red = shift toward orange
    Yellow + green = slight shift toward green
    Yellow + orange = slight shift toward orange
    Yellow + violet = some neutralization
    Blue + red = shift toward violet

    Blue + yellow = shift toward green
    Blue + violet = slight shift toward violet
    Blue + green = slight shift toward green
    Blue + orange = some neutralization

Secondaries:
    Orange + red = shift toward red
    Orange + yellow = shift toward yellow
    Orange + blue = some neutralization
    Orange + green = some neutralization
    Orange + violet = some neutralization
    Green + yellow = shift toward yellow
    Green + blue = shift toward blue
    Green + red = some neutralization
    Green + orange = some neutralization
    Green + violet = some neutralization
    Violet + red = shift toward red
    Violet + blue = shift toward blue
    Violet + yellow = some neutralization
    Violet + orange = some neutralization
    Violet + green = some neutralization

Browns and neutrals:
    Brown + any chromatic color = shift toward added color
    White + any chromatic color = tint of added color
    Gray + any chromatic color = shift toward added color
    Black + any chromatic color = deep shade of added color
    Any chromatic color + brown = some neutralization
    Any chromatic color + white = shift toward tint
    Any chromatic color + gray = reduction of intensity
    Any chromatic color + black = reduction of intensity

Colors of woven textiles offer many opportunities to select fabrics in which yarns of several colors are combined to produce a tone that may appear uniform but that actually has a component of contrasting color. A seemingly red fabric, for example, may have woven into it some yarn strands of another color, blue or green perhaps, and so will be useful in achieving the subtlety of color relationship through the admixture of varied hues. An upholstery fabric that is dominantly blue, for example, but that has some red strands will relate well to other tones of red or pink present in adjacent locations. Carpeting that incorporates yarns of varied color tones can also provide a similar mediating effect that promotes harmonious color relationships.

A checklist of color problems and possible means of avoidance or remedy follows:

Too much color. The obvious remedies involve substitution of schemes that favor neutral or monochromatic tones. Restriction of strong color tones to limited areas or to accent roles are also routes to schemes that are safer and less strident.

Harsh or clashing color relationships. Possible alternatives include use of analogous colors or introduction of colors that incorporate small admixtures of other colors present in the same scheme.

Dull or drab color. Remedies include avoidance of institutional green or buff and introduction of accents of strong, chromatic color.

Problematic colors, especially black and purple. Caution in the use of the colors and limitation of area or restriction to accent uses will avoid tones that may be found objectionable by many viewers.

Color in random or confused relationships lacking in clear impact. This is a common result of unplanned color in which elements are chosen without thought to color interaction. Systematic color planning, making use of preestablished color elements, is needed to bring about coherence and organization in color terms.

In all of these situations, color planning through charting and assembly of color sample groupings is the primary means of converting disturbing, chaotic, or clashing color into schemes that embody relationships which are satisfying and pleasant.

16
Special Situations

Certain issues that may surface in interior design work call for special consideration. This chapter includes some discussion of a number of such matters.

OUTDOOR/INDOOR SPACES

While interior design might not seem to be concerned with spaces that are not fully enclosed, interior designers are, in practice, often involved in projects that include enclosed courtyards, decks, patios, terraces, greenhouses, and rooftop spaces where color planning is no less significant than in rooms. Visible sky acts as a ceiling for open portions of such spaces and presents a changing color element ranging from the characteristic blue, through the grays and white of clouds and overcast, to the pinks and oranges of sunsets, and the near black of the night sky. Where there are overhanging roofs or shelters, their under surface becomes another ceiling element, usually white or near white. Awnings can be elements of bright solid color or striping. The surfaces of walls and parapets are most often of architectural construction

materials such as brick or concrete which can be left in natural color or, possibly, painted. Brick or concrete walls are often cemented or stuccoed, providing a surface that may be left its own gray or tan or can be painted in stronger color. Floor surfaces may be concrete, but are best surfaced with suitable material such as tile, slate, or flagstone. Outdoor wood decks may be left in natural wood, which will weather to gray in time. Outdoor furniture also offers opportunities for color in the cover fabrics of cushions or seats, in frame elements, and in tabletops. Living plants are likely to be important elements in outdoor spaces and their green tones and the colors of their containers are additional elements to be considered. (See Figure 16.1.)

With so many elements to be dealt with, it is reasonable to consider any outdoor space in much the same way as an interior room, going through similar steps in choosing colors in the abstract and proceeding to material selections and specification. The bright light of the out-of-doors often encourages selection of bright colors that relate well to sky and plant colors, but neutral or near neutral color can also be effective in leaving strong color to the natural environ-

Figure 16.1 A semioutdoor room in a seaside house introduced as "Holiday House" presented by the magazine of that name. George Nelson was the architect.

mental surround that is usually visible from partially or totally open outdoor spaces.

CHANGEABLE COLOR

While the color schemes of most interiors are thought of as permanent and fixed, at least until a major renovation takes place, it may be advantageous for some interiors to provide ways in which color changes can be made from time to time. This is most often managed by planning major color in items that can be changed with relative ease. A typical example would be the use

of upholstered furniture that can be slipcovered, bed covers that can be easily substituted, or wall-hung tapestries, weavings, or artwork that is easily replaced by alternatives. Reasons for desiring such changes may include the following:

Seasonal changes to respond to alternatively hot and cold weather
Changing functions, such as alternative use of a space as gymnasium and dining room or auditorium and exhibit hall
Desire for frequent change as a stimulant to commercial activity, as in

certain types of retail facilities where a new appearance can dramatize an advertised sale or other event

Need to change the setting for exhibited materials, as in gallery or museum exhibit spaces

Desire for the stimulus of a new look in residential interiors

In all of these cases, it is necessary to identify ways of making color changes that will not be overly costly or disruptive. The seasons of the year are made part of the Christian religious practices of many church denominations, and such changes are facilitated through the use of the cloths and hangings called *vestments* with strong colors for each season, such as the white and gold of Christmas, the purple of Lent, and other colors for specific church observances. A similar approach has often been used in residential design where darker upholstery colors for winter are obscured by light-colored slipcovers in summer. Bed covers, blankets, and cushions are equally suitable for seasonal change. Many early-American coverlets were woven so as to offer darker colors on one side and light colors on the reverse: dark blue with a thin white pattern on the winter side, mostly white with blue patterns on the reverse for summer.

Wall hangings, banners, and readily changeable artwork offer similar possibilities for change whether seasonal or simply for variety. More extensive color change as needed in gallery and exhibit spaces housing changing events may call for full re-painting of walls. More complex mechanical means of changing color through shifting wall surfaces and alternative furniture are rarely used, but are possibilities in which the techniques of stage design might be adapted to more routinely functional interiors.

Use of colored lighting is another technique that can be borrowed from stage design. While strongly colored light is not generally satisfactory for normal ambient light, colored light focused on a particular surface can bathe that area in color while making little change in general lighting. In a restaurant or store, for example, if most color is kept near neutral and general lighting is subdued, a major wall area can be chosen for lighting with variable-colored light similar to stage lighting. The lighted wall can then be changed to any desired color tone to act as a dominant, chromatic color setting the color quality of the space.

ACCESSORIES

Small objects, functional or strictly ornamental, can introduce strong color (usually as accent) into an interior. Objects chosen without thought as to color can be disruptive to a planned color scheme, but well-chosen objects can be highly effective. In an office space with largely neutral color, for example, desk accessories such as letter trays and desk organizers of a consistent strong color can enliven the total effect of the space in a simple way (see Figure 16.2). Flower arrangements and live plants are also elements that can contribute to a color environment in a favorable way if planned with color in mind and maintained on a regular basis.

Table settings in both restaurant and residential dining areas are a favorite way of introducing strong color into an otherwise quiet color environment (see Figure 16.3). In each of these cases, the use of accessories as a source of color will also offer easy changeability as previously discussed. The interior designer must be wary of the fact that, unless such color use is planned and controlled, introduction of strong color in randomly chosen items can dilute and upset the effectiveness of planned color. In many work places, in school classrooms, and in residential interiors, it is not uncommon to see a clutter of displays, posters, objects, and strongly colored accessories

Figure 16.2 An open office space with reserved color enlivened by desk accessories in a uniform tone of red in the offices of Dial Finance in Des Moines, Iowa. John Pile was the designer. (*Photo by Norman McGrath.*)

generating an effect of confusion that undermines the success of planned color. If it is anticipated that display of objects or of graphic materials will be required, it is best to provide a specific location where such materials can be grouped and contained so that their presence will not defeat the effectiveness of planned color. Cases or shelf units that support and contain objects, tackboards, or enclosed display surfaces can be designed and placed in a way that acommodates such varicolored materials in concentrated locations.

ARTWORKS

The role of works of art, paintings, sculpture, weavings, and certain craft productions in relation to interior color calls for some special consideration. Small works, framed paintings, prints, photographs, and

Figure 16.3   A colorful table setting in the Britannia dining room of the oceanliner Queen Elizabeth II. (*Photo by John Pile.*)

small sculptural objects may be considered in the same way as accessories. Larger and more important works, however, become a factor in the color of the interior space where they are placed (see Figure 16.4). If a single work will have an important role, through size or placement, its color must be considered as part of the resultant color scheme. Several possibilities exist for establishing a satisfactory relationship to such a work. If, for example, a large painting with strong color is to be hung in a certain location, it is possible to choose one of several plans for relating to that work.

1. The color or colors of the painting may be used as a starting point in developing a color scheme that will relate well through use of similar or closely related color.

2. An opposite strategy is to select color that will contrast strongly with the color or colors of the artwork. A painting with a dominant red tonality, for example, may suggest a scheme otherwise dominated by green, thus creating a contrasting scheme in which the painting becomes, if it is large, the complementary element that balances the other color tones present. If small, such a work can be viewed as a contrasting accent color within an otherwise monochromatic or analogous scheme.

Figure 16.4   A large painting from a corporate art collection gives color focus to an office reception area at Dial Finance in Des Moines. John Pile was the designer. (*Photo by Norman McGrath.*)

3. An artwork with strong color or with varied color may be used as the primary color in a space that is otherwise neutral or achromatic in color. White or off-white, tones of gray, or near-neutral cream, beige, or tan that neither repeat nor contrast with the color of the art allow the work to take over the role of providing color.

Artwork that is not strongly chromatic in color places no pressure on other color choices, of course, and can be added into any color scheme without problems. Where a number of works having different color characteristics are to be present (as in a museum or gallery space or in any other space where a collection will be displayed), the third plan of using color that is achromatic or neutral is usually considered to be the best plan of action. The use of white or any other very light tone is not necessarily the best choice though, because, as discussed earlier, the high reflectivity of such light background color may create excessive brightness contrast, to the detriment of the art on display. Middle tones of subdued color are likely to be more effective in providing a suitable color environment for the display of art. If a single artwork will be prominent, but will be frequently changed, a similar color plan is likely to provide a setting that will not be problematic whatever the dominant color of the art may be.

Where art is to be commissioned for use in a particular space (a mural, for example, or a fixed-in-place sculpture), it is possible to work toward good color relationships in several ways. The artist commissioned to execute a work will usually be asked to provide a sketch or small scale study that will reveal the intended color. The interior designer can then use the color information from that sketch or study as a given element in developing the related environmental color according to any of the plans previously suggested. An alternative plan begins with the overall color plan for the space and provides it to the commissioned artist and leaves the decisions about color relationship to the judgment of that artist. Whether this order of events is practical depends to a large degree on the preference and temperament of the artist involved. Some artists may resent and resist being asked to work in relation to colors that have been predetermined and will insist that the color of the setting be adjusted to their work rather than the reverse. Commissioning of artwork that will be achromatic in color (as with sculpture in neutral-colored stone or metal, or woven hangings using neutral-colored fibers) will, of course, leave complete freedom for all related color decisions (see Figure 16.5).

HISTORIC RESTORATION

Some interesting problems arise where interiors of historic buildings are to be preserved or restored. It is usually suggested that original color be retained or restored, but determining original color can present difficulties. Since color is the element of interior design that is most easily changed, existing color in an older interior is rarely the original color. Surfaces are repainted, drapery and furniture replaced and changed over a period of time, and there

is likely to be no record of what the original colors were. Research can be undertaken to seek out some original color. For example, paints can be scraped carefully to remove overcoatings until the earliest layer is discovered, but even this plan is not totally effective. The bottom layer of paint may be a primer or undercoating, and whatever layer is considered to be original may have faded or undergone chemical changes over time that altered its color. Natural wood colors tend to darken with age or, in some cases, may have lightened through the bleaching action of sunlight. Textiles are even more vulnerable to fading, bleaching, and color shifting. Fabrics and rugs are likely to be replaced as necessitated by wear, with records of earlier color lost. Where the search for information on original color proves unsuccessful, the designer is forced to turn to available information on the color practice of the period and location in question and to make decisions about color in the light of whatever such information can be obtained. Existing preserved interiors in older buildings or in museum rooms can be consulted, but it must be remembered that colors in these spaces may also not be truly original, having been subjected to the same patterns of fading, color shifting, redecoration, and, possibly, a mistaken effort at restoration some time in the past. (See Figure 16.6.)

It should also be noted that original color is only one of several choices that can be thought of as having equal validity. An interior space can be given color treatment representative of any chronological point in its history and still have historic validity. The colors of the rooms of the White House in Washington, for example, would be historic whether they were original, the colors applied during the rebuilding after the fire set by the British in 1812, the colors of Abraham Lincoln's day, or the colors used during the reconstruction done during Harry Truman's presidency. Some of the great cathedrals of Europe, now gener-

Figure 16.5 In the New York showroom of the Olivetti Corporation, a commissioned bas-relief wall sculpture in soft gray-beige tones of sand sets a neutral tonality against which brighter colors stand out. The wall is the work of Constantino Nivola in a space by BBPR of Milan. (*Photo by John Pile.*)

ally in the colors of natural stone, were probably painted in strongly chromatic colors originally or at some later time in history. Victorian efforts at restoration that attempted to use strong color now seem to have been mistaken and represent Victorian taste rather than original medieval practice. Such problems and uncertainties leave the designer working in preservation and restoration with many decisions that must be made on the basis of good judgment rather than slavish attempts at authenticity which cannot be guaranteed to be successful either historically or aesthetically. If original color now appears less attractive aesthetically than some later

color treatment, it becomes a serious question whether restoration to original status is wise. Even the effects of wear and dirt are, after all, the results of historic survival so that restoration to "like new" appearance is often unsatisfactory and disturbing, as demonstrated when well-known works of art are cleaned and suddenly

Figure 16.6 Restoration of a landmark space: the main banking room of the Bowery Savings Bank in New York, a 1923 project by the firm of York and Sawyer as renewed by the firm of Swanke Hayden Connell Architects. (*Photo by Otto Baitz, courtesy of Swanke Hayden Connell Architects.*)

made bright and harsh in color tonality that can be quite shocking.

Balancing these concerns means that the designer working in preservation and restoration must take responsibility for arriving at decisions that are appropriate to the age and character of the space being worked on. This may mean an attempt to return to original status, but alternatively, it can mean an effort to return to or retain the color of some later time that can also be historically valid. It is also possible to elect to retain some of the evidences of age— one expects an old building or an old room to look old, and freshly renewed color may not meet this expectation.

It should be noted that a number of manufacturers are now supplying products intended for use in restoration that, with more or less accuracy, offer the materials and color of products now generally considered obsolete for modern use. Paints, floor coverings, wallpapers, and textiles are available in considerable variety in designs and colors that reproduce historic materials. While use of reproductions of historic furniture designs is generally considered questionable when authentic antiques are available, for the more fugitive materials such as textiles, there is no viable alternative to using modern products that reproduce or reasonably substitute for whatever may have been original.

PROJECTED LIGHT

The use of light, possibly strongly colored light, as a means of making color readily changeable in certain situations has been previously mentioned. Another possibility of generally limited usefulness is the projection of fully colored images onto otherwise blank surfaces such as walls and ceilings. Photographic images, such as the familiar color slides, when projected, can transform a surface into a complex, detailed simulation of almost any reality. The projection of an accurate image of the night sky onto a dome surface is well known as the surprisingly convincing simulation of reality in a planetarium. Similar projection of outdoor images can transform a wall into a landscape, an architectural interior or simply provide a solid color or color pattern.

Some designers have managed demonstrations in which the interior of a small room is suddenly made to resemble the interior of a vast space or of some historic interior. This is a variation on a similar technique often used in modern stage design in which a backdrop is projected on a white surface making possible scenery of great complexity and a high degree of realism while, at the same time, making changes of scene easy and rapid. Several problems associated with projected color have made its use uncommon. The equipment for projection is costly, lamp life is short while lamp replacement is expensive and inconvenient, and there must be a suitable location for the projector or projectors. There must also be a clear space for the projector beam so that objects (such as pieces of furniture) or people do not cast disturbing shadows and so that the glare of the projected light beam cannot shine in the eyes of anyone in the space. Some of these problems can be avoided by rear screen projection, sometimes used in theater applications, but the space for this is not usually available in functioning interiors. As a result of such difficulties, projected color remains a limited and largely experimental technique.

17
Color in Current Practice

In this chapter, the ways in which a number of highly regarded design professionals work with color is presented with some examples of their work and some comments on their various approaches. Perhaps the most striking observation that this survey produces is an awareness of the great variety in approach. This is not only variety in end results; but also in method of work. Some designers have offered comments on their method, others have left their methods to be deduced from the visible results.

The designers whose work appears here represent six differing types of involvement in interior design, and each also demonstrates a particular approach to color. There are here: (1) a well-known architect known for use of color that onlookers relate to post-modernism, (2) an interior designer who often develops color systems, (3) an interior and architectural designer with a special interest in furniture design, (4) a designer and teacher with a unique way of teaching and working with color, (5) an architect who deals with color interiors in his own work, and (6) a large design firm with a varied practice.

The primary lesson to be learned here is that there is no one way to use color and work with color. Any method, any approach can be successful if it leads to results that are appropriate and satisfying.

MICHAEL GRAVES

Michael Graves is an American architect currently practicing in Princeton, New Jersey. He was trained at the University of Cincinnati and at the Graduate School of Design at Harvard. He was a winner of a Prix de Rome fellowship in 1960 and established his practice in 1964. He first became known for his work as a member of the group called "The New York Five," often informally known as "The Whites" in response to the geometric, white painted forms that were typical of their architectural work.

By the 1970s, Graves's work had moved away from the austere style of The Five and toward the direction that has become known as Postmodernism—a term not much favored by Graves himself. It is a direction that has opened up a free and imaginative use of color, particularly in inte-

Figure 17.1   A portion of a courtyardlike space in a furniture showroom for Sunar Hauserman in Houston, Texas. Intense color is used freely in the ceiling forms and in the bases of the columns. (*Photo by Charles McGrath, courtesy of Sunar Hauserman.*)

Figure 17.2   A nurses' station with treatment rooms beyond in the offices of Ear, Nose and Throat Associates in Fort Wayne, Indiana. Color is used as metaphor: yellow for sunlight, blue for sky, and green for plants. (*Photo by Balthazar Korab.*)

riors. Graves's attention turned to the use of color for symbolic meaning or metaphor. Colors were used as symbols or references—for example, blue referred to sky or water, yellow to sunlight, green to growing plants, and red to the idea of wall. The interiors for the medical practice of Ear, Nose and Throat Associates in Fort Wayne, Indiana of 1971 demonstrate Graves's use of this symbolism.

Graves's later work has been less doctrinaire in its use of color but has continued to be adventurous in use of varied color tones, including pastels and secondary colors, in ways that have been influential in opening up the color preferences of other designers. The varied use of color in recent work of both interior designers and architects is due in large measure to this aspect of Graves's work.

Figure 17.3 In the same medical offices, each treatment room includes an original mural painting by the architect, Michael Graves, filled with lively color. (*Photo by Balthazar Korab.*)

Figure 17.4   An adult lounge–reading area in the San Juan Capistrano (California) Library. Subtle pastel colors, pale greens, some deeper green, and blue-green in furniture upholstery establish an ambience that is calm and contemplative. (*Photo by Paschall/Taylor, courtesy of Michael Graves, architect.*)

Figure 17.5 A gallery for the display of classical antiquities in the Michael Carlos Museum at Emory University in Atlanta, Georgia. In this space the deep terra-cotta wall color helps to set off the objects on display. (*Photo by Steven Brooke Studios, courtesy of Michael Graves, architect.*)

Figure 17.6   In the lobby of the Humana Building in Louisville, Kentucky, a variety of marbles are used to define spaces with color. Michael Graves was the architect with John Carl Warnecke and Associates as the associated architect. (*Photo by Paschall/Taylor, courtesy of Michael Graves, architect.*)

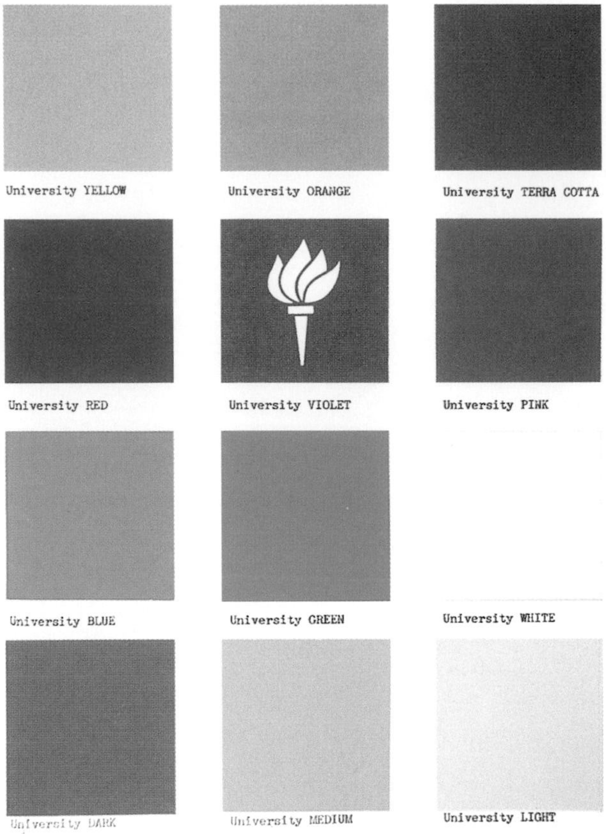

University YELLOW   University ORANGE   University TERRA COTTA

University RED   University VIOLET   University PINK

University BLUE   University GREEN   University WHITE

University DARK   University MEDIUM   University LIGHT

Figure 17.7 A color system developed for New York University (NYU) is summarized here in a page for a manual outlining the system. The key colors are shown in a square with the theme purple containing a white torch, a symbol for the university.

SUZANNE SEKEY

Suzanne Sekey is a designer who has worked in interior, architectural, and graphic design for several prominent architectural firms, as a partner in an interior design practice, and, most recently, in independent practice. Her training was at the Art Students League and the Design Laboratory in New York. She then worked as a designer in the offices of Donald Deskey, George Nelson, Warner-Leeds, Skidmore, Owings and Merrill, I.M. Pei and Partners, Marcel Breuer, and Richard Meier before becoming a partner with Harold Leeds in Leeds Associates. Since 1978 she has headed her own firm. In most of the many projects on which Sekey has worked, her involvement has included responsibility for selection of color.

For larger projects including hotels, college, university, and health care facilities,

Sekey has developed color systems—that is, a selection of related colors in materials and paint that can be used in varied ways throughout a project. Such a system makes possible varied use of color while insuring that all colors used will have a harmonious relationship. In working with such systems, Sekey has developed a standard sample format of 3 inch squares that can be grouped in a nine by nine inch square configuration which can display up to nine material or color samples (or any smaller number) in edge to edge relationship. Schemes can be planned and modified easily by exchanging samples while maintaining a consistent format.

In a number of Sekey's projects, a key or theme color is selected with other color tones chosen to achieve a relationship with the theme and to offer variety. In other situations, varied color relationships are

Figure 17.8   The group of standard colors selected for the NYU system are shown here as swatches on a ring, each with a number.

Figure 17.9   The standard nine-inch-square box with three-inch-square samples available to arrange in any desired grouping. The center block contains a rainbow arrangement of the full range of colors.

used to identify departments or other units within an organization or, in multifloor installations, to provide a key identifying color for each floor. In large projects with many repeated units (such as the bedrooms of a hotel or health care facility), a small number of schemes have been used to create variety while maintaining a degree of standardization. Such color system approaches are highly effective in organizing the elements of large and complex projects.

Figure 17.10   Nine of the standard colors arranged in a fresh grouping.

Figure 17.11   Nine carpet colors, related to the key colors of the system shown here in the standard nine-inch-square box.

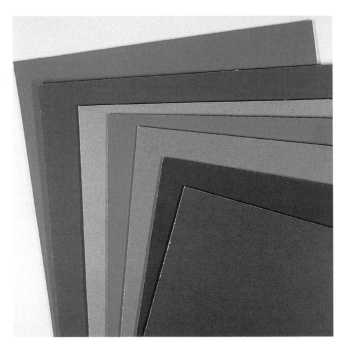

Figure 17.12   A grouping of standard colors that are part of a system developed for Baruch College of The City College of New York. Each sample is a nine-inch square, available to be used with three by three inch samples in making up proposed color schemes.

Figure 17.13   A grouping of nine samples from the Baruch College system.

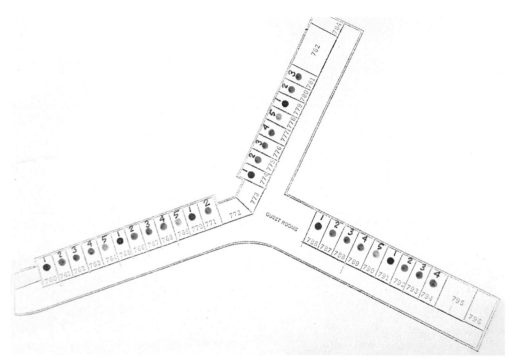

Figure 17.14 A diagrammatic plan of a portion of one floor of a hotel project. Five standard color schemes are provided for guest rooms. The location where each scheme is to be used is indicated by a key color symbol.

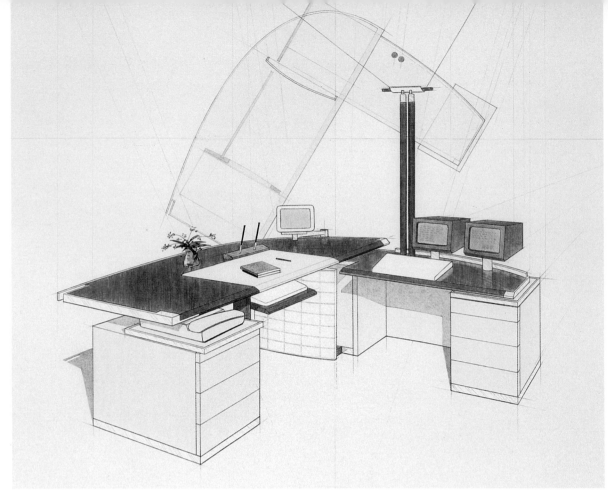

Figure 17.15   A lightly drawn plan and a color perspective of an office furniture group in a design development study by Norman Diekman.

NORMAN DIEKMAN

Norman Diekman is a New York interior and architectural designer whose practice includes an extensive involvement in furniture design. He was trained in the architectural school of Pratt Institute in Brooklyn and then worked as a designer in the offices of Philip Johnson, Lee Harris Pomeroy, and Skidmore, Owings and Merrill before opening his own office in 1970. Diekman was drawn into an emphasis on furniture design through a long-lasting relationship in the development of furniture for Ward Bennett distributed by Brickell Associates. Since 1984, Diekman has been a designer for Stow & Davis/Steelcase while continuing a private practice as an interior and architectural designer. He has also been active as a lecturer and teacher at Parsons School of Design, the New York School of Interior Design, and Pratt Institute.

Diekman's design working method is characterized by the use of drawings, particularly color drawings in which furniture is often the key to both form and color development. He is a master draftsman and his plan and elevation drawings, as well as perspectives, can be viewed as artworks in their own right, quite independently of their role as tools for design realization.

A Diekman project will often move from line drawing of furniture to color images that then grow into fully developed designs for space, in which color plans, elevations, and perspectives combine to define what will become a realized space in rich and unique color.

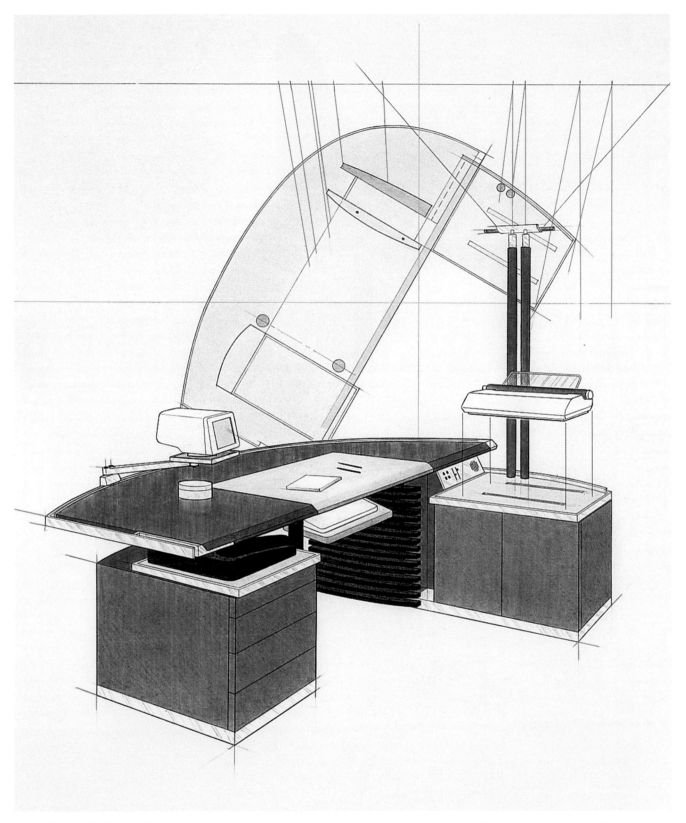

Figure 17.16 Further development of the same furniture grouping by Diekman with revisions and additional color.

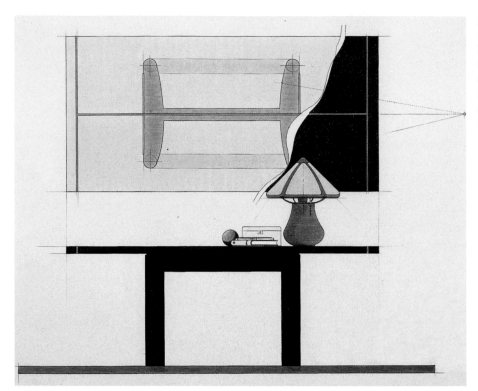

Figure 17.17   Furniture design development by Diekman. A plan (top/bottom view) above with an elevation below with the lamp and accessories added to give scale.

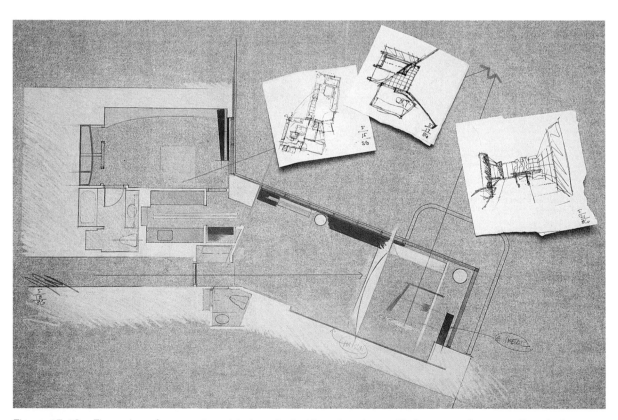

Figure 17.18   Floor plan of an apartment being studied in color along with three small perspective study sketches.

Figure 17.19   A more finished version of the apartment plan in which Diekman has shown developing furniture concepts.

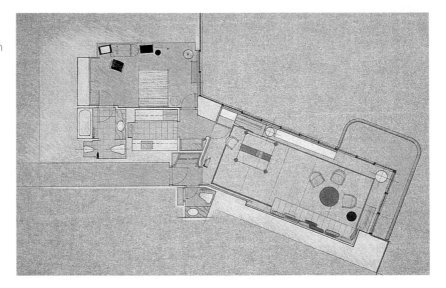

Figure 17.20   A perspective study in which the table shown in the developed plan appears and is shown in a superimposed top view.

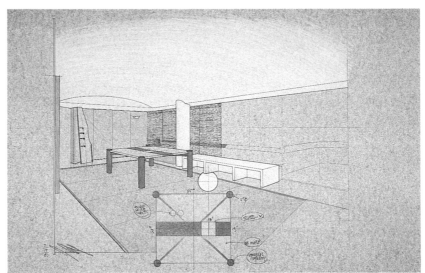

Figure 17.21   Another view of the same room looking in the opposite direction.

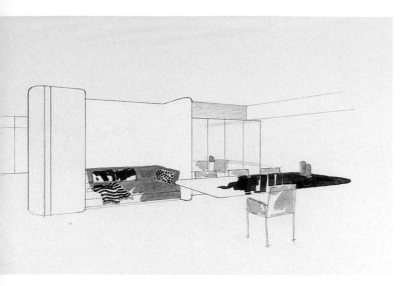

Figure 17.22 A Diekman perspective study in neutral color tones and white on yellow tracing paper.

Figure 17.23 A completed interior, an apartment living room by Norman Diekman. Warm color tones generate a sense of comfort and relaxation.

Figure 17.24   A contextual color study in which photo images of a cubic volume have been cut and clustered in a circular grouping in a deliberate attempt to obliterate existing form so as to isolate color.

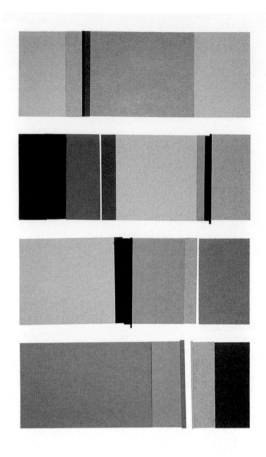

Figure 17.25   Bands of color derived from the contextual study have been made up into "color sentences" as a basis for the next step in forming abstract color sketches.

SHASHI CAAN

Shashi Caan is an architectural and interior designer and an active teacher of design in New York. She grew up in India and Scotland and took degrees in environmental design at the Edinburgh College of Art and in industrial design and architecture at Pratt Institute in Brooklyn. She has worked professionally with Spencer Alexander Associates in London, with Knoll International, and with the offices of major design firms such as Swanke Hayden Connell in New York. She is now active as a senior designer with the New York office of Gensler Associates. She is also a teacher of design, light, and color at Pratt Institute and the New York School of Interior Design and is affiliated with the School of Visual Arts in New York.

Along with her work on interior design and space planning projects, Caan has developed an interesting and highly personal approach to color, which is a basis for her teaching as well as her own design practice. She is critical of the tendency in modern practice to separate design as form from thinking about light and color and to treat color as a matter of afterthought to be added after the other design components are complete. To move toward a better integration of light and color with other aspects of design, she has developed an

Figure 17.26 Abstract sketches derived from the color sentences which were in turn derived from the contextual study. These generate an understanding of contrasts, proportions, scale, light, and color.

Figure 17.27 Charts developed from the abstract arrangements moving closer to actual designed volumes which reflect the integration of light color and form.

Figure 17.28 A further development into a chart that approaches a plan and elevation (maquette) chart for the color of a specific space.

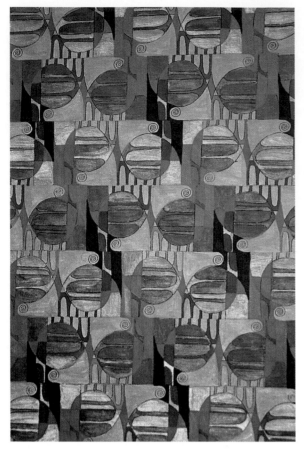

Figure 17.29 Color pattern developed in a comparable sequence to preceding project, here forming a textile design.

Figure 17.30 Another textile design in a different palette of color.

approach that begins with a "*contextual color study*" in which the color of a real environment is studied in an abstract clustering of color images made from photographs of an existing space. From such a study, she extracts "*color sentences*" that take the form of bands of color grouped in relationships proportional to the colors of the original space. These lead to the development of abstract color sketches in such forms as circles or squares of color blocks. These, in turn, form the basis for conceptual forms that move toward design representations which are close to actual designed volumes integrating light, color, and form for real spaces. These are suitable to form a basis for color plans that provide literal guidance for final color selection and use.

This methodology has proven highly effective in Caan's actual design practice and has been extremely useful as a basis for her teaching of design and color to design students.

Figure 17.31 Integration of color in a reception space, designed by Shashi Caan in the firm of Swanke Hayden Connell Architects. The space is part of an office group for a major law firm in Miami, Florida. *(Photo by Dan Forer, courtesy of Shashi Caan.)*

Figure 17.32   Stuarts, a New York restaurant in which monochromatic, nearly achromatic color generates a sense of subdued elegance. Walls and columns are a light cream color. Floor and ceiling are a warm, almost neutral gray. Chairs are black. Lively color is introduced by the clothing of patrons when the room is occupied. (*Photo by Paul Warchol.*)

Figure 17.33   In the cafe Word of Mouth, neutral background tones are dominated by the thematic red tone used for furniture and woodwork details. Green marble tabletops offer a complementary contrast to the ubiquitous red. (*Photo by Norman McGrath.*)

ALFREDO DE VIDO

Alfredo De Vido is a New York architect with an active and varied practice that includes residential, institutional, and commercial projects ranging from smaller houses to college buildings, stores, restaurants, hotels, and churches. De Vido received his training as an architect at Carnegie-Mellon University, at Princeton, and (in town planning) at the Royal College of Fine Arts in Copenhagen. He has been in practice in New York since 1975 working with a small staff. He has won many awards and his work is frequently published. He is the author of several books and a frequent lecturer at architectural schools.

Whenever possible, De Vido acts as the interior designer for his architectural projects and has produced many assignments that are primarily or totally within the field of interior design. In interiors, De Vido has developed a strong and highly personal color sense that is special to his practice.

While it is not possible to detect any formula, most De Vido interiors use color that is drawn from the natural tones of the materials in use along with an extensive use of white. His interiors usually are, however, strongly chromatic in color feeling through the use of strong colors in certain areas or for particular elements. Furniture in a restaurant, merchandise on display in a store or showroom, or a particular surface in a residential interior become the locations for strong color which enlivens an otherwise simple color surround of natural, neutral, and achromatic color.

Figure 17.34 In this solar house in New Jersey, white paint, gray floors, and other near-neutral tones are relieved by the fireplace and end wall painted a gray-blue and by pale violet tones in the cushions of upholstered furniture. (*Photo by Peter Aron.*)

Figure 17.35   In the De Vido's own New York apartment, living room walls are pale yellow, doors and wood-work are natural pine wood. The dining room–library, seen through the open doors, gains color from books and objects that fill the open shelves. The rugs are colorful orientals. (*Photo by Norman McGrath.*)

Figure 17.36   Living area of a house on Long Island. The largely neutral color forms a backdrop for the owners' collections of art and primitive artifacts. Paint color is used for limited areas of architectural and decorative detail. (*Photo by Paul Warchol.*)

Figure 17.37 Off-white walls and a wood ceiling in this small garment showroom for the New York firm of Tess provide a quiet setting for the colors of items on display. The left-hand wall is mirrored, doubling the image of the space, the bright green neon sign, and the chair rail painted blue-green. (*Photo by Frederick Charles.*)

Figure 17.38   This church, the chapel of Mount St. Dominic in Caldwell, New Jersey, is a renovation of an older building. White and neutral tones of natural materials generate a sense of calm and dignity. (*Photo by Paul Warchol.*)

Figure 17.39   Brilliant color in a series of receding planes in a showroom for the Artemide lighting firm in Miami, Florida. (*Photo courtesy of Vignelli Associates.*)

VIGNELLI ASSOCIATES

Vignelli Associates is a New York firm headed by Massimo and Lella Vignelli, Italian-born architects and designers. Both Vignellis are graduates in architectural design from the University of Venice. In 1965, Massimo Vignelli with partners founded a New York office, named Unimark. In 1971, he formed Vignelli Associates with his wife Lella as a partner. The firm has grown large and has a varied practice including graphic design and packaging, product design, and interior design for a number of offices, showrooms, and even a New York church.

Throughout the work of the Vignellis, in every field, there is a strong and emphatic use of color—most often bright, chromatic color used with considerable daring and great skill. In many instances, the Vignelli work in interiors is part of a more extensive program that may include graphic, packaging, and product design so that there is a unity of concept and relationships in the use of color throughout the visible aspects of a particular client's projects. The brilliant yellow that is the theme color for the furniture firm of Kroin, for example, is used in advertisements and brochures and in showroom interiors in a way that generates a memorable continuity.

Figure 17.40   Subdued color in a showroom for the Steelcase Design Partnership in Grand Rapids, Michigan. (*Photo courtesy of Vignelli Associates.*)

Although full of the energy and business skills that may be thought of as typically American, the Vignelli use of color seems to retain some of the sense of brightness and adventure that suggests a surviving quality of Italian *brio* and spirit.

Vignelli design has received many awards and honors ranging from the Compasso D'Oro award of 1964 to an honorary joint doctoral degree from the Parsons School of Design, where Massimo Vignelli has been a frequent teacher.

Figure 17.41 A retail shop interior. Barney's in New York. White and neutral color tones set off merchandise, in this case men's clothing. (*Photo by Aurelia Amendolqa, courtesy of Vignelli Associates.*)

Figure 17.42 An orange-red wall as accent adjacent to a white wall that forms a background for display of colorful clothing at Designer's Collezione at Pasona, Japan. (*Photo courtesy of Vignelli Associates.*)

Figure 17.43   Effects of color and lighting make an otherwise austere space lively and stimulating in the Hauserman showroom in Los Angeles, California. (*Photo courtesy of Vignelli Associates.*)

Figure 17.44   The interior of St. Peter's Church, adjacent to the Citicorp Center in New York, utilizes the natural colors of materials and white with added accents of bright color in specially designed textiles used for seating cushions. (*Photo by John Pile.*)

Figure 17.45   In the Vignelli Associates' New York offices, restrained color is used with metallic surfaces for some walls and, here, for a table base. The view is looking from a hallway into Massimo Vignelli's office. (*Photo by Luca Vignelli, courtesy of Vignelli Associates.*)

18
A Portfolio of Color Schemes

This chapter offers a collection of color schemes in abstract form—the form that was the subject of Chapter 6. A variety of uses ranging from casual to some systematic exercises are suggested. By simply leafing through this section, it is possible to have some reaction to each scheme which may offer hints or stimuli toward producing others that will serve well for projects that come to hand. One or another scheme can simply be borrowed and put to use, but, in the process of borrowing, it will become clear that a more creative process becomes inevitable. The materials to match one or another color will not quite match, or a small shift of color may seem more appropriate—before long a whole new scheme will emerge, built on the beginnings suggested by the colors here.

More methodical uses can include any (or all) of the following:

1. *Critical evaluation.* How successful is each scheme seen in the abstract? Can it be improved by changing one or more colors, by changing the areas of some of the colors?

2. *Appropriate use.* Each scheme is developed to be suitable for certain uses. Are the uses suggested in the captions appropriate? What other sort of functional spaces could also use such a scheme? Where would it be less appropriate or totally inappropriate?

3. *Material selection.* What materials would be best for the various elements of a space, and which of these materials would appear in what colors?

4. *Color scheme classification.* To which of the theoretical color scheme types does each of the following schemes belong? Is a scheme an example of:

   Monotone color
   Monochromatic color
   Analogous color
   Complementary color
   Split-complementary color
   Triad color
   Tetrad color

   or is it a variation on one of these types or even a scheme that defies all classification? Are there modifications or departures from theoretical color relationships?

Figure 18.1　A triad color scheme originally used in the showroom of a paint company. The floor is hardwood boarding finished in a brown tone. Part of the ceiling was black with areas of orange and blue adjacent. Walls were white and several other bright colors. Such a scheme is inherently lively and active.

Figure 18.2　Soft colors that might be considered for a bedroom. The floor is blue, the ceiling white, walls a medium gray. Furniture is natural wood, the bed cover a dull rose.

5. *Color scheme approach.* Does each scheme suggest one of the practical approaches suggested in Chapter 8? Is the scheme neutral, natural, or functional, or is it a variation on one of these types (neutral-plus, for example) or an example of color that does not fit any of these approaches?

6. *Color scheme improvement.* Can the scheme be improved by substitution of different colors or by changing the relative areas of colors?

7. *Color scheme creation.* Can a new scheme surface as a result of starting from one of the schemes proposed here that will be creative, original, and best-suited to whatever project may be at hand?

Suggestions here are, in the end, merely intended as sources to stimulate fresh and original work in which color will be central to achievement of results which are both practical and aesthetically satisfying.

Figure 18.3   A near monochromatic scheme in which
achromatic colors dominate
with the dark blue and dull
red offering some variety. As
originally used, the scheme
served a large, loftlike living
space with a blue area rug
and upholstery in soft red
tones.

Figure 18.4   A high-key, near
monochromatic scheme with
floor and ceiling in similar
tones, walls close to white.
Furniture, trim, and other
details are in warm tones
except for small accessory
items that include small areas
of black. The gentle color of
such a scheme tends to
maintain a pleasant warmth
during long periods of occupancy.

Figure 18.5   A scheme close
to totally achromatic except
for the bright blue-green. As
originally used, in a loft space
occupied by a musician, a
grand piano in traditional
black stood on a dark-gray
floor. The ceiling was black,
and walls were white with
some areas of gray and blue-
green. Columns, prominent in
this space, provided the
strong color that made the
space characteristically cool
in overall impact.

Figure 18.6 Pale and delicate colors include a beige floor covering, off-white walls and ceiling, and soft tones of yellow and blue in furniture covering and window treatment. Such a reserved scheme suggests a fashion orientation that might be appropriate to a bedroom, dressing area, or bath, or might be considered for an office space for a style-related business organization.

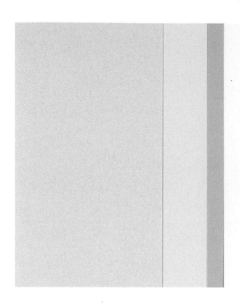

Figure 18.7 Low-key color suited to a conference room, library, or study where a quiet or studious atmosphere is called for. The floor uses a black rug placed on a dark-brown wood floor. The ceiling is white, the walls a greenish tone of yellow. Dark green, brown, and tan appear in furniture and other details.

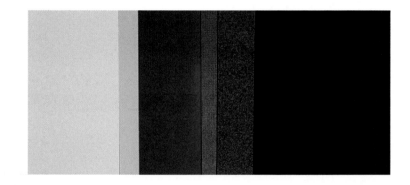

Figure 18.8 A strong, warm-colored scheme originally used in an early-American house bedroom. The walls are pink, the floor wide wood boards painted red. Furniture is in tones of brown. The bed covering is one of several quilts in which tones of red and pink appear along with areas of white or near white. The ceiling is painted a light tan.

Figure 18.9 Color as used in a postmodern interior. Floors are in tones of green, the lighter tone an area rug placed on floors painted in the darker green. Walls are white, the ceiling gray. The dull orange and yellows are the colors of wood furniture using veneers and solid woods in natural finishes.

Figure 18.10 A warm color scheme using browns and reds in furniture and fabrics, a light-tan tone for walls, and white for the ceiling. The floor uses an oriental rug, also with tones of red on a black surround. The white band represents a trim color. This range of color would be well suited to living or office spaces where the traditional flavor of comfort expressed through warmth is sought.

Figure 18.11 A cool color scheme with tones of blue and green together with white and a few limited areas of black. This would be suitable color for living spaces in a warm climate or for spaces where intense southern sun would be a daytime constant.

Figure 18.12 Subtle color including pastel tones and violets, often thought of as problematic. Postmodernism has been more hospitable to such color than the usual thinking of either traditional or modernist interior design.

Figure 18.13 Grays and black form a nearly achromatic scheme except for the addition of the pink accent color. A scheme as limited as this is best suited to spaces used for brief times such as vestibules, elevator cabs, or bathrooms.

Figure 18.14 Dominating brown tones with a medium-tan ceiling suggest the qualities of a study, library, or somewhat formal office. An interior using wood as a primary material (for floor and paneled walls) will generally lead to a scheme of this type. The red and green used in elements of furniture can relieve any sense of dullness or gloom.

Figure 18.15 A tan-yellow floor covering (wood, tile, or carpet) is used here with white walls, an off-white ceiling, and woodwork trim painted in a tone of violet. The blue and dark green are present in furniture and upholstery fabrics.

Figure 18.16 The brown of a natural wood floor, dull-yellow walls with white trim and moldings, and a sand-beige ceiling appear here with the reddish-brown of mahogany furniture. Furniture upholstery and window drapery are in yellows relating to the wall color. This is a scheme suitable to a public meeting hall, a courtroom, or a church where a balance between dignity and restraint and brightness are sought.

Figure 18.17 A residential living space with walls paneled in wood finished in a light tan. The floor is blue-gray with a darker area rug. Blue and green appear in furniture cushions. The brown is the tone of the stone of a fireplace. The ceiling is the light-tan tone. Cool and warm tones are present in near-equal emphasis. The warm tones are desaturated yellows and so stand next to green in the color wheel. Since the range of hues is from yellow through green to limited use of blue, the scheme is an example of analogous color relationships.

Glossary

achromatic: Color produced by the reflection of light without chromatic color content. Black, white, and grays are achromatic colors.

additive color: Color produced by the addition of light of various colors.

additive primaries: The primaries of additive color are red, green, and blue.

analogous colors: Colors that are adjacent or close in their position in the spectrum and on the color wheel.

chroma: The purity or saturation of a color tone.

color temperature: A number indicating the warmth or coolness of the color of light expressed in degrees kelvin (k or kelvins).

color wheel: The arrangement of the colors of the spectrum in a circle or wheel form in their rainbow or spectrum order.

complementary colors: Colors positioned on opposite sides of a color wheel such as red and green, yellow and violet, or blue and orange.

continuous-spectrum light: Light in which all of the visible energy wavelengths are present. Daylight and incandescent electric light exhibit a continuous spectrum.

CRI (color rendering index): A number indicating the ability of a particular source of illumination to give a correct evaluation of the color of objects and surfaces.

discontinuous-spectrum light: Light in which only some visible energy wavelengths are present. Gaseous-discharge lamps deliver a discontinuous spectrum. Fluorescent lamps mix continuous and discontinuous spectra.

double-complementary color: Four hues in two complementary pairs. Two hues on one side of a color wheel are used with two hues on the other side of the color wheel, each complementary to one of the opposite hues.

fluorescent light: A light source that mixes light from glowing gases within a lamp and light from fluorescent materials used to line the lamp. Most fluorescent lamps are tubular although some are available in globe shapes.

full-spectrum light: Light from a source that delivers all wavelengths of light energy present in daylight including both visible and invisible radiation.

halogen light: *See* **tungsten-halogen light.**

HID light: An abbreviation for *high-intensity discharge* light. HID lamps use mercury, sodium, or metal-halide to produce a highly efficient form of electric illumination.

hue: The characteristic of a color identified with a particular color name and with a particular position in the spectrum or color wheel. The three primary hues are red, yellow, and blue; the three secondaries are orange, green, and violet.

incandescent light: The common type of electric light source in which illumination is produced by a heated, glowing wire (usually tungsten) within a sealed globe or bulb from which air has been evacuated.

maquette: An interior floor plan with surrounding elevations placed in contact with the plan so that, when cut out and folded, a three-dimensional simulation of a space is created.

mercury light: An electric light source using mercury gas in a sealed tube which produces a discontinuous-spectrum light when excited by electric current. A bluish color is characteristic.

metal-halide light: A type of HID light source that produces economical illumination of high intensity.

monochromatic color: Color of a single hue.

monotonal color: Color of one particular hue, chroma, and value.

Munsell color system: A widely used color system in which all possible colors are identified by the three attributes: hue, value, and chroma.

Ostwald color system: A color system using four primaries to organize all possible colors according to hue, value, and saturation.

primary color: A color hue that cannot be produced by mixture of other hues. The additive primaries (of light) are red, green, and blue; the primaries of subtractive color are red, yellow, and blue.

quaternary colors: Color hues positioned between tertiary hues and adjacent primaries or secondaries in the spectrum or on a color wheel.

radiation: The transfer of energy by electromagnetic wave action. Color is a phenomenon of light radiation.

reflectance: The proportion of incident light which is reflected by an illuminated surface expressed as a percentage.

saturation: *See* **chroma**.

shade: A color tone which has been darkened by an admixture of gray, black, or a complementary hue.

sodium light: A gaseous-discharge light source in which sodium gas in a sealed tube is activated by passage of an electric current. Sodium light has a discontinuous spectrum producing an orange color tone.

spectrum: The band of electromagnetic energy arranged in order of wavelength. The visible spectrum can be seen by passing white light through a prism breaking it up into the spectrum colors of red, orange, yellow, green, blue, and violet, which appear in that order.

split-complementary color: Use of complementaries in which one hue is opposite to two hues on the other side of the color wheel that are equidistant from the complementary of the first color.

subtractive color: The colors of surfaces and objects that result from the absorption of spectrum colors so that only certain hues are reflected.

tertiary colors: Color hues positioned between primaries and secondaries in the spectrum or on a color wheel.

tetrad color: Colors of the four hues positioned at the quarter points around the circumference of a color wheel.

tint: A color made lighter by the addition of white or another light color to the pure hue.

triad color: Colors of three hues placed at equidistant points around the circumference of a color wheel.

tungsten-halogen light: An incandescent light source that uses metal halides in compact bulbs or tubes providing a high-intensity illumination.

value: The lightness or darkness of a color in relation to its position on a scale ranging from white to black.

Bibliography

Albers, Josef. *Interaction of Color.* New Haven, Conn.: Yale University Press, 1971.

Birren, Faber. *Creative Color.* New York: Van Nostrand Reinhold, 1965.

———. *Color and Human Response.* New York: Van Nostrand Reinhold, 1984.

———. *Color for Interiors, Historic and Modern.* New York: Whitney Library of Design, 1963.

———. *Color Psychology and Color Therapy.* New Hyde Park, N.Y.: University Books, 1961.

———. *Color for Interiors.* New York: Whitney Library of Design, 1963.

Eiseman, Leartrice, and Lawrence Herbert. *The Pantone Book of Color.* New York: Harry N. Abrams, 1990.

Evans, Ralph M. *An Introduction to Color.* New York: John Wiley & Sons, 1959

Garau, Augusto. *Color Harmonies.* Chicago: University of Chicago Press, 1993.

Gerritsen, Frans. *Theory and Practice of Color.* New York: Van Nostrand Reinhold, 1975.

———. *Evolution in Color.* West Chester, Pa.: Schiffer Publishing, 1988.

Gerstner, Karl. *The Spirit of Colors.* Cambridge, Mass.: MIT Press, 1981.

von Goethe, Johannes W. *Color Theory* (Translation by C. L. Eastlake of *Farbenlehre*). Cambridge, Mass.: MIT Press, 1970.

Graves, Maitland. *Color Fundamentals.* New York: McGraw-Hill Book Company, 1952.

Halse, A. O. *The Use of Color in Interiors.* New York: McGraw-Hill Book Company, 1968.

Itten, Johannes. *The Art of Color.* New York: Van Nostrand Reinhold, 1961.

———. *The Elements of Color.* New York: Van Nostrand Reinhold, 1970.

Kobayashi, Shigenobu. *A Book of Colors.* Tokyo: Kodansha International, 1987.

Kuehni, Rolf G. *Color: Essence and Logic.* New York: Van Nostrand Reinhold, 1983.

Küppers, Harald. *Color: Origin, Systems, Uses.* London: Van Nostrand Reinhold, 1973.

Lamb, Trevor, and Janine Bourriau, eds. *Colour: Art and Science.* Cambridge, England: Cambridge University Press, 1995.

Mahnke, Frank H., and Rudolph H. Mahnke. *Color and Light in Man-made Environments.* New York: Van Nostrand Reinhold, 1987.

Marberry, Sara, and Laurie Zagon. *The Power of Color.* New York: John Wiley and Sons, 1995.

Munsell, A. H. *A Color Notation.* Baltimore: Munsell Color Company, 1929.

Ostwald, Wilhelm. *The Color Primer.* New York: Van Nostrand Reinhold 1969.

Sharpe, Deborah T. *The Psychology of Color and Design.* Chicago: Nelson-Hall, 1974.

Varley, Helson, ed. *Color.* Los Angeles: Knapp Press, 1980.

Williamson, Samuel. *Light and Color in Nature and Art.* New York: John Wiley and Sons, 1983.

Wright, W. D. *The Measurement of Color.* New York: Van Nostrand Reinhold, 1969.

Index

About the Author

John F. Pile is a professional interior design consultant practicing in New York City. A graduate in architecture from the University of Pennsylvania, he has been honored by the Graham Foundation and the Mellon Fund. His clients have included Citibank, ITT, Knoll International, and Alfred University. A professor of design at Pratt Institute since 1948, John Pile has authored or co-authored more than 20 books in his field, including *Dictionary of 20th Century Design, Furniture: Modern and Postmodern,* and *Perspective for Interior Designers.* He lives in Brooklyn Heights, New York.